VOICES FROM
THE GREAT WAR

——————

PETER VANSITTART

PIMLICO

Published by Pimlico 2003

2 4 6 8 10 9 7 5 3 1

First published in Great Britain by Jonathan Cape 1981
First Pimlico edition 1988
Second Pimlico edition 2003

Pimlico
Random House, 20 Vauxhall Bridge Road,
London SW1V 2SA

Random House Australia (Pty) Limited
20 Alfred Street, Milsons Point, Sydney,
New South Wales 2061, Australia

Random House New Zealand Limited
18 Poland Road, Glenfield,
Auckland 10, New Zealand

Random House South Africa (Pty) Limited
Endulini, 5A Jubilee Road, Parktown 2193, South Africa

Random House UK Limited Reg. No. 954009

A CIP catalogue record for this book
is available from the British Library

ISBN 1-8441-3415-6

Papers used by Random House UK Limited are natural,
recyclable products made from wood grown in sustainable forests.
The manufacturing processes conform to the environmental
regulations of the country of origin

Printed and bound in Great Britain by
Bookmarque Ltd, Croydon, Surrey

Dedicated with much love
to
Claudia and Peregrine Worsthorne

CONTENTS

INTRODUCTION

It is sometimes very hard to tell the difference between history and the smell of skunk.

Rebecca West

This is a very personal book about what I still call the Great War. As a small boy in Southsea, I saw streets disfigured by ragged, un-wanted ex-soldiers, medalled, but ill, blind, maimed, selling matches, bootlaces, notepaper, trundling barrel-organs or standing with a melancholy dog or monkey beside a decrepit hurdy-gurdy. Whether they were pleading or abusive, resigned or menacing, they appalled me. Their wretchedness suggested that, in overthrowing Germany, they had earned some monstrous penalty now being inexorably exacted.

Meanwhile, new recruits still marched, bugles called, drums beat, and in the Solent still loomed the grey, momentous ships of the Grand Fleet: *Rodney*, *Nelson*, *Hood*, *Repulse* – soon to be exposed as being as archaic as iguanodons. Half glimpsed through winter haze, glittering in summer suns, they seemed an iron wall ready to blow invaders to bits, invulnerable as the Prince of Wales himself.

The dark dormitories of boarding school intensified the War for me. Though over, I somehow felt it was still going on. Common rumour had it that mysterious potentates were up to no good. George V had a Maltese wife, Queen Mary a wooden leg, and the Pope a bathroom cupboard crammed with the wives of his predecessors: these were commonplace, for, in the Brussels' market place, the Kaiser, all Highest, Supreme Warlord, was slicing off the right hands of Belgian schoolboys. He had British corpses boiled down into soap, so that our red repellent squares of Lifebuoy acquired a sick glamour: or into edible fats, making us consider whether the suet pudding, already disgusting, might have been a cavalry officer. The Kaiser, he strode and clanked, glowered and threatened, through the vast halls of sleep. Even today, journalists mention him, and expect to be understood. One boy's father knew that, for insulting the Kaiser, a youth had been compelled to cycle over a Norwegian cliff: another had seen the Canadian crucified at Amiens, on imperial orders. Everyone knew that, if jostled on the street by a civilian, a German officer must at once cut him down, failing that, then resign his commission and, if belonging to one of the Kaiser's favourite regiments, shoot himself in the right temple.

The Kaiser, so forbidding and evil, was simultaneously a painted devil, target for the puerile and ribald. He was a nervous man, sleeping with a revolver by his bed, and, ominous for a Warlord, with one arm deformed.

Kaiser Bill went up the hill
To play a game of cricket,
The ball went up his trouser leg
And hit his middle wicket.

Kitchener's Army in Belgium, where Wellington's had been before them, had sung:

Poor Kaiser Bill is feeling ill,
The Crown Prince he's gone barmy,
And we don't care a fuck
For old von Kluck
And all his bleedin' great army.

He had been Victoria's favourite grandson, loathed by Edward VII. 'Willy was always fond of yachting,' Uncle Edward remarked, when shown the Imperial High Seas Fleet so ominously assembled at Kiel. Years later, in 1940, when the Nazis invaded Holland, the Kaiser, exiled, old, forgotten, refused Winston Churchill's offer to send the RAF to fly him to Britain. 'Inherently trivial and with no sense of proportion,' Churchill wrote, in a relatively compassionate summing up.

By 1930 I had learnt, from older boys, that the mistreated and forgotten could turn terrible. In 1918–19 wild mobs had been shot down in Liverpool, the Army had mutinied in Shoreham, the Canadians at Rhyl and a British military soviet had been established at Calais. 'Bloody Friday' in Glasgow saw tanks and machine guns in George Square.

Simultaneously I was acquiring a new vocabulary, still imprecise, seldom reassuring, but enlarging the world, showing its nastier side, very different from such majestic utterances as *Esplanade*, *Ambassador*, *George Bernard Shaw*, *Throne of the Heavenly Grace*, *Rickshaw Boy*, *Mazawattee Tea*, and those evocative titles inscribed on the green, mottled panes of fairy-tale houses from which I was excluded: *Private*, *Public*, *Saloon*, *Wines from the Wood*, *Bottle and Jug*, *Ales and Stout*. The darker words joined the names of school meals – *White Baby*, *Worms*, *House on Fire*, *Hardbaked Tombstone*, *Deadman's Leg*, *Old Hundreds*, *Cat's Illness*, and *Stuff*. I now ruminated over *Uhlan* – spiked helmets against an ashen hill, lances scratching the summer sky of 1914 – *Bosche*, *Minnie Werfers*, *Hun*, *Kibosh*, *Zeppelin*, *Over the Top*, *Napoo*, *Whizz Bangs*, *Dug Out*, *Dawn Patrol*, *Fatherland*, *Hard Tack*, *Crump*, *Conshie*, *Q-Ships*, *Brass Hat*, *Big Bertha*, and, with her not-in-front-of-the-children aura, *Mademoiselle from Armentières*. Such words still occasionally slip out of me, the young looking up with expressions more often reserved for interesting but doomed animals. The innocuous *trench* gained the sinister force of *tumbril*. Certain place names not usually heard in geography lessons created a spectral landscape: *Mons*, *Somme*, *Wipers*, *Passchendaele*. 'His father was drowned at *Jutland*,' was repeated like a glum chorus.

Every November, Armistice Day came round, curiously complementary to Guy Fawkes Day. Bonfires had sunk, flags rose, hymns resounded, as we gathered before the War Memorial on which an embossed sword was already turning green, as if septic from the bodies it had slashed. We pored over bound volumes of *Punch*, the *Illustrated London News*, the *Times History of the War*, unconsciously preparing for the classics, *The Case of Sergeant Grisha*, *All Quiet on the Western Front*, *The World Crisis*, *Good Bye to All That*, and, for me especially, C. E. Montague's *Rough Justice*, Richard Aldington's *Death of a Hero*, and the early talkie, *Hell's*

Angels, with its zeppelins over London. More strange names assembled: *Rasputin*, *Ludendorff*, *Mata Hari*, *von Tirpitz* with his two beards, *Captain Boy Ed*, *Falkenhayn*, *Hohenzollern*, *Château Thierry* – one unpronounceable foreign name is as good as another, Churchill said – and *von Kluck*, 'Old One O'Clock' the Tommies called him, as, in the Crimea, their grandfathers had transmuted the French General Canrobert into 'Bob Can't'.

We learnt to mock generals. Unlike jolly admirals, few generals really endeared themselves to the British. Cromwell and Marlborough seemed cold, as did Wellington, quite wrongly. I respected Lord George Townshend, at Lauffeld, when a German brother-officer's head was shattered. 'I had not realised', said Townshend, wiping his sleeve, 'that Shieger had so many brains.' Unfairly, no doubt, generals seemed at one with the Elizabethan, Sir John Smythe, of whom Leicester, himself scarcely a Hannibal, complained: 'After the muster, he entered into such strange cries for ordering of men and for fight with weapons as made me think he was not well. God forbid that he should have charge of men who know so little as I dare say he does.' Later, in South Africa Sir Redvers Buller was described by Churchill as 'a characteristic British personality. He looked stolid. He said little, and what he said was obscure. He was not the kind of man who could explain things, and he never tried to do so. He usually grunted, or nodded, or shook his head, in serious discussion.' Of Lord Chelmsford, Philip Guedalla declared that he had chief command 'because he was the son of a distinguished lawyer whom the family incompetence had compelled the Prime Minister to exclude from the Woolsack eleven years previously. The cogency of the reason will be readily apparent to any student of the English system.'

Great War generals, on all fronts, would remind me of Bertie Wooster's aunt, 'like a tomato struggling for self-expression'. After impressive careers on horseback, they seemed perpetually confused by technology. Foch declared in 1910 that aircraft were all very well for sport, but useless for the army. None, perhaps, was quite so subjective as the Greek general, fighting the Turks in 1922, and so convinced that his legs were made of glass that he refused to leave his bed, a precaution for which his troops were ungrateful. During the Second World War 'Cassandra', the newspaper columnist, wrote, 'Generals are trained like race horses to behave like asses', but this is an unsatisfactory assessment of Montgomery, Alexander,

Mountbatten, Slim, Eisenhower, Patton, Rommel . . .

Certain incidents proved for me unforgettable. In *Hindenburg, the Wooden Titan*, John Wheeler-Bennett described the gigantic wooden effigies of the old field-marshal erected throughout war-time Germany. To assist war funds, citizens bought nails and hammered them into their stolid father-figure, a Freudian ambivalence indeed. The ex-Empress Eugénie allegedly read aloud the outlines of the Versailles Treaty over the tombs of her husband and son, forty-nine years after Sedan where, symbolically, the Great War surely began. My friend, William Coldstream, on Birchington beach in August 1914, was ordered to remove his box-kite from the sky. 'This country is AT WAR!' At my school, in 1914, the proprietor received a parcel from a parent in India which contained a loaded pistol with which to shoot his two sons if the Germans landed. I imagined, with misgivings, the announcement, short but emphatic, after morning prayers: 'Last Sunday's church collection was threepence short, a disgraceful occurrence. I now wish to see the Marshal brothers in the cellar. At once. For a very few minutes.'

In many schools, new boys would be welcomed by some picture of a dead khaki warrior, entitled with the Latin tag that so angered Wilfred Owen.

If in some smothering dreams you too could pace
Behind the wagon that we flung him in,
And watch the white eyes writhing in his face,
His hanging face, like a devil's sick of sin;
If you could hear, at every jolt, the blood
Come gargling from the froth-corrupted lungs,
Obscene as cancer, bitter as the cud
Of vile, incurable sores on innocent tongues, –
My friend, you would not tell with such high zest
To children ardent for some desperate glory,
The old Lie: *Dulce et decorum est*
Pro patria mori.

A master would, in a knowing way, refer to 'the Fourth Balkan War', but for the rest of us it remained the Great War, a monstrous frieze of myth and legend, romantic falsehoods and despicable truths, still breeding within the torments of the defeated, the disappointments of the victors, the sufferings of the world, all evoked within seconds by some sentimental but unforgettable tune. 'It's a long way to Tipperary . . . ' survived like a password into a dark, unspeakable cult. I would know of the gruesome mobile brothels; young women chirping from tawdry stages, 'We don't want to lose you but we think you ought to go'; vicious harpies presenting young men with white feathers, one harridan hissing at G. K. Chesterton, 'Why aren't you out at the Front?' to which he replied, patting his own uncompromising circumference, 'Madame, I *am* out at the front.' Horses disembowelled; Tommies and Jerries fixed on the No Man's Land wire, as if in some ghoulish spider trap. Execution posts, each with its drooping body. Officers with gloves and swords, glossy as conkers, such as Colonel Forbes Robertson, admired by Conan Doyle as 'one of the heroes of Cambrai, who earned the coveted Cross by fighting on horseback like some knight of old, and repeatedly restoring the line when it was broken.' The doubtless apocryphal story of Warden Spooner, 'Ah! Now tell me, was it you or your brother who was killed at the Front?' Flanders poppies; John McCrae's 'In Flanders fields the poppies blow'; roses of Picardy; mournful stations groaning with departing troop trains; unending casualty lists; the generals' great paunches; the statesmen's beards of unpredictable design and almost passionate profusion; the lonely Tsar; the troubled eyes of the father in that recruiting poster, 'What did you do in the Great War, Daddy?' The thin glare of Very Lights and the men slipping off duck-boards into insatiable mud incessantly churned by shells which sucked them down forever. And, above all, the 10 million dead, the 20 million wounded or missing, 150,000 Serbs dead of typhus, seven times that number of Armenians massacred, the 74,779 American gas victims.

Ironies abounded. The wise and gentle G. M. Trevelyan, in 1914, hoped that England would hit hard and thus have more influence in a treaty that would not crush Germany, 'who is our ultimate bulwark against "the barbarian" with whom we are necessarily allied at this moment.' Then, in 1917, rejoicing, 'Russia is free! I can think of nothing else, feel nothing else.'

This book is eclectic, I hope, vigorously so: I have chosen to concentrate more upon the war fought on the ground than at sea or by air. In addition, considerations of space and translation necessarily limit the contributions of the British Dominions, India and the Balkans. The complex causes of the war and the nature of the

Versailles Treaty would have demanded a different book. I agree with A. J. P. Taylor, that the controversies over the origins of the First World War helped to bring about the Second. If the selection seems inordinately masculine, this is almost wholly to the discredit of the men.

The contents are arranged chronologically: a reader can follow the war's broad course and discern the larger patterns, notably the frustrations of trench war stretching from the Alps to the North Sea, and the consequent and bloody dream of the breakthrough – which, in the equally horrible but more fluid Eastern Front, periodically occurred. More important, it is an anthology into which to delve at random and, I hope, to find the suggestive and the moving.

The Great War 'freed' a number of peoples. To look at most of them today makes a bitter verdict on necessary alliances, magnificent fortitude, a scalding waste of spirit.

PETER VANSITTART

PRELUDE

My dear Winston, the experiences of a long life have convinced me
that nothing ever happens.

> Sir William Harcourt, 1895

The Moon shines with so blue a light
Over the City,
Where a decaying generation
Lives cold and evil –
A dark future prepared
For the pale grandchild.

> Georg Trakl

Remembering with Pride
    Jack Judge Who in this Street and Building was
inspired to write and compose
    the immortal Marching Song
'It's a long way to Tipperary'.
    He was also the first to sing it
in public – at the Grand Theatre, opposite,
    January 31st 1912.

> Plaque in Corporation Street, Stalybridge, Cheshire

Here, richly, with ridiculous display,
    The Politician's corpse was laid away.
While all of his acquaintance sneered and slanged
    I wept: for I had longed to see him hanged.

> Hilaire Belloc

END OF THE WORLD

The bourgeois' hat flies off his pointed head,
The air re-echoes with a cry.
Men leap from the roof, hit the ground,
And at the coast – one reads – the seas are rising.

Storm is here, the savage seas hop
On the land and smash thick dams.
Most people have a cold.
Trains fall from bridges.

>   Jakob van Hoddis, 1910

I look upon the People and the Nation handed on to me as a
responsibility conferred upon me by God, and I believe, as it is
written in the Bible, that it is my duty to increase this heritage for
which one day I shall be called upon to give an account. Whoever
tries to interfere with my task I shall crush.

>   Kaiser Wilhelm II

The Kaiser

When William talked loosely about coming to lunch on an island in
the lake of Hamburg, the city fathers, instead of reminding him that
their guest house was actually on a peninsula, built a new pavilion
complete with flower beds on an artificial island in the middle of the
lake. William had only to say to Bülow that 'your light trousers are
enough to upset the best weather forecast' and an obsequious
Chancellor hurried off to change.

>   Michael Balfour

There was a type existing then that I imagine has largely vanished
from later suburbs. This was the decent family man, husband,
father, rate-payer, who would be suddenly compelled to break all
the rules, dismiss all responsibilities, vanishing from home and
office, unaccountably behaving like a gold-miner new from the
diggings and going off on a tremendous 'binge', nobody knew
where.

>   J. B. Priestley

The enormous expansion of wealth in the peaceful years between 1908 and 1914 brought not happiness but fear, and fear so powerful that it could be expressed only in images of fear and destruction. When war came, it was almost universally accepted as something foreseen and foretold. Even those who loathed the notion of it acquiesced in it as inevitable, and it is not foolish to conclude that what ultimately brought the war was not the ambitions and fears of Germany, but a death-wish in the peoples of Europe, a half-conscious desire to break away from their humdrum or horrifying circumstances to something more exciting or more exalted.

    C. M. Bowra

There is not a single tenet of the National Socialist Party programme of February 1920 or of its later amendments which was not propagated in the political literature before 1914. Moreover, there was an element of emergency, of impatient waiting for the day, in the atmosphere of Wilhelmian Germany which was noted with alarm by many writers. It was in this spirit of expectancy that the outbreak of the war in August 1914 was greeted by most politicians and intellectuals, among them almost all literary men.

    J. P. Stern

Zabern: 1913

Yet for a while the irrational forces of nationalism were in balance against the more rational forces of industrialism: prior to the First World War collective reason seemed even to have the upper hand. People migrated freely across national frontiers, without regard to occupation and status and without using passports. which were needed only in the surviving despotisms of Russia and Turkey . . . A common sense of law and order prevailed over large parts of the planet, to a now-astonishing degree: peace, security, continuity reigned as under the Antonines. So deep had become respect for the personality, so sure was the sense of individual freedom, that when a single lame cobbler was attacked by a German officer in Zabern, because the humble man had not yielded the sidewalk to him, a cry of outrage rose throughout the world – not least in Germany, where the Reichstag censured the government by a vote of 293 to 54.

    Lewis Mumford

Men's minds seem to have been on edge in the last two or three years before the war in a way they had not been before, as though they had become unconsciously weary of peace and security. You can see it in things remote from international politics – in the artistic movement called Futurism, in the militant suffragettes of this country, in the working-class trends towards Syndicalism. Men wanted violence for its own sake, they welcomed war as a relief from materialism. European civilization was, in fact, breaking down even before war destroyed it.

> A. J. P. Taylor

In 1914, Europe had arrived at a point in which every country except Germany was afraid of the present, and Germany was afraid of the future.

> Lord Grey

The Germans went to war in 1914 because we had no clear policy. They thought, moreover, that even they could not goad into action another country without a policy, the United States.

> Lord Vansittart

We muddled into war.

> David Lloyd George

It is not too much to say that Aehrenthal, Austrian Foreign Minister, 1908–12, by his policy of annexation, was indirectly the cause of the Great War.

> Lord Hardinge

The state of mind of Sazonov, Russian Foreign Minister, contributed greatly to that over-agitated handling of the Serbo-Austrian crisis which precipitated the final catastrophe during the tragic days of July, 1914.

> L. Albertini

1914

The year 1914 in America seemed the crest of a wave of passionate idealism among young people, and of passionate selfishness among middle-aged people. The idealism showed itself in two ways; in liberal humanitarian propaganda, and in such an outburst of poetry as no nation has seen since the Elizabethan age in England. Upon both these lovely and gracious growths the cloven hoof of the war crushed down with exterminating violence.

> John Cowper Powys

Let the names of imperial cities
Caress the ears with brief meaning.
It's not Rome the city that lives on,
It's man's place in the universe.

Emperors try to rule that,
Priests find excuses for wars,
But the day that place falls empty
Houses and altars are trash.

> Osip Mandelshtam

JUNE 28

Archduke Franz Ferdinand, heir to the Austro-Hungarian Empire, and his wife, are assassinated by Slav nationalists at Sarajevo.

Here, in this historic spot, Gavrilo Princip was the initiator of Liberty on the day of St Vitus, the 28th of June, 1914.

> Memorial at Sarajevo to the killer

Sophie, Sophie, don't die. Live, for the children's sake . . . It's nothing, it's nothing . . .

> Franz Ferdinand, dying

No one has ever managed to show that the Serb government had any connexion with the plot. Indeed, it was easy to guess that an Austrian Archduke would be shot at if he visited Sarajevo on 28 June, Serbia's national day . . . The plot was the work of six high-minded national idealists. Two of them are still alive. One is a professor at Belgrade University; the other curator of the museum at Sarajevo.

> A. J. P. Taylor, 1956

Professor Poprovic, Custodian of Sarajevo Museum, died in June 1980. Professor Cubrilovic is still living in Belgrade (August 1980).

In the train at the Saint-Lazare station, I read in the *Latest News* the murder of the Archduke, heir to the throne of Austria-Hungary, and his wife at Sarajevo. She [my wife] pouted with indifference. 'Look at Poucette,' she said to me, 'the little darling likes being in a train.'

> André Maurois

Then came the summer of 1914, and suddenly all appeared different, inwardly and outwardly. It became evident that our former well-being had rested on unsafe foundations, and thus there now began a time of wretchedness, the great education. The so-called time of testing had come, and I cannot declare that it found me better prepared, worthier, or superior to any others. What distinguished me from the rest during those days was only that I lacked the great compensation so many of them felt: enthusiasm.

> Hermann Hesse

JULY 5

At Potsdam, Germany promises absolute backing for Austria-Hungary's undisclosed demands on Serbia, accused of complicity in the Sarajevo murders. Russia warns of her support for Serbia if these demands are unreasonable.

JULY 23

Austria-Hungary sends an ultimatum to Serbia, demanding a reply within two days.

JULY 25

Influenced by Russia, Serbia accepts the bulk of the ultimatum, at The Hague, suggesting the rest be referred to international arbitration. Rejected. Refusing further peace overtures, Austria moves troops to the Serb frontier.

A great moral victory for Vienna, all grounds for war disappear.

Kaiser Wilhelm II

By such means Serbia was trapped and the whole of Europe doomed. Count Berchtold [Austrian Foreign Minister] and his friend Conrad von Hotzendorf [Chief of the General Staff], who were resolved upon hostilities, persuaded the Hungarian Minister, Count Tisza, to withdraw his opposition, and gained the consent of the old Emperor Franz Josef by a totally false statement that Serbian troops had fired on the Austrian garrison of a Danubian port; and the final declaration of war was dispatched on July twenty-eighth. The consequences were clearly foreseen by the plotters against peace. If Austria attacked Serbia and stretched out its hand to the Black Sea, Russia was bound to intervene; for Russia did not want . . . to have the Austrian Empire as neighbour on another front, and it could not like to see Slavs subject to Teutons. Germany must join in on the pretext of aiding Austria, not because it had yet developed an appetite for Russian territory, though that was to come later, but because it could now find a pretext for attacking France, who was Russia's ally, and was showing dangerous signs of having recovered its strength after the defeat of 1870. Immediately millions of people were delivered over to the powers of darkness and nowhere were these more cruel than in Serbia.

Rebecca West

This will take the attention away from Ulster, which is a good thing.

Prime Minister H. H. Asquith, *to Lady Ottoline Morrell*

JULY 25

Sir Edward Grey proposes a peace conference, at which Britain, France, Germany and Italy would mediate between Vienna and St Petersburg. Declined by Germany.

JULY 28

Austria declares war on Serbia.

Winston, who has a pictorial mind brimming with ideas, is in tearing spirits at the prospect of a war, which to me shows a lack of imagination.

>   Prime Minister H. H. Asquith

Everything tends towards catastrophe and collapse. I am interested, geared up and happy. Is it not horrible to be built like that? The preparations have a hideous fascination for me. I pray to God to forgive me for such fearful moods of levity. Yet I wd do my best for peace, and nothing wd induce me wrongfully to strike the blow.

>   Winston Churchill

In Paris, Jean Jaurès pleads for peace.

The Tsar Telegraphs the Kaiser

In this most serious moment I appeal to you to help me. An ignoble war has been declared to a weak country. The indignation in Russia shared fully by me is enormous. I foresee that very soon I shall be overwhelmed by the pressure brought upon me and be forced to take extreme measures which will lead to war. To try and avoid such a calamity as a European war, I beg you in the name of our old friendship to do what you can to stop your allies from going too far.

>   Nicky

The Kaiser Telegraphs the Tsar

With regard to the hearty and tender friendship which binds us both
from long ago with firm ties, I am exerting my utmost influence to
arrive at a satisfactory understanding with you. I confidently hope
you will help me in my efforts to smooth over difficulties that may
still arise. Your very sincere and devoted friend and cousin,

> Willy

England alone carries the responsibility for peace or war, no longer
us.

> Kaiser Wilhelm II

JULY 30

Jaurès is assassinated.

Jaurès' murder is just the beginning, war unchains instincts, all
forms of madness.

> Victor Adler, *to Trotsky*

Tsar Nicholas II orders general mobilisation.

JULY 31

I am thirsty for a man's work to accomplish, and it will in full
measure be awarded me.

> Ludendorff

Frivolity and weakness are going to plunge the world into the most
frightful war.

> Kaiser Wilhelm II

Now Tsarism has attacked Germany, now we have no choice, now
there is no looking back.

> Kurt Eisner

JULY, 1914

All month a smell of burning, of dry peat
Smouldering in the bogs.
Even the birds have stopped singing,
The aspen does not tremble.

The god of wrath glares from the sky,
The fields have been parched since Easter.
A one-legged pilgrim stood in the yard
With his mouth full of prophecies.

'Beware of terrible times . . . the earth
opening for a crowd of corpses.
Expect famine, earthquakes, plagues,
And heavens darkened by eclipses.

'But our land will not be divided
by the enemy at his pleasure:
the Mother-of-God will spread
a white shroud over these great sorrows.'

        Anna Akhmatova

JULY 31

The American Ambassador in Berlin

Acting on my own responsibility, I sent the following letter to the Chancellor:

'Your Excellency, – Is there nothing that my country can do? Nothing that I can do towards stopping this dreadful war? I am sure that the President would approve any act of mine looking towards peace – Yours ever, James W. Gerard.'

To this letter I never had any reply. On August 1, at five pm. the order for mobilisation was given, and at 7.10pm. war was declared by Germany on Russia, the Kaiser proclaiming from the balcony of the Palace that 'he knew no parties any more.'

Of course, during these days, the population of Berlin was greatly excited. Every night great crowds of people paraded the streets singing 'Deutschland Über Alles,' and demanding war. Extras, distributed free, were issued at frequent intervals by the news-papers, and there was a general feeling among the Germans that their years of preparation would now bear fruit, that Germany would conquer the world and impose its 'Kultur' upon all nations.

On August 2 I called in the morning to say good-bye to the Russian Ambassador. His Embassy was filled with unfortunate Russians who had gone there to seek protection and help. Right and left men and women were weeping, and the whole atmosphere seemed that of despair.

James W. Gerard

AUGUST 1

Germany declares war on Russia.

[In St Petersburg] a quickly organised gang smashed a side-door of the [German] Embassy. I could see flashlights and torches moving inside, flitting to the upper storeys. A big window opened and spat a great portrait of the Kaiser at the crowd below. When it reached the cobblestones, there was just enough left to start a good bonfire. A rosewood grand piano followed, exploding like a bomb; the moan of broken strings vibrated in the air for a second and was drowned: too many people were trying to outshout their own terror of the future . . . A new crowd carrying the portrait of the Tsar and singing a hymn was advancing slowly . . . the bonfire was being fed by the furniture, books, pictures and papers which came hurtling through the windows of the Embassy. The emblazoned crockery of state came crashing, and the shattering sound whipped the crowd into a new wave of hysteria. A woman tore her dress at the collar, fell on her knees with a shriek, and pressed her naked breasts against the dusty boots of a young officer in campaign uniform.

'Take me! Right here before these people! Poor boy . . . you will give your life . . . for God . . . for the Tsar . . . for Russia.

Sergei Kourakoff

There is an accumulative cruelty in a number of men, though none in particular is ill-natured.

Rudyard Kipling

AUGUST 1

A Russian communist in Berlin

Can't stop trembling, suffering as for the death agony of a loved one. So this is war! When we first conceived of it, we imagined that at once the shadow of the red spectre would spring up from behind its shoulders. But this submissive bewilderment, this silence from the Party, is enough to drive one mad.

Alexandra Kollontai

Austria

The war that began in 1914 and has been going on ever since revealed its nature to me through two experiences. Awkward young soldiers were being pelted with flowers by women and girls. The streets of Graz were full of excited people marching towards the Sudbahnhof. Their patriotism reeked of alcohol. Over and over came the roar: 'Death to all Serbs! Long live the Emperor! Down with traitors!' Outside the station, in the middle of a knot of howling, screaming, insane people, a man was dragged to the ground, trampled upon, torn limb from limb. 'A Serbian spy!' someone called out. 'A Serbian spy!' went the cry from one mouth to another as the remains of a human being were retrieved from the murderous mob.

Ernst Fischer

AUGUST 3

Germany declares war on France, and invades neutral Belgium and Luxembourg.

GERMANY INVADES
FRANCE — ACTION OF
ENGLAND AWAITED.
British Government to Announce its Attitude in House of Commons Today – Luxembourg is taken.
Efforts to Stop War go on.
London (Sunday, midnight) The political situation is bad, but not hopeless. In spite of everything the British Cabinet is continuing the exertions to stop the war though the sudden movement of German troops has made this difficult.

Curiously enough whilst Austria is actually negotiating at St Petersburg, Germany has declared war against Russia and has thrown her troops across the French frontier. The fact, therefore, remains that while a state of war exists between Germany and Russia, without any overt act, Germany has violated French territory without declaring war.

> *Christian Science Monitor*, Boston

Sunday Schools
    Pray for Peace.
New York
Thirty million members of the World's Sunday School Association, scattered throughout the world, were to pray for peace Sunday . . .

> *Christian Science Monitor*, Boston

I naturally replied that whatever might be said of the political aspect of the matter, a soldier need think only of his orders, and that for officers more than all other ranks the maxim 'My Country Right or Wrong' holds good.

> Prince von Bülow, ex-Imperial Chancellor, *on the German invasion of Belgium*

Failure of British Foreign Policy?

In England the Sarajevo murder attracted little attention at first. To the ordinary man it was only another example of Balkan savagery, while even the Government appears to have been too preoccupied with the crisis in Ireland to appreciate its full significance. As the days passed and the threat of a European war grew louder the overwhelming mass of the British people remained indifferent: Serbia was not popular and it was extremely difficult to persuade anyone that it was necessary to go to war on her behalf.

Difficult or not, it had to be done once it became clear that France was going to be involved, if only because the Anglo-French military and naval arrangements, of which the people knew nothing, were in fact as binding as any formal treaty. They were kept in the dark right up to the end. Sir Edward Grey, the Foreign Secretary, solemnly announced in the House of Commons on June 11th:

'If war arose between European Powers, there were no un-

published agreements which would restrict or hamper the freedom
of the Government or of Parliament to decide whether or not Great
Britain should participate in a war. That remains as true today as it
was a year ago. No such negotiations are in progress and none are
likely to be entered upon so far as I can judge.'

It was a statement outstandingly untruthful and misleading even
by the standards of British Liberalism, since Sir Edward knew, what
was concealed even from the House of Commons, that Britain was
pledged to protect the North Coast of France from naval attack in
the event of war.

The attitude of the Government in the days before the War could
hardly have been more calculated to make its outbreak certain.
France and Russia knew that Britain would intervene on their
behalf. Germany was allowed to believe that there was at least some
good chance of Britain remaining neutral. Whatever may have been
the intention behind this attitude, its result was to encourage both
sides to stand out stubbornly for terms that could not possibly be
conceded.

A. L. Morton

AUGUST 2

A British View

A nation's first duty is to its own people. We are asked to intervene
in the Continental war because unless we do we shall be 'isolated'.
The isolation which will result for us if we keep out of this war is
that, while other nations are torn and weakened by war, we shall not
be, and by that fact might conceivably for a long time be the
strongest Power in Europe, and, by virtue of our strength and
isolation, its arbiter, perhaps, to useful ends . . .

The last war we fought on the Continent was for the purpose of
preventing the growth of Russia. We are now asked to fight one for
the purpose of promoting it. It is now universally admitted that our
last Continental war – the Crimean War – was a monstrous error
and miscalculation. Would this intervention be any wiser or likely to
be better in its results?

On several occasions Sir Edward Grey has solemnly declared that
we are not bound by any agreement to support France, and there is
certainly no moral obligation on the part of the English people so to
do. We can best serve civilization, Europe – including France –

and ourselves by remaining the one Power in Europe that has not
yielded to the war madness. This, I believe, will be found to be
the firm conviction of the overwhelming majority of the English
people.

> Norman Angell, *to 'The Times'*

AUGUST 3

House of Commons

Of the men who rose in melancholy succession to counsel a standing
aloof from the war, a desertion of France, a humble submission to
the will of Potsdam in the matter of Belgium's neutrality, one wishes
to speak fairly. Many of them are men who have gloatingly threatened us with class warfare in this country – warfare in which rifles
and machine guns should be used to settle industrial disputes; they
have seemed to take a ghoulish pleasure in predicting a not-far
distant moment when Britons shall range themselves in organized
combat, not against an aggressive foreign enemy, but against their
own kith and kin. Never have they been more fluent with these hints
and incitements than during the present sessions; if a crop of violent
armed outbreaks does not spring up one of these days in this country
it will not be for lack of sowing of seed. Now these men read us
moral lectures on the wickedness of war. One is sometimes assured
that every man has at least two sides to his character; so one may
charitably assume that an honest quaker-like detestation of war and
bloodshed is really the motive which influences at the present
moment some of these men who have harped so assiduously on the
idea – one might almost say the ideal – of armed collision between
the classes. There are other men in the anti-war party who seemed
to be obsessed with the idea of snatching commercial advantages
out of the situation, regardless of other considerations which
usually influence men of honour.

> Saki

It had struck five on the last afternoon before the world broke, and
the sun was now going down on a number of things besides landscapes. Twilight soon, and hesper would light up the lamps of the
sky for the last evening's reign of the British gold pound over all the
pleasant places of Europe: Mürren, Marienbad, Venice, Cortina –

its bright orb had reigned regally throughout them, levying for us islanders the kindly fruits of the Continental earth.

The old England, too, the one that was still feudal at heart, had come to her death-bed at last. Only six or seven hours now and all her ancient belfries, from Winchester up to Durham and Carlisle, would be tolling their twelve strokes apiece for her passing. She died hard, the glorious old jade. A little wicked in her time, and now wizened, she lay handsome tonight, with the fine bones showing well through the skin that was turning to wax. At any rate for what was left of that lustrous Tuesday in August, people would stay in the classes to which it had pleased God or some other authority to call them; cows would stand still to be milked; ale would be good at twopence a glass; and all the young men whom you liked would remain alive, with two arms to them each, and two legs, to employ in such tranquil pursuits as lawn-tennis in sunny gardens over the shining waters of the Thames, if it were their blest portion – or else to stretch them on hot turf among roses, as Victor and Auberon did at this moment, utterly at peace, as it still seemed, with all men and the gods, in spite of the current talk about war.

C. E. Montague

AUGUST 4

I 'attended' at the Palace in Berlin. In the room where the Court balls had been held in peace times a certain number of the members of the Reichstag were assembled. The diplomats were in a gallery on the west side of the room. Soon the Emperor, dressed in field-grey uniform, and attended by several members of his staff, entered the room. He walked with a martial stride, and glanced toward the gallery where the diplomats were assembled, as if to see how many there were. Taking his place upon the throne and standing, he read an address to the members of the Reichstag. The members cheered him and then adjourned to the Reichstag, where the Chancellor addressed them, making his famous declarations about Belgium, stating that 'necessity knew no law,' and that the German troops were perhaps at that moment crossing the Belgium frontier . . . The Socialists had not been present in the Palace, but joined now in voting the necessary credits.

James W. Gerard

I still feel as though in a dream – and yet one ought to be ashamed for not having considered it possible or seen that the disaster must come. What an affliction! How will Europe look, inwardly and outwardly, when it is over? Personally, I shall have to prepare myself for an utter change in my standard of life. If the war long continues I shall doubtless be what is termed 'ruined'. In God's name! What significance has this against the revolution, the spiritual revolution which such great events must bring with them? Should we not feel grateful for such a totally unexpected chance to witness such mighty things? My chief feeling is of immense curiosity – and, I confess, the deepest sympathy for this loathed, enigmatic and fated Germany, which, if it scarcely ranks 'civilization' as man's chief estate, has at least assumed the responsibility of destroying the world's most degraded police-state.

Thomas Mann, *to Heinrich Mann*

War might drive a man till he dropped: it could be a dangerous and bloody business; we believed, however, that it still offered movement, colour, adventure, and drama. Later, when the murderous, idiotic machinery of the Western Front was grinding away, of course all was different.

J. B. Priestley

I esteem the moral values of war, on the whole, rather highly. To be torn out of a dull capitalistic peace was good for many Germans and it seems to me that a genuine artist would find greater value in a nation of men who have faced death and who know the immediacy and freshness of camp life.

Hermann Hesse, *to Volkmar Andreä*

Germany is the only possibility for the further spiritual development of man.

General Count von Moltke the younger

Just for a word, 'neutrality' – a word that in wartime has so often been disregarded – just for a scrap of paper, Great Britain is going to make war on a kindred nation, which desires nothing better than to be friends with her.

Dr Theobold von Bethmann-Hollweg, German Imperial Chancellor

On Receiving News of the War

Snow is a strange white word;
No ice or frost
Has asked of bud or bird
For Winter's cost.

Yet ice and frost and snow
From earth to sky
This Summer land doth know;
No man knows why.

In all men's hearts it is:
Some spirit old
Hath turned with malign kiss
Our lives to mould.

Red fangs have torn this face,
God's blood is shed.
He mourns from his lone place
His children dead.

O ancient crimson curse!
Corrode, consume,
Give back this universe
Its pristine bloom.

                Isaac Rosenberg

Readers should refuse service from a German or Austrian waiter.

                Daily Mail, London

August 5

No nation has ever entered into a great struggle – and this is one of
the greatest in history – with a clearer conscience and a stronger
conviction that it is fighting not for aggression or the advancement
of its own interests, but for principles whose maintenance is vital to
the civilised world.

            Prime Minister H. H. Asquith, *addressing the House of
            Commons*

Rally Round the Flag – Every Fit Man Wanted.

> Recruiting Poster

AUGUST 6

Lord Kitchener of Khartoum, 'K of K', appointed Minister of War.

K grew very arrogant. He had flashes of genius but was usually stupid. He could not see any use in Munitions. He was against tanks. He was against Welsh and Irish divisions. He refused the flags which the ladies worked. He obstructed us in all things and ruined the Dardanelles. But he was a great force in recruiting. This Asquith said of him, 'He is not a great man. He is a great poster.'

> Sir Arthur Conan Doyle

I had a close view, finding him older and greyer than the familiar pictures of him. The image I retained was of a rather bloated purplish face and glaring but somehow jellied eyes, an image not of an ageing man, already bewildered by, reeling under, the load of responsibility he refused to share, but of some larger than life yet now less than life figure, huge but turning into painted lead. It was a frightening and not pleasing image, and a year later, when we heard he had been drowned, I felt no grief, for it did not seem to me that a man had lost his life: I saw only a heavy shape, its face now an idol's, going down and down into that northern sea. Yet it was he – and he alone – who had raised us new soldiers out of the ground. This, not anything he did in Egypt and the Sudan, was a stroke of genius; he created armies when all the others, mischievous clowns like Henry Wilson or the huntin'-and-shootin' Cavalry Captains pretending to be generals, said he was an obstinate old fool and laughed at him. Here I was, I still am, on his side. But the image that remained after that inspection, of something immensely massive and formidable but already hardening and petrifying, nearer to death than to life, haunted me and to my disquiet for a long time. Even when at last we reeled through a cleft in the Downs, saw the sea and gave a cheer, straightened our shoulders for the final miles along the clean and twinkling edge of it, swinging through Hythe and Sandwich, that image was there, the eyes glaring out of death not life.

> J. B. Priestley

Yesterday we heard noise of explosions destroying inconvenient houses at Harwich . . . We also heard thunder; and the children affirm that they distinctly heard the noise of firing – not explosions.

Report of action in North Sea in evening papers . . . I agree that Russia is the real enemy, and not Germany, and that a *rapprochement* between England and Germany is a certainty . . . I think that the belligerency of England is a mistake for England . . . Sir Edward Grey's astounding mistake in his big speech, was the assertion that the making of war would not much increase our suffering. It will enormously increase it. The hope for us is the honesty and efficiency of our administration. The fear of France springs from the fact that the majority of French politicians are notoriously rascals, out for plunder. The corruption of Russian administration is probably even worse . . . If Germany is smashed in this war, the man most imperilled will be the German Emperor. If she is not smashed the man most imperilled may be the Tsar.

      Arnold Bennett

Upon the wall at the corner of Marlborough House as it was then, I saw a large bill; it was an unusual place for an advertisement and I stopped to read it. It was a Royal Proclamation. I forget what matter it contained; what struck me was the individual manner of the wording. King George was addressing 'My people.' There was no official 'we' and 'our' about it.

I had been so busy with the idea of civilization fighting against tradition, I had been so habituated to the liberal explanation of the monarchy as a picturesque and harmless vestigial structure, that this abrupt realization that the King was placing himself at the head of his people was like a bomb bursting under my nose. My mind hung over that fact for a moment or so.

'Good God!' I said in the greatest indignation, 'What has he got to do with our war?'

I went on my way digesting it.

'My people' – me and my sort were *his* people!

So long as you suffer any man to call himself your shepherd sooner or later you will find a crook round your ankle. We were not making war against Germany; we were being ordered about in the King's war with Germany.

      H. G. Wells

We should have been prepared for this war. Our Socialist guides had instilled in us the idea that capitalism, in its struggle for markets, inevitably produced war. Old Man Jackson in high school had warned us that war would come while we were still young. We had grown up in the shadows of war, near and far. Had it not been for the Russo-Japanese clash, my family might never have come to America.

But we were not a bit prepared. News of the European war came to us with the unexpected violence of an earthquake . . . Abstract truth was one thing, reality another. From the distance, through deliberately confusing news dispatches, we observed the battle of nations growing more fierce, spreading like wildfire from land to land, devouring more and more men. Humanity, we said, echoing our elders, was bleeding. We began to wonder whether it wasn't bleeding to death. We drew closer to America where peace prevailed, where the don in the White House urged us to remain neutral in our sympathies for the contending powers.

> Joseph Freeman

AUGUST 8

It is not the German people who are the enemy. It is the tyranny which has held them in its vice, the tyranny of personal government armed with a mailed fist, the tyranny of a despotic rule, counter-signed by Krupps.

> *Daily News*, London

Black and hideous to me, the tragedy that gathers and I'm sick beyond cure to have lived on to see it. You and I, the ornaments of our generation should have been spared this wreck of our belief that through the long years we have seen civilization grow and the worst become impossible. The tide that bore us along was then all the while moving to *this* as its grand Niagara – yet what a blessing we didn't know it. It seems to me to undo everything, everything that was ours, in the most horrible retroactive way – but I avert my face from the monstrous scene.

> Henry James, *to Rhoda Broughton*

A god at last.

> Rainer Maria Rilke

Eastern Front

Russian advance into East Prussia helps save Paris and the Allied cause in the West.

AUGUST 9

ALSACE INVADED

FRENCH DASH OVER THE FRONTIER.

LIEGE STILL HOLDING OUT

>   *The Times*, London

AMERICANS ILL-TREATED IN GERMANY

Mr Archer M. Huntington, honorary president of the American Geographical Society, and his wife have been arrested in Nuremberg by the German police, and are now held prisoners as spies . . . Mr Huntington was stripped naked in being searched and his wife was subjected to insults and indignities.

>   *The Times*, London

AUGUST 10

Germans enter Antwerp.

Now it is you I will praise, Banner, that, ever since childhood,
I gazed surmisingly after and guessingly greeted
as the streaming files carried you off asleep:
tremblingly greeted, as though you might dream of my greeting.
You, now awake in battles, flaming with life like a bride
that suddenly wakes, and, full of amazement, remembers
she's loved, leaps up, and with flowing
hair and gown, resplendently billowing maiden,
storms the night-guarded hill, leaving her feelings behind.
Revealed at last! . . .

>   Rainer Maria Rilke

Isn't it luck for me to have been born so as to be just the right age and just in the right place – not too high up to be worried – and to enjoy it to the most!

>   Julian Grenfell

INTO BATTLE

The naked earth is warm with spring,
    And with green grass and bursting trees
Leans to the sun's gaze glorying,
    And quivers in the sunny breeze,
And life is colour and warmth and light,
    And striving evermore for these;
And he is dead who will not fight;
    And who dies fighting has increase.

      Julian Grenfell

My own attitude towards the conflict was simple and clear. In my eyes it was not Austria fighting to get a little satisfaction out of Serbia but Germany fighting for her life, the German nation for its 'to be or not to be', its freedom and its future . . .

    Now began for me, as for every German, the greatest and most unforgettable period of my life. Compared with the events of that mighty struggle, all the past fell into empty oblivion. I think with pride and sorrow of those days and back to the weeks of the beginning of our nation's heroic fight, in which kind fortune allowed me to partake.

      Adolf Hitler

Despite all my hatred and aversion for war, I should not have liked to have missed the memory of those first days. As never before thousands and thousands felt what they should have felt in peace-time – that they belonged together.

      Stefan Zweig

Chosen daughter of the Lord,
Spouse-in-Chief of the ancient sword,
There's the menace of the Word
In the Song on your bugles blown,
England –
Out of heaven on your bugles blown!

      W. E. Henley

How glad I am that tomorrow I shall at last be able to join in the campaign. At last I shall be playing my part, proving with my life what I think and feel.

>Ernst Toller

We are Fred Karno's army,
    The ragtime infantree,
We cannot fight, we cannot shoot
    What bleeding use are we?
And when we get to Berlin
    The Kaiser he will say
Hoch! Hoch! Mein Gott!
    Vot a bloody rotten lot,
Vot a bloody rotten lot are they!

Now, God be thanked Who has matched us with His hour,
And caught our youth, and wakened us from sleeping,
With hand made sure, clear eye, and sharpened power,
To turn, as swimmers into cleanness leaping,
Glad from a world grown old and cold and weary,
Leave the sick hearts that honour could not move,
And half-men, and their dirty songs and dreary,
And all the little emptiness of love!

>Rupert Brooke

All my Libido is for Austria-Hungary.

>Sigmund Freud

AUGUST 15

Dissent in London

Sir

Against the vast majority of my countrymen, even at this moment, in the name of humanity and civilization, I protest against our share in the destruction of Germany.

A month ago Europe was a peaceful comity of nations; if an Englishman killed a German, he was hanged. Now, if an Englishman kills a German, or if a German kills an Englishman, he is a patriot, who has deserved well of his country. We scan the newspapers with greedy eyes for news of slaughter, and rejoice when we read of innocent young men, blindly obedient to the word of command, mown down in thousands by the machine-guns of Liège. Those who saw the London crowds, during the nights leading up to the Declaration of War saw a whole population, hitherto peaceable and humane, precipitated in a few days down the steep slope to primitive barbarism, letting loose, in a moment, the instincts of hatred and blood lust against which the whole fabric of society has been raised. 'Patriots' in all countries acclaim this brutal orgy as a noble determination to vindicate the right; reason and mercy are swept away in one great flood of hatred; dim abstractions of unimaginable wickedness – Germany to us and the French, Russia to the Germans – conceal the simple fact that the enemy are men, like ourselves, neither better nor worse – men who love their homes and the sunshine, and all the simple pleasures of common lives; men now mad with terror in the thought of their wives, their sisters, their children, exposed, with our help, to the tender mercies of the conquering Cossack.

And all this madness, all this rage, all this flaming death of our civilization and our hopes, has been brought about because a set of official gentlemen, living luxurious lives, mostly stupid, and all without imagination or heart, have chosen that it should occur rather than that any one of them should suffer some infinitesimal rebuff to his country's pride. No literary tragedy can approach the futile horror of the White Paper. The diplomatists, seeing from the first the inevitable end, mostly wishing to avoid it, yet drifted from hour to hour of the swift crisis restrained by punctilio from making or accepting the small concessions that might have saved the world, hurried on at last by blind fear to loose the armies for the work of mutual butchery.

And behind the diplomatists, dimly heard in the official documents, stand vast forces of national greed and national hatred – atavistic instincts, harmful to mankind at its present level, but transmitted from savage and half-animal ancestors, concentrated and directed by Governments and the Press, fostered by the upper class as a distraction from social discontent, artificially nourished by the sinister influence of the makers of armaments, encouraged by a whole foul literature of 'glory', and by every text-book of history with which the minds of children are polluted.

England, no more than other nations which participate in this war, can be absolved either as regards its national passions or as regards its diplomacy . . .

It thus appears that the neutrality of Belgium, the integrity of France and her colonies, and the naval defence of the northern and western coasts of France, were all mere pretexts. If Germany had agreed to our demands in all these respects, we should still not have promised neutrality.

I cannot resist the conclusion that the Government has failed in its duty to the nation by not revealing long-standing arrangements with the French, until, at the last moment, it made them the basis of an appeal to honour; that it has failed in its duty to Europe by not declaring its attitude at the beginning of the crisis; and that it has failed in its duty to humanity by not informing Germany of conditions which would insure its non-participation in a war which, whatever its outcome, must cause untold hardship and the loss of many thousands of our bravest and noblest citizens.

Bertrand Russell, *to the 'Nation'*

We are fighting not for shadowy political advantages, not for the lust of power, not for the hegemony of Europe, but for our very existence as an independent nation . . . we say quite simply that the German Fleet must be swept from the face of the seas.

Editorial in Horatio Bottomley's *John Bull*

At least the thing will be over in three weeks.

Lieutenant Bernard Montgomery

AUGUST 20

Kitchener's 'First Hundred Thousand' stationed at Maubeuge.

Mr Kaiser, Mr Kaiser,
You're the cause of all the trouble,
Cause of all the crime.
When the Gunners get to France
They will make the Germans dance.
It's all through Mr Kaiser all the time.

A Volunteer

I returned to my old farm at Akenfield for 11s. a week, but I was unsettled. When the farmer stopped my pay because it was raining and we couldn't thrash, I said to my seventeen-year-old mate, 'Bugger him. We'll go and join the army.'

Leonard Thompson, *to Ronald Blythe*

Apart from a few traction engines for pulling heavy siege guns, the B.E.F. was completely unmechanised until, at the last moment, a couple of Royal Engineer officers were sent to commandeer a few score brewery lorries. No provision had, of course, been made for a supply of magnetos, and the disgraceful story of how the war office obtained them by secret trading with the Bosch Company of Stuttgart has never yet, I believe, been told.

Robert Graves

Where are our uniforms?
    Far, far away.
When will our rifles come?
P'r'aps, p'r'aps some day.
And you bet we shan't be long
Before we're fit and strong;
You'll hear us say 'Oui, oui, tray bong'
    When we're far away.

They had heard that the German Army had a General von Kluck, and this prompted them to sing to the tune of 'The Girl I Left Behind Me':

'Oh, we don't give a fuck
For old von Kluck
An' all his fuckin' Army!'

In spite of their schoolboyish demeanour, they were not all young men – very far from it: freely interspersed among young and pink faces were those with a hint of double-chin and thickening jowls; when they removed their stiff-peaked 'cheesecutter' caps one could discern heads which were getting thin on top, as gentlemen's hairdressers have it, and others which were unashamedly balding. Many upper lips were heavily moustached, and on the left breasts of

a number of tunics could be seen ribbons of well-nigh forgotten wars
– the Sudan, South Africa, the North-West Frontier of India.

    Tim Carew

. . . that mysterious army of horsemen, ploughmen and field workers who fled the wretchedness of the land in 1914. The army had
provided – along with the railways – an escape route for many
years before this, but it was the First World War which swept Len
and his contemporaries off the hated land to conditions which
forced the countrymen to decide to halt a system of degradation
when they returned.

    Ronald Blythe

It is not true, as some young critics of the First War British high
command have suggested, that Kitchener's army consisted of brave
but half-trained amateurs, so much pitiful cannon-fodder. In the
earlier divisions like ours, the troops had months and months of
severe intensive training. Our average programme was ten hours a
day, and nobody grumbled more than the old regulars who had
never been compelled before to do so much and for so long. It was
only in musketry that we were far behind the Regular Army, simply
because we had to wait for months for the rifles we would eventually
use.

    J. B. Priestley

It is not good when people no longer believe in war. Pretty soon
they no longer believe in many other things which they absolutely
must believe in if they are to be decent men.

    Thomas Mann

Only the victory of Germany will guarantee the peace of Europe.

    Thomas Mann

Don't *grouse*. However irksome the duty, remember that others
have been put to the same inconvenience – and worse – scores of
times before. Try to do what you have to do cheerfully. It is all in a
day's work.

Don't lose your temper at games. It is painful both to the other players and to the onlookers, and invariably to your disadvantage.

Don't use bad language or deal in strange oaths. The habit is easily acquired, but became bad form shortly after the withdrawal of our Army from Flanders.

> From *The Young Officers 'Don't' or Hints to Youngsters on Joining* by Major-General D. O'Callaghan, C.V.O. (1907) (still being issued in 1914)

You shape like a whore at a christening!

You're slower than the second coming of Christ.

Fix bayonets! Don't look down! You'd soon find the hole if there was a fucking tart on it.

> Sergeant-Majors' clichés

One must first overcome the inner *Schweinehund*.

> Manfred von Richthofen

Honour has come back like a king to earth.

> Rupert Brooke

AUGUST 21

General Samsonov's Russian army invades Germany.

AUGUST 23

The British, under Sir John French, fight in the Battle of Mons. Joffre the French Commander-in-Chief, orders a retreat.

In 1914, when Joffre and French were Commanders-in-Chief, many people were truly delighted that each name contained six letters and that the last three of the first name and the first three of the second were identical.

> E. M. W. Tillyard

My old man's a dustman,
He fought at the Battle of Mons,
He killed ten thousand Germans
With only a couple of bombs.
One lay here, one lay there, one lay round the corner,
And one poor sod with his leg hanging off
Was crying out for water.

Madame, your beer's no bon,
Madame, your beer's no bon.
Your pomme de terre frits,
They give us the squits,
Madame, your beer's no bon.

Japan joins the Allies.

AUGUST 26–31

The Eastern Front

Russians defeated at Tannenberg by Hindenburg, Ludendorff and Hoffmann.

While from the German bivouacs scattered among the forest rose the hymn of the Battle of Leuthon, Samsonov [commander of the Russian 2nd Army] accompanied by five staff officers hastened on foot through the darkness toward the Russian frontier. At length, exhausted, he began to lag and ultimately disappeared. What his fate was is unknown, but it is believed that he shot himself.

> J. F. C. Fuller

I beg most humbly to report to your Majesty that the ring round the larger part of the Russian Army was closed yesterday. The 13th, 15th, and 18th Army Corps have been destroyed. We have already taken more than 60,000 prisoners, among them the Corps Commanders of the 13th and 15th Corps. The guns are still in the forests and are now being brought in. The booty is immense . . .

> General Paul von Hindenburg

AUGUST 28

They are beginning to face the possibility of a siege of Paris, in which case we might be cut off. If that should happen, endure it with courage, for our personal desires are nothing in comparison with the great struggle that is now under way.

Marie Curie, *to her daughter Irene*

I went to put on my uniform which my father wanted to see. The Infantry still wore blue tunics and red trousers. Mine had been got out of a wardrobe the day before and smelled of camphor. The puttees felt uncomfortable on my legs. My father looked me over with the severity of an old soldier. 'You must polish up your buttons.' He was sad at my leaving but full of hope for France and happy to see a son of his taking part in the war of revenge of which he had dreamed ever since 1871.

André Maurois

It's a fearful nuisance, this war, I think the perfect place is at the Front – we'll starve or die of suspense anywhere else . . .

By the time you get this the war will have only just begun, I'm afraid. Europe will have just stepped into its bath of blood. I will be waiting with beautiful drying towels of painted canvas and precious ointments to smear and heal the soul; and lovely music and poems. But I really hope to have a nice lot of pictures and poems by the time all is settled again, and Europe is repenting of her savageries.

Isaac Rosenberg, *to Edward Marsh*

Herbert bicycled in from Cambridge one day with the evening paper announcing the fall of Namur. My brothers and I were delighted at the speed with which it had fallen because the prolonged defence of Liège had threatened a speedy determination of the war. As long as the war continued, we might one day be involved, and the world of Henty seemed to come a little nearer. Perhaps there would be an invasion, as in William Le Queux's famous documentary novel, and Berkhamsted Common, I believed, would be ideal for the exploits of one young *franc-tireur*. Indeed, there were dramatic incidents even in Berkhamsted. A German master was denounced to my father as a spy because he had been seen under the railway bridge without a hat, a dachshund was stoned in the High Street, and once my uncle Eppy was summoned at night to the police station and asked to lend his motor car to help block the Great North Road down which a German armoured car was said to be advancing towards London.

                    Graham Greene

AUGUST 31

The Western Front

FROM THE LITTLE CAR

On the 31st day of August in the year 1914
I left Deauville shortly before midnight
In Rouveyre's little car

Including his chauffeur there were three of us

We said goodbye to a whole epoch
Furious giants were looming over Europe
The eagles were leaving their eyries expecting the sun
Voracious fishes were swimming up from the abysses
Nations were rushing together to know each other through and
    through
The dead were trembling with fear in their dark dwellings

                    Apollinaire

SEPTEMBER

The Austrian Front

To horse! The bugle gave the signal. Out again, to war! The dashing cavalry – to war! First of all we attended Mass, which was celebrated at a field-altar. Then, when the salute was fired, the horses became restive and swords leapt from their scabbards like a single flash of lightning. Officers to the front! Silence. My horse stood two paces ahead of my troop, dead straight in line with the other cadets. I was lucky; my horse stood as quiet as a statue, man and mount cast in bronze. The regiment ceased to breathe. The Prussian Field-Marshal von Mackensen, the chin-strap of his shako, the shako of the Death's-Head Hussars, martially pushed up on his chin, his dolman – bordered with leopard skin – decoratively flung back over one shoulder, and mounted on his high-bred Arab dapple-grey, came riding along our lines there on parade, his entourage following him. Mackensen himself gave me an order – and I, lost in admiration of the splendid spectacle, which reminded me of my boyish enthusiasm for Napoleon and his generals, did not hear it properly and promptly forgot it. They said he always had a French chef with him, for he liked to give magnificent dinners in his temporary headquarters, which was also the headquarters of our own troops since we had suffered our great strategic set back. Beside the Imperial German helmets, eagle-crowned, gold and silver braid, glittering orders and stars, the Imperial-Royal Austro-Hungarian generals held their own with the gleaming blue plumes in their cocked hats. On either side the staff officers could be recognized by the red stripes on their trousers. I had to take a message to the staff mess, where the table seemed, so far as I could see, to be plentifully provided and where, modestly separate from that of the loftier war-lords, there was also a table for the chaplains. The latter all wore black, most of them with a large cross bobbing on their breast. The war of religion between the seven confessions represented in our army, the Gospels' message of love for one's neighbour, seemed to be settled over the wine and the not entirely dry bread for the shepherds of souls – which set my mind at rest. An equal, a peer among his peers, there was the rabbi among them too, with his own personal reasons for rejoicing. The German Supreme Command had sent a special call to Jewry to make common cause with the Germans. 'To my beloved Israelites!' Ah, the darling man, General Ludendorff! A heart of gold! What goodness came gushing forth from the source of German strength and joy!

Oskar Kokoshka

SEPTEMBER 3

CITIZENS OF PARIS

The Members of the Republican Government have left Paris: they will give fresh impetus to National Defence.
I have been empowered to defend Paris against the invader.
This task I shall carry out to the end.

Gallieni, Military Governor of Paris

SEPTEMBER 6

Opening of the Battle of the Marne.

SEPTEMBER 7

This day is the decisive one. One whole army, stretching from Paris to upper Alsace, has been fighting in a battle since yesterday. If I had to give my life today to gain victory, I would relinquish it with rapture, as thousands of our comrades in arms have already done. What rivers of blood have flowed, what nameless sorrow has overwhelmed the countless innocents whose houses and farms have been burnt down and destroyed – I am often overcome by a sense of horror when I think of it, and I have the feeling that I may be called to account for all these ghastly disasters.

General Count von Moltke, *to his wife*

The German defeat saves Paris. The Germans retreat to the Aisne.

We have lost the war. It will go on for a long time but it is already lost.

Crown Prince Wilhelm

SEPTEMBER 8

The terrible difficulty of our situation often stands like a black wall in front of me, seeming quite impenetrable.

General Count von Moltke

Von Moltke had been selected by the Kaiser because he imagined that his name would have a terrifying effect on neighbouring countries. In this we discover the key which unlocks the whole system of the German Higher Command, which was as royally rotten as the French was politically corrupt. After 1870, as after 1763, the German army rested on its laurels . . . Von Moltke in 1914, was 68 years old, out-of-date, and soused in the staff ideas of his uncle, which he copied slavishly.

J. F. C. Fuller

SEPTEMBER 10

A violent propaganda campaign was urged on all [private] schools to show the extent of German guilt.

'Brave little Belgium,' read the posters. 'Nearly 2,000 years ago Julius Caesar wrote, "the bravest of all the Gauls are the Belgians". He knew, he had fought against them.'

'A few years ago Belgian oarsmen astonished the rowing world by winning at Henley Regatta the "Grand Challenge", the blue ribbon of all fresh-water rowing.'

'And in these recent weeks the brave little nation, nerved by the love of liberty, held up for many long and priceless days, under the steel cupolas of the Liège forts and elsewhere, the might of Germany, and has won for herself the immortal glory which belongs to a people who prefer freedom to ease, to security, even to life itself.'

'Truly God has chosen the weak things of the world to confound the things that are mighty.'

Members [of the Independent Association of Preparatory Schools] reported: 'that boys had not returned to school after the summer holidays, school fees were not being paid, boys already entered did not come, and that owing to fears of air-raids boys were being withdrawn and parents disclaiming liability for fees.'

      Arthur Harrison

Kaiser Bill went up the hill
To see the British Army,
General French jumped out of a trench
And made the cows go barmy.

      Children's Song

At long last the day came when we left Munich on war service. For the first time I saw the Rhine, as we journeyed westwards to stand guard before that historic German river against its traditional and grasping enemy. As the first soft rays of the morning sun broke through the light mist and disclosed to us the Niederwald statue, with one accord the whole troop train broke into the strains of *Die Wacht am Rhein*. I then felt as if my heart could not retain its spirit.

      Adolf Hitler

SEPTEMBER 12

> Retreat of Germans
> > On Extreme Left of
> > > The Allies Continues.

Despatches from London and Bordeaux say that Anglo-French are
Rapidly Driving Back *Right* Wing of Invaders.

Centre Situation Unchanged.

> *Christian Science Monitor*, Boston

> German General
> > Reports Defeat
> > > Near the Marne.

> *Christian Science Monitor*, Boston

King Peter [of Serbia] hobbled up to some troops that were waver-
ing under artillery fire to which their army had no answer, and said
to them, after the manner of a Homeric general, 'Heroes, you have
taken two oaths, one to me, your king, and one to your country.
From the first I release you, from the second no man can release
you. But if you decide to return to your homes, and if we should be
victorious, you shall not be made to suffer.'

> Rebecca West

SEPTEMBER 13

In the Battle of the Aisne the Battalion was to acquire a Victoria
Cross. Private George Wilson, former Edinburgh newspaper seller,
won the supreme award for a one-man charge on a German
machine-gun section: a marksman of some repute, he shot the
officer in command and three of the crew with four slow and
deliberate shots from his rifle, and despatched the remaining two
with his bayonet.

> Tim Carew

SEPTEMBER 14

It may be – I do not know and I do not profess to understand – that
this is the great Audit of the Universe, that the Supreme Being has

ordered the nations of the earth to decide who is to lead in the van of human progress. If the British Empire resolves to fight the Battle cleanly, to look upon it as Something More than an ordinary war, we shall realise that it has not been in vain, and We, the British Empire, as the Chosen Leaders of the World, shall travel along the road of Human Destiny and Progress, at the end of which we shall see the patient figure of the Prince of Peace pointing to the Star of Bethlehem which leads us on to God.

Horatio Bottomley, at the London Opera House

SEPTEMBER 19

We have been living in a sheltered valley for generations. We have been too comfortable, too indulgent, many perhaps too selfish. And the stern hand of fate has scourged us to an elevation where we can see the great everlasting things that matter for a nation; the great peaks of honour we had forgotten – duty and patriotism, clad in glittering white, the great pinnacle of sacrifice pointing like a rugged finger to heaven.

David Lloyd George

AT THE EASTERN FRONT

Like the wild organs of winter storms
Is a people's dark wrath,
The crimson wave of the battle,
Of leafless stars.

With broken brows, with silver arms,
To dying soldiers waves the night.
In the shades of the autumnal ash tree
Sigh the spirits of the slain.

Thorny wilderness strangles the town.
From bloodstained steps the moon
Harries the frightened women.
Wild wolves have broken through the gate.

Georg Trakl

Dying Values

The historian, Henri Pirenne . . . this Belgian was torn away from his home and his university by the invading Germans: his rights and immunity as a non-combatant and a scholar were violated and he was sent to a concentration camp. That single act of violence was enough to awaken the protest throughout the world: Scandinavian scholars, in the shadow of German might, protested as valiantly as the Americans; and finally, in response to a combined appeal from the Pope and the President of the United States, Pirenne was given decent conditions of lodgings by himself, in a German village, and an opportunity to work on a book. Respect for human liberty was still strong enough to command the actions of an autocratic enemy government.

Lewis Mumford

SEPTEMBER 23

Great Allied Triumph; Foe's Right Crushed.
Deadly German Sea-Victory Stuns England.

2 German Submarines
    Sunk in Daring Attack
        On 3 British Cruisers

All England tonight is shaken by the news of the great naval disaster in the North Sea when five German Submarines sank three British Cruisers . . .

A dispatch from the front in France . . . says:
'The German right, commanded by General von Kluck, has been turned by the allies between Peronne and Saint Quentin on the ninth day of the great battle of the Aisne.
    Nine miles of trenches are filled with the dead.'

Los Angeles Examiner

SEPTEMBER 27

I think one must resist, if it comes to a push. But I admit it's a difficult question. One solution is to go and live in the United States of America. As for our personal position, it seems to me quite sound and coherent. We're all far too weak physically to be of any use at all. If we weren't we'd still be too intelligent to be thrown away in some really not essential expedition, and our proper place would be the National Reserve. I suppose God has put us on an island, and Winston has given us a navy, and it would be absurd to neglect the advantages – which I consider exactly to apply to able-bodied intellectuals.

On the whole I don't care much about England's being victorious (apart from personal questions) – but I should object to France being crushed. Mightn't it be a good plan to become a Frenchman?

> Lytton Strachey, *to James Strachey*

SEPTEMBER 29

'British Greed Would Drag U.S. INTO WAR,' German View.
   Noted Teuton Warns
      America of Dangers
         If Kaiser is Beaten.

Dr Bernhard Dernburg, Former Secretary
Of State for the German colonies, says
that England will attempt to dictate to
the entire World if the Allies Win War.

British imperialism has gained enormously. It has gobbled up whatever has been worth having in the World. You cannot expect they will sit still in the future when they need something.

I put this before the American public very seriously. If Great Britain gets the enormous addition to its power she will use it. Her theory has always been to fight to the next best man. Who that will be after Germany is crushed nobody can have any great doubt.

So America has the greatest interest in having a strong central power in Europe. That is the only way she can keep out of the general struggle . . .

> *Los Angeles Examiner*

I have six sons fighting . . . I did all in my power to keep peace, but your enemies would not have peace and now we will have to crush them to the ground.

> Wilhelm II, *to Danish pastor*

I adore war. It's like a big picnic without the objectlessness of a picnic. I've never been so well or happy. No one grumbles at one for being dirty.

Julian Grenfell, killed May 26, 1915

Julian's love of war he himself explained in terms of his being allowed to be dirty: he meant this physically, but psychologically it was relevant too. For the first time a generation brought up to be clean and bright and obedient could, without guilt, be fierce and babyish and vile . . . Julian's men felt the 'reality' of war too: this curse was not just aristocratic. War was a freedom both from society and from social fantasies: it was the one area in which there were standards of excellence other than those of snobbishness, bitchiness and money.

Nicholas Mosley

THE CIVILIAN

On a morning in late October 1914 a woman walked along Whitehall with determined steps and positioned herself three feet away from the mounted Household Cavalry sentry at the entrance to Horse Guards Parade. The sentry eyed her out of the corner of his eye without any particular interest: in his five years' service he had grown used to admirers; it was all part of the day's work.

But this particular lady was no admirer of the Household Cavalry. She was a female of waspish tongue and nature; a fervid patriot, who distributed white feathers to men of military age wearing civilian clothes. The fact that once, later in the war, she presented one to a recipient of the Victoria Cross deterred her not at all – the country's young men had to be made aware of their responsibility to King and Country. To add emphasis to this admirable theory, she demanded in ringing tones of the sentry why he was not with a fighting regiment.

The sentry stared straight in front of him, but his lips under his moustache just perceptibly moved. He was, in fact, prophesying such a fearful fate for the militant lady that had she heard him she would have swooned there and then. As it was, she brandished her umbrella at the sentry and strode off to sow the seeds of patriotism elsewhere.

Tim Carew

Hell hath no fury like a noncombatant.

C. E. Montague

OCTOBER 29

Turkey joins the Central Powers.

When Turkey closed the Straits to Russia in 1914, she cut her off from world trade and drove her, whether she would or no, to the policy of 'socialism in a single country'. In the perspective of history, Bolshevism may well appear as nothing more than the economic consequences of the closing of the Straits.

A. J. P. Taylor

NOVEMBER

Don't you think that the chance for the Jewish people is now within the limits of discussion at least? I realize, of course, that we cannot 'claim' anything, we are much too atomized for that; but we can reasonably say that should Palestine fall within the British sphere of influence, and should Britain encourage a Jewish settlement there, as a British dependency, we could have in twenty or thirty years a million Jews out there, perhaps more, they would develop the country, bring back civilization to it and form a very effective guard for the Suez Canal.

Chaim Weizmann, *to C. P. Scott*

NOVEMBER 3

Von Moltke is replaced by Falkenhayn.

He lived on until 1916; he saw the war pass beyond the scope of mere armies, however big. People's war, with hate and fear instead of policy, and total national wealth as an instrument, had been born out of his failure to wield Germany's sword in a single killing stroke.

Corelli Barnett

NOVEMBER 6

A Letter from Munich

Everything visible has again been thrown into the tumultuous abyss to be melted down. The Past is relinquished, the Future shudders,

the Present lacks foundations, but the hearts, should not they have
the power to soar and hover among the mighty clouds? At the start
of August I was flayed by the apparition of War, of the War
God . . . now the war has long become invisible to me. A visiting
spectre, no more a god but a god's being released over the peoples.
All that is left now is for the soul to endure it, agony and catastrophe
are perhaps no more common than before, only more real, more
active, more visible. For the misery in which humanity has daily
existed since time began cannot really be increased by any event.
But there may yet be a development in our understanding of the
unspeakable wretchedness of our human life and perhaps all this is
leading us to it; so much calamity – as though new dawns were
seeking distance and space for their unfolding.

> Rainer Maria Rilke, *to Elizabeth and Karl von der Heydt*

NOVEMBER 10

Lord Kitchener, Mr Asquith, and Mr Churchill on the WAR.

> War Speeches At
>   Lord Mayor's
>   Banquet
>
> Empire Fighting for Its
>   Existence.
>
> 1,250,000 Training
>
> Navy's Pressure: "The
>   Doom of Germany."

Lord Kitchener: 'I have no complaint whatever to make about the
response to my appeals for men. But I shall want more men and still
more, until the enemy is crushed . . . The men at the Front are
doing splendidly.'

> *Daily Graphic*, London

NOVEMBER 10–18

First Battle of Ypres – 'Wipers'.

Far, far from Wipers I long to be,
Where German snipers can't snipe at me.
Damp is my dug-out,
Cold are my feet,
Waiting for the whizz-bangs
To send me to sleep.

I had a comrade,
None better could you find,
The Drum called us to battle,
He marched by my side.

                    German Marching Song

You take the high road
And I'll take the duck-boards
And I'll be at Wipers before you,
Both me and Major Hand
We will inspect the band
On the bonny, bonny banks of Hill Sixty.

REMORSE

Lost in the swamp and welter of the pit,
He flounders off the duck-boards; only he knows
Each flash and spouting crash, – each instant lit
When gloom reveals the streaming rain. He goes
Heavily, blindly on. And, while he blunders,
'Could anything be worse than this?' – he wonders,
Remembering how he saw those Germans run,
Screaming for mercy among the stumps of trees:
Green-faced, they dodged and darted: there was one
Livid with terror, clutching at his knees . . .
Our chaps were sticking 'em like pigs . . . 'O hell!'
He thought – 'there's things in war one dare not tell
Poor father sitting safe at home, who reads
of dying heroes and their deathless deeds.'

                    Siegfried Sassoon

NOVEMBER 27

Battleship Blown Up With Great Loss of Life at Sheerness.

H.M.S. Bulwark Rent
    Asunder by Explosion
of Internal Magazine

Between 700 and 800
    Men have perished.

Daily Mirror, London

DECEMBER 17

*The German navy bombards Scarborough, Hartlepool and Whitby,
the first shells to fall on Great Britain.*

CHRISTMAS DAY

Scots and Huns were fraternizing in the most genuine possible
manner. Every sort of souvenir was exchanged, addresses given and
received, photos of families shown, etc. One of our fellows offered a
German a cigarette; the German said, 'Virginian?' Our fellow said,
'Aye, straight-cut:' the German said, 'No thanks, I only smoke
Turkish!' . . . It gave us all a good laugh. A German NCO with the
Iron Cross – gained, he told me, for conspicuous skill in sniping –
started his fellows off on some marching tune. When they had done
I set the note for *The Boys of Bonnie Scotland where the heather and
the blue bells grow,* and so we went on, singing everything from
Good King Wenceslaus down to the ordinary Tommies' song, and
ended up with *Auld Lang Syne,* which we all, English, Scots, Irish,
Prussians, Württembergers, etc, joined in.

                Captain Sir Edward Hulse

DECEMBER 30

Flanders

On New Year's Eve, we exchanged the time having agreed to fire
some shots at midnight. The night was cold. We sang, they applauded (our lines were only some two hundred feet apart). We

played the mouth organ, they sang to our music, and then we
applauded. I called over to ask whether they had some musical
instruments, on which they produced a set of bagpipes (they were a
Scots Guards regiment, with short kilts and bare legs). They played
their poetic tunes and sang. At midnight both sides fired shots in the
air. Our artillery too fired a few rounds; I do not know their target:
tracer bullets, usually so lethal, soared like harmless fireworks. Men
were waving torches and cheering. We had prepared grog and
drank a toast to Kaiser Wilhelm and the New Year.

> German Soldier

THE OLD HOUSES OF FLANDERS

The old houses of Flanders,
They watch by the high cathedrals;
They overtop the high town-halls;
They have eyes, mournful, tolerant, and sardonic, for the ways of
    men
In the high, white, tiled gables.

The rain and the night have settled down on Flanders;
It is all wet darkness; you can see nothing.
Then those old eyes, mournful, tolerant, and sardonic,
Look at great, sudden, red lights,
Look upon the shades of the cathedrals;
And the golden rods of the illuminated rain
For a second . . .

And those old eyes,
Very old eyes that have watched the ways of men for generations,
Close for ever.
The high, white shoulders of the gables
Slouch together for a consultation,
Slant drunkenly over in the lee of the flaming cathedrals.

They are no more, the old houses of Flanders.

> Ford Madox Ford

The Kaiser, Champion of Kultur

Here is cultured William, see!
An enlightened soul was he.
He killed the doves and broke the chairs,
And threw the grey cat down the stairs,
And, oh! far worse than all beside,
He hurt his Mary till she cried.
Such stores of 'Kultur' Will possessed,
That he'd to spare for all the rest
(Particularly dark Louvain
Sunk in the barbarous inane),
And he vowed the world should be
Just as full of it as he.
Helped by Mr Krupp of Essen,
Everyone should learn the lesson,
Spread by missionary Huns
Well equipped with bombs and guns.

       E. V. Lucas

1915

Here we dead lie because we did not choose
   To live and shame the land from which we sprung.
Life, to be sure, is nothing much to lose,
   But young men think it is, and we were young.

    A. E. Housman

The War is going to be my opportunity.

    Horatio Bottomley

The Russians lose one million men on the Eastern Front. The Turks deport 1,750,000 Armenians to Mesopotamian deserts. 600,000 die, another 600,000 vanish. The British, Australians and New Zealanders lose 252,000 at the Dardanelles between April and December.

Trench war continues in the West with the battles of Neuve Chapelle and Loos. Germany pushes into Russian Poland, Galicia and Lithuania, inflicting hideous losses on the courageous but ill-equipped Tsarist armies. Serbia and most of Belgium are overrun.

The British blockade was angering neutrals, but anti-German feelings were growing in America, which applauded such films as The Kaiser, Beast of Berlin, *and in which Erich von Stroheim quickly became famous as the brutal Prussian officer, 'the man you love to hate'.*

The Western Front – trenches, barbed wire and fortified lines – was now firmly established from the Flanders shores to Switzerland, shifting with local fortunes but remaining virtually unbroken until the last weeks, despite terrifying attempts on both sides to break through and deliver a knock-out. The Eastern Front was more fluid, and despite two courageous Russian offensives in Poland, always tending to the advantage of Germany and Austro-Hungary, already her virtual satellite. With Turkey and Bulgaria joining the Central Powers, and Italy the Allies, and stalemate in the West, 1915 saw Anglo-French schemes to win a final victory not on the Western Front but in Turkey and the Balkans.

A diversionary allied attack on Turkey, at the Dardanelles, would relieve the Russians in the Caucasus, and subdue incipient Russian unrest, while deflecting the war from the stalemate on the Western Front.

I don't know what is to be done. This isn't war.

>   Lord Kitchener

Between the battle of Tannenberg in August 1914 and Riga in September 1917, Germany conquered most of Poland and much of European Russia, extinguished the independent Baltic states, humiliated Italy and reduced Austria to clientage. It was as if Frederick the Great and Moltke the Elder had been telescoped into four years.

>   John Keegan

I know the truth – give up all other truths!
No need for people anywhere on earth to struggle.
Look – it is evening, look, it is nearly night:
What do you speak of, poets, lovers, generals?

The wind is level now, the earth is wet with dew,
The storm of stars in the sky will turn to quiet.
And soon all of us will sleep under the earth, we
Who never let each other sleep above it.

>   Marina Tsvetayeva

JANUARY

The Zeppelins have been to Sandringham, but the King and Queen had left a few hours earlier. No panic; people are reconciled to the fact that these visits will be repeated, and the effect they are having is no greater than that of a railway accident. It is a mistake to think that the morale of this country can be subdued. While this lasts, people are merely laying bets for and against Zeppelins.

> ex-Empress Eugénie, *to the Duke of Alba*

France's war against Prussia in 1870, led by Eugénie's husband, Napoleon III, led to overwhelming and humiliating French defeat, the loss of Alsace-Lorraine, an unending desire for revenge and, in Versailles itself, the proclamation of the German Empire.

During the war, Britain suffered 111 air raids, with 1413 dead. Germany lost 720 over Britain.

JANUARY 9

Bavarian Progress

The greater part of the devilry in the Vosges seems to have been the work of Bavarians. At Gerbéviller they proceeded to avenge their losses on the civilian population. They burst into the houses, shooting, stabbing, and capturing the inhabitants – sparing neither age nor sex – and burning and sacking the houses. A woman aged 78 was shot and her body afterwards shamefully profaned.

> Official French report on German atrocities

With pride and joy I look upon the brave Bavarian army, which has confirmed its ancient renown and in glorious battles has proved itself a worthy member of the German army. My confidence is immutable that the overwhelming defeat of our enemies will enable me to lead my people forward on the road to economic and cultural development.

> King Ludwig III of Bavaria

Beneath God's smiling sun
The gentlest women in the world
Shall overthrow the Hun.

> Recruiting Poster for the Women's Land Army

The trouble with Germans is not that they fire shells, but that they engrave them with quotations from Kant.

> Karl Kraus

JANUARY 14

At the Albert Hall

Why is the red blood flowing – why do the women weep?
Why have our dear, long-lost brothers gone to their long, last sleep?
Come, comrade, come – consider: let's look things in the face,
For this war is more than a war, mate, it's a call to the human race.
Listen! Don't you hear it, ringing through the land?
Prepare and be ye ready, my Audit is at hand!
How do your books to mine stand, are all the entries made?
Is anything unsettled, are all the first debts paid?
The Audit will be searching – and this will be the best –
What have you done for England, have we given of our best?
And when the Audit's finished, what are you going to do?
And you, behind the counter, and you – and you – and you?

            Horatio Bottomley

Discipline

Discipline in the old British army was severe, if not occasionally
actually brutal. True, the soldier no longer feared the lash, the
normal deterrent prior to 1881, when flogging was abolished. But
dirty cavalrymen were forcibly scrubbed in horse troughs in icy
water with hand scrubbers; idle drummer boys ran the risk of six of
the best from the drum-major on the bare rump; misdemeanours
were sometimes corrected by senior N.C.O.s without any reference
to company office; soldiers sentenced to a spell in detention barracks rarely went back to sample it a second time. There was the
possibility of Field Punishment Number One – the malefactor was
tied by hands and feet to a gunwheel in an attitude of crucifixion –
and even the firing squad for cowardice or desertion in the face of
the enemy.

            Tim Carew

I don't want to join the bloody Army,
I don't want to go unto the War,
I want no more to roam,
I'd rather stay at home
Living on the earnings of a whore.

I, Madam, am the Civilization they are fighting for.

> Philip Guedalla

The Dardanelles

In an effort to smash the paralysis of trench warfare on the Western Front, and to succour the Russians, fast weakening after gigantic losses, the First Lord of the Admiralty, Winston Churchill, against much opposition, persistently urged attacking Turkey, the back door of the Central Powers, at the Dardanelles, the Straits of Gallipoli, near the site of ancient Troy. Here, he argued, the end could be brought to a war already prolonged to shocking length. Nearly half a million British and French troops landed. Had they succeeded, they would have secured vital food supplies to Russia and released her southern armies; by enabling the capture of Constantinople they would have awed the entire Islamic world; German influence in south-east Europe would have been eliminated, thus preventing Bulgarian entry into the war on her side. The difficulties were immense, but such prizes were so great as to be virtually unlimited. The end of the Great War in 1915 might well have prevented the Bolshevik revolution, and certainly the accession of Adolf Hitler.

In 1915, soon after I left Oxford for London to do war-work there, I was sent on some errand to the War Office in Whitehall. As I was entering, I saw, facing me, a notice-board on which there was posted a list of officers recently reported killed, and, at the same moment, two women passed me. They had just read on the board the announcement of a death. One of the two was weeping bitterly; the other was talking rapidly and emphatically – as if her hurrying words could overtake and perhaps retrieve the cruel loss that had been suffered by her companion. I can see those two poor women's faces as clearly today in my mind's eye as, on that day, I saw them in the life. While I still have life and strength, I must work for the abolition of the wicked institution that was the cause of that terrible sorrow.

> Arnold Toynbee

FEBRUARY 4

Germany announces a submarine blockade of Britain, to include neutrals.

Nearly every red-blooded human boy has had war, in some shape or
form for his first love; if his blood has remained red and he has kept
some of his boyishness in after life, that first love will never have
been forgotten. No one could really forget those wonderful lead
cavalry soldiers; the horses were as sleek and prancing as though
they had never left the parade-ground, and the uniforms were
correspondingly spick and span, but the amount of campaigning
and fighting they got through was prodigious. There are other
unforgettable memories for those who had brothers to play with and
fight with, of sieges and ambushes and pitched encounters, of the
slaying of an entire garrison without quarter, or of chivalrous,
punctilious courtesy to a defeated enemy. Then there was the slow
unfolding of the long romance of actual war, particularly of European war, ghastly, devastating, heartrending in its effect, and yet
somehow captivating to the imagination. The Thirty Years' War,
was one of the most hideously cruel wars ever waged, but, in
conjunction with the subsequent campaigns of the Great Louis, it
throws a glamour over the scene of the present struggle. The thrill
that those far-off things call forth in us may be ethically indefen-
sible, but it comes in the first place from something too deep to be
driven out; the magic region of the Low Countries is beckoning to us
again, as it beckoned to our forefathers, who went campaigning
there almost from force of habit.

>   Saki

In Germany, a Woman Writes to her Son, a Great Novelist and Author of 'The Blue Angel'

My dear, good Heinrich, do not attack your fatherland for now
defending itself with *all its strength* – it desired only to show loyalty
to its own allies and was pushed into this struggle which may kill it –
or so the enemy wishes. Some distinguished diplomats had seen the
war coming even *earlier* because Germany was becoming too big
and powerful; hence the Allied Entente. We would have been good
friends to them perhaps, if, like Switzerland, Denmark, Holland or
Scandinavia, we had been willing to stay neutral – but always in
fear of the more powerful. No, it would be agreeable now if the
entire world belonged to the Germanic peoples – and if England
mends her ways she could join us.

>   Julia Mann, *to Heinrich Mann*

MARCH 10–12

Battle of Neuve-Chapelle. 11,000 British and Italian casualties.

We licked 'em on the Marne
And whacked 'em on the Aisne,
We gave 'em hell at Neuve Chapelle
And we'll bloody well do it again.

MARCH 23

The Kiplings, neither of them, look so well as they did at Kessing-land. He is greyer than I am now and he says his stomach has shrunk, making him seem smaller. I expect that anxiety about the war is responsible. Their boy John, who is not yet eighteen, is an officer in the Irish Guards and one can see that they are terrified lest he should be sent to the Front and killed, as has happened to nearly all the young men they knew.

> H. Rider Haggard

All men must die but it is given to few to die for their country.

> Epitaph, 1915, to Colonel Breakspear, in Henley Church

British and Imperial dead in the Great War totalled some 1,900,000.

APRIL 1

One of our men flew over the Lille aerodrome and dropped a football. All the Germans rushed for cover, imagining that a bomb was coming down, but when, after many enormous rebounds, the ball at length came to rest, they approached it cautiously, and on it they read:

'April Fool! Gott Strafe England!'

> Captain P. A. Thompson

First Day in a Berlin Prison

They took me in the 'Black Maria', but that didn't disturb me unduly: I had already experienced it once in Warsaw. The situation was so strikingly similar that it started a train of humorous thoughts. There was one difference, though: the Russian gendarmes treated me with great respect as 'a political', whereas the Berlin police said they didn't care a snap of the finger what I was, and thrust me in with the rest of my new 'colleagues' without further ceremony. Ah well, that's a matter of minor importance, and life has to be taken with serenity and a grain of humour. You mustn't get exaggerated ideas about my heroism, though and I'll admit that when I had to undress and submit to a bodily examination for the second time that day the humiliation almost reduced me to tears. Of course, I was furious with myself at such weakness, and I still am when I think of it. But the first night the thing that made a deeper impression on me than the fact that I was once again in a prison cell, snatched from the land of the free, was – Guess what it was? That I had to go to sleep without a night-dress and without being able to comb my hair. And to display my classical education: do you remember the first scene in Schiller's 'Mary Stuart'? Mary's trinkets are taken from her, and Lady Kennedy observes sadly: 'To lose life's little gauds is harder than to brave great trials.' Look it up; Schiller puts it rather better than I do. But heavens! where are my errant thoughts leading me? Gott strafe England! And forgive me that I compare myself to an English Queen.

Rosa Luxemburg

APRIL 15

This night there was an air-raid on Southwold, Lowestoft etc., a Zeppelin passed over the town about 20 to 12 without dropping bombs and either this or another come back from London an hour later and we were awoken by a terrific explosion and immediately heard the loud whirring of the engines apparently over the west part of the Town, very quickly another explosion occurred and shook the whole place . . . Some amusing yarns went about, one of our fishermen was said to have looked out of his window and seen the Zeppelin so close that he was going to knock it down with a stick only his wife said, 'For God's sake don't do that, think of the children.' Another of an old lady who was a bit of a midwife at Reydon outside whose garden a bomb was dropped making a hole 6 feet deep, she and the old man were in bed and she said, 'Well, if they do want me in a hurry they needn't have knocked all the windows in,' and they picked glass out of the old boy's beard for a week after.

Ernest Read Cooper

APRIL 22

Germans pioneer poison gas at the Second Battle of Ypres.

It is with a feeling of loathing that the chronicler turns to narrate the next episode of the war, in which the Germans, foiled in fair fighting, stole away a few miles of ground by the arts of the murderer. So long as military history is written, the poisoning [gas attack] of Langemarck will be recorded as an incident by which warfare was degraded, and a great army, which had been long honoured as the finest fighting force in the world, became in a single day an object of horror and contempt.

Sir Arthur Conan Doyle

Gas! GAS! Quick boys! – An ecstasy of fumbling.
Fitting the clumsy helmets just in time;
But someone still was yelling out and stumbling;
And flound'ring like a man in fire or lime . . .
Dim, through the misty panes and thick green light,
As under a green sea, I saw him drowning.

In all my dreams, before my helpless sight,
He plunges at me, guttering, choking, drowning.

Wilfred Owen

The flowers left thick at nightfall in the wood
This Eastertide call into mind the men,
Now far from home, who, with their sweethearts, should
Have gathered them and will never do again.

Edward Thomas

APRIL 26

To detach Italy from her pledge to the Central Powers, the Allies sign the secret Treaty of London, promising her Trieste, the Trentino, the German Tyrol.

APRIL 23

Death of Rupert Brooke, in the Aegean

A voice had become audible, a note had been struck, more true, more thrilling, more able to do justice to the nobility of our youth in arms engaged in this present war than any other – more able to express their thoughts of self-surrender, and with a power to carry comfort to those who watch them so intently from afar. The voice has been swiftly stilled. Only the echoes and the memory remain: but they will linger.

                    Winston Churchill

I have been fighting for two months and I can now gauge the intensity of life . . . this war is a great remedy. In the individual it kills arrogance, self-esteem, pride. It takes away from the masses numbers upon numbers of unimportant units, whose economic activities become noxious as the recent trades crises have shown us.

                    Henri Gaudier-Brzeska, *to P. Wyndham Lewis*

I am feeling the weight of the war much more since I came back here – one is made terribly aware of the waste when one is here. And Rupert Brooke's death brought it home to me. It is deadly to be here now, with all the usual life stopped. There will be other generations – yet I keep fearing that something of civilization will be lost for good, as something was lost when Greece perished in just this way. Strange how one values civilization – more than all one's friends or anything – the slow achievement of men emerging from the brute – it seems the ultimate thing one lives for. I don't live for human happiness, but for some kind of struggling emergence of mind. And here, at most times, that is being helped on – and what has been done is given to new generations, who travel on from where we have stopped. And now it is all arrested, and no one knows if it will start again at anything like the point where it stopped. And all the elderly apostates are overjoyed.

                    Bertrand Russell, *to Ottoline Morrell*

APRIL 29

A deposition by Captain Bertram, 8th Canadian Battalion, was carefully taken down by Lieut. McNee. Captain Bertram was then in the Clearing Station, suffering from the effects of the gas and from a wound. From a support trench about 600 yards from the German lines he had observed the gas. He saw, first of all, a white smoke rising from the German trenches to a height of about 3 feet. Then, in front of the white smoke appeared a greenish cloud, which drifted along the ground to our trenches, not rising more than about 7 feet from the ground when it reached our first trenches. Men in these trenches were obliged to leave, and a number of them were killed by the effects of the gas.

Daily Chronicle, London

MAY 1

The Germans issue a general warning to those about to travel in the unarmed liner Lusitania, *suggesting that the ship was carrying contraband goods, and was thus liable to be torpedoed.*

MAY 2

Eastern Front

Russians are defeated at Gorlice Tarnow.
Warsaw falls.

MAY 7

The Lusitania, *carrying some 173 tons of rifle ammunition, and accused by the Germans of secreting planes, tanks and guns, is sunk off Ireland by Kapitänleutnant Walther Schweiger, of submarine U-20.*

1198 drowned, out of 1959, including 139 Americans. Fury and outrage erupted in U.S.A. The Germans issued a commemorative medal, inscribed 'Business as Usual' and 'No Contraband Goods'.

As at the sinking of the Titanic, *muddle, inefficiency and absence of passenger drill caused chaos. Many drowned ignorant of how to secure their life jackets. A woman passenger had to take over from an irresolute officer. A lifeboat sailed with only three occupants leaving 'swarms of men, women and children twisting like flies and wrigglers on a lily pond'. A woman gave birth in the water. One man kept afloat on a corpse, a second was sucked into a funnel, then shot out by an underwater explosion, a third found he was lowering himself on to the churning propellers.*

As the liner tilted sharply downwards, the fantail soared a hundred feet into the air, exposing four nearly motionless propellers, as well as the immense sixty-five ton rudder. And, to complete the nightmare, she stopped there, frozen still, her forward motion suddenly and strangely arrested. A long, lingering moan arose and lasted many moments, as though the waters were wailing in horror.

A. A. and Mary Hoehlling

MAY 8

An Extraordinary Success.

Frankfurter Zeitung

MAY 9

Few of Liner's 1273 Victims Found; 120 Americans Dead, Sinking of the Lusitania is Defended by Germany; President Sees Need of Firm and Deliberate Action.

New York Times

There was no acute feeling of fear whilst one was floating in the water. I can remember feeling thankful that I had not been drowned underneath, but had reached the surface safely, and thinking that even if the worst happened there could be nothing unbearable to go through now that my head was above the water. The life-belt held one up in a comfortable sitting position, with one's head lying rather back, as if one were in a hammock. One was a little dazed and rather stupid and vague. I doubt whether any of the people in the water were acutely frightened or in any consciously unbearable agony of mind. When Death is as close as he was then, the sharp agony of fear is not there; the thing is too overwhelming and stunning for that. One has the sense of something taking care of one – I don't mean in the sense of protecting one from death; rather of death itself being a benignant power. At moments I wondered whether the whole thing was perhaps a nightmare from which I would wake, and once, half laughing, I think – I wondered, looking round on the sun and pale blue sky and calm sea, whether I had reached heaven without knowing it – and devoutly hoped I hadn't.

Viscountess Rhondda

MAY 10

Modern history affords no such example of a great nation running amok and calling it military necessity.

New York World

Like a prairie fire indignation and the bitterest resentment is sweeping today over the American continent. The only question is: Will this universal feeling of horror and mingled grief for the innocent victims of the greatest crime in history overwhelm the Government and force it into a declaration of war? Already many voices are raised counselling calmness and presence of mind in face of what is admitted even in Washington to be the gravest crisis which has confronted this country since the outbreak of the Spanish-American War. I have found no one – even the soberest and most experienced judges of the nation's psychology – who dares predict what the outcome will be.

Daily Mail, London, from the New York correspondent

It will have no other effect than to strengthen humanity in waging a relentless war to the death and to round up the enemy as one rounds up a beast escaped from a menagerie which is flinging itself upon every passer-by.

M. Pichon, *Le Petit Journal*, Paris.

The example of America must be a special example. The example of America must be the example not merely of peace because it will not fight, but of peace because peace is the healing and elevating influence of the world and strife is not. There is such a thing as a man being too proud to fight. There is such a thing as a nation being so right that it does not need to convince others by force that it is right.

President Woodrow Wilson

British and American Babies Murdered by the Kaiser.

Daily Mail, London

Given, for the sake of argument, that Germany was wholly responsible for this war – was the state of Europe *before* the war so wonderful, was it so worth preserving that it deserves the title of abominable for having caused its downfall? Was this state of things not greatly more understood to be impossible, unmaintainable, intolerable? The balance of European power – but it was the European impotence. It had been more than once its disgrace; and if this impotence of the Continent, swaying in jealous and strained balance, had for long served one politically outside Europe, yes, anti-Europe world-power, it was nowhere written that the same service should last like that for eternity. Have a little courage, gentlemen, to think clearly.

Thomas Mann, *to the 'Svenska Dagbladet', Stockholm*

May 11

A German Painter Writes from the Western Front

I have such a passion for painting! I am continually working at form. In actually drawing, and in my head, and during my sleep. Sometimes I think I shall go mad, this painful, sensual pleasure tires and torments me so much. Everything else vanishes, time and space, and I think of nothing but how to paint the head of the resurrected Christ against the red constellations in the sky of Judgment Day . . . Or, how shall I paint Minkchen now, with her knees drawn up and her head leaning on her hand, against the yellow wall with her rose, or the sparkling light in the dazzling whiteness of the anti-aircraft shell-bursts in the leaden, sun-drenched sky and the wet, clear-cut, pointed shadows of the houses, or, or – I could write four pages like this if it were not time to go to sleep if I'm ever to paint even the hundredth part of it all.

Max Beckmann

May 13

London's anger at the sinking of the Lusitania burst in a violent storm upon the heads of Germans yesterday. German shops were pillaged by huge and riotous crowds which the police were unable to control and men known to be Germans who showed themselves in public places were very roughly handled. The trouble began at Smithfield, where, in spite of the boycott, a number of German butchers drove up in order to obtain supplies of meat. The meat porters in a body mobbed them and hustled them out of the market.

Another German was chased across Farringdon Street into Holborn by some 300 people. He attained a marvellous speed, and the men perched on the vans and wagons shouted sporting phrases at him. 'Strafe him, boys!' shouted one stout porter, who was unable to join in the chase. The chase was long and stern, but eventually the German found sanctuary on an omnibus in Holborn, and the porters, who were by this time reinforced by every office and errand boy within running distance, returned to the market in a body, singing 'Tipperary'.

The English butchers and slaughterers, now reinforced, proceeded to a German barber's shop a few doors from Aldgate Station, and gave him a thrashing. The shop of an Austrian barber in High Street, Aldgate, was next attacked, the mob setting about the manager, whom they seized and flung into the road. The mob looted the shop, taking possession of razors, shaving-pots, cigarettes and cigars, and practical jokers among the crowd commenced free shaving operations.

Daily Mirror, London

MAY 15

This war for which Germany had prepared conscientiously and out of distrust, but which it would not have wanted if one had not forced it to want it: why did Germany recognize and welcome it when it broke upon us? – because she recognized in it the herald of her Third Reich. – What is her Third Reich then? – It is the synthesis of *might* and *mind*, of might and spirit – it is her dream and her demand, her highest war aim – and not Calais or the 'enslavement of peoples' or the Congo.

Thomas Mann, *to the 'Svenska Dagbladet', Stockholm*

MAY 21

The trenches wound in meandering lines and white faces peered from dark dug-outs – a lot of men were still preparing the positions, and everywhere among them there were graves. Where they sat, beside their dug-outs, even between the sandbags, crosses stuck out. Corpses jammed in among them. It sounds like fiction – one man was frying potatoes on a grave next to his dug-out.

The existence of life here had really became a paradoxical joke.

For that matter it's by no means certain that it is not one in fact, when we think of the circle of flame that blazed round us. In point of fact even that is not needed. When my mother died the world seemed just the same to me as it does now. The mystery of corpses pervading everything . . .

Max Beckmann

MAY 22

S.S. [Siegfried Sassoon] and I have great difficulty in talking about poetry and that sort of thing together as the other officers of the batt. are clearly terribly curious and suspicious – If I go into his mess and he wants to show me some set of verses he says, 'Afternoon, Graves, have a drink . . . , by the way I want you to see my latest recipe for rum punch.' The trenches are worse than billets for privacy. We are a disgrace to the batt. and we know it: I don't know what the C.O. would say if he heard us discussing the sort of things we do. He'd probably have a fit.

Robert Graves, *to Edward Marsh*

When I write of the birth of fear I have in mind something more deeply rooted, that has nothing to do with the stage fright of the novice who does not know if he is going to act badly or well, something that is born of time and stress, which a man must watch lest it come to influence what he does. It appears only in men who have been scarred by months of war; unless the initial plunge is into a battle or intense shelling it may be months before the ordinary man has any trouble. His discovery of danger does not come at once; often it does not come for a long time. At first he has a strange feeling of invulnerability – a form of egotism – then it is suddenly brought home to him that he is not a spectator but a bit of the target, that if there are casualties he may be one of them.

In this sense I find fear mentioned in my diary only once before the spring of 1915, and then only as we might describe a man seized with a fit in the street, something bizarre that was not part of our lives. But as the war dragged on, and fear was no longer an occasional and exotic visitor but a settler in our midst, I got into the habit of watching for signs of wear and tear, that a man might be rested before he was broken.

Lord Moran

MAY 25

Italy enters the war, against the Central Powers.

Watch

A whole night,
thrown down beside a friend,
himself slaughtered,
his grinning mouth turned to the full moon,
I, with his convulsed hands reaching into my silence,
have written letters filled with love.

I have never felt so drawn towards life.

> Giuseppe Ungaretti

A sigh of relief was emitted by all Italians on learning that hostilities
had been opened against Austria. This day has been looked forward
to for 49 years, since peace was forced upon Italy by Germany in
1866, thereby preventing the Italians from avenging their naval
defeat at Lissa.

> *Manchester Guardian*

For our part, every word forced from our throats would be too
much. Let us not utter words of complaint but grind our teeth and
use other weapons than words to the new enemy.

> *Vossische Zeitung*

The Dardanelles. Tremendous Struggle in Progress. Turks 200,000
Strong.

> *Manchester Guardian*

The Moon shines bright on Charlie Chaplin,
His boots are cracking, for want of blacking,
And his khaki trousers they want mending,
Before we send him
    To the Dardanelles

The Turkish guns served by German artillerymen at the Dardanelles were of British manufacture and delivered by Zaharoff.

> Donald McCormick

The Gallipoli campaign of 1915 was the most imaginative, the most controversial and – in its possibilities – the most important single operation in the whole course of the two world wars. By the end of 1914, the German onrush across France had been stopped in the Battle of the Marne, and in the east the Russians, though dreadfully hit, were still just able to hold their ground. The Gallipoli campaign was an attempt to break this deadlock, and bring the war to a rapid end by a decisive outflanking movement from the south which would enable the British and the French to join hands with their Russian allies in the Balkans. When it failed, Europe was condemned to four senseless years of slaughter in the trenches, from which it has not yet recovered, and in the east there followed the long campaign in the Mesopotamian desert, the collapse of Russia, the revolution, and the setting up of the Soviet Republic as we know it today. Within the short nine months of its duration the Gallipoli adventure drew together all the threads of war: the most modern weapons and the greatest ships, the latest inventions like the submarine and the aeroplane, the worst and some of the most brilliant strokes of generalship; and so long as the issue hung in doubt so did the fate of half a dozen kingdoms and governments. There was something too in the very setting of the battle – Mount Ida and the ruins of Troy, the Hellespont of Byron and Hero and Leander – that seemed to bring the young soldiers to an extreme pitch of romantic heroism, so that there was nothing which they would not dare and no hopeless prospect of death for which they would not volunteer.

Alan Moorehead

A Suffolk man at Gallipoli

We arrived at the Dardanelles and saw the guns flashing and heard the rifle-fire. They heaved our ship, the River Clyde, right up to the shore. They had cut a hole in it and made a little pier, so we were able to walk straight off and on to the beach. We all sat there – on the Hellespont! – waiting for it to get light. The first things we saw were big wrecked Turkish guns, the second a big marquee. It didn't make me think of the military but of the village fêtes. Other people must have thought like this because I remember how we all rushed up to it, like boys getting into a circus, and then found it all laced up. We unlaced it and rushed in. It was full of corpses. Dead English-

men, lines and lines of them, and with their eyes wide open. We all
stopped talking. I'd never seen a dead man before and here I was
looking at two or three hundred of them. It was our first fear.
Nobody had mentioned this. I was very shocked. I thought of
Suffolk and it seemed a happy place for the first time . . .

We set to work to bury people. We pushed them into the sides of
the trench but bits of them kept getting uncovered and sticking out,
like people in a badly made bed. Hands were the worst; they would
escape from the sand, pointing, begging – even waving! There was
one which we all shook when we passed, saying, 'Good morning', in
a posh voice. Everybody did it. The bottom of the trench was
springy like a mattress because of all the bodies underneath. At
night, when the stench was worse, we tied crêpe round our mouths
and noses. This crêpe had been given to us because it was supposed
to prevent us being gassed. The flies entered the trenches at night
and lined them completely with a density which was like moving
cloth. We killed millions by slapping our spades along the trench
walls but the next night it would be just as bad. We were all lousy
and we couldn't stop shitting because we had caught dysentery. We
wept, not because we were frightened but because we were so dirty.

We didn't feel indignant against the Government. We believed
all they said, all the propaganda. We believed the fighting had got to
be done. We were fighting for England. You only had to say
'England' to stop any argument. We shot and shot. On August 6th
they made a landing at Suvla Bay and we took Hill 13 again, and
with very few casualties this time. We'd done a good job. The trench
had been lost yet again, you see. When we got back for the third
time we found a little length of trench which had somehow missed
the bombardment. There were about six Turkish boys in it and we
butchered them right quick. We couldn't stay in the trench, we had
to go on. Then we ran into machine-gun fire and had to fall flat in the
heather, or whatever it was. Suddenly my mate caught fire as he lay
there. A bullet had hit his ammunition belt. Several people near
jumped up and ran back, away from the burning man and the
machine-gun fire. I could hear the strike of the gun about a foot
above my head. I lay between the burning man and a friend of mine
called Darky Fowler. Darky used to be a shepherd Helmingham
way. I put my hand out and shook him, and said, 'Darky, we've got
to go back. We must go back!' He never answered. He had gone. I
lay there thinking how funny it was that I should end my life that

night. Then my mate began to go off like a firework – the fire was exploding his cartridges. That did it! I up and ran.

Leonard Thompson, *to Ronald Blythe*

From 'The Dead'

Pressed close against each other
The dead without hatred or flag
The hair stiff with congealed blood
The dead are all on one side.

René Arcos

Everyone save the wilfully purblind now realises that, in the words of the German official account, 'Churchill's bold idea was not a fine-spun fantasy of the brain', and that the real sufferers from delusions were the commanders on the Western Front . . . We too now know, as the Germans did in the war, how feasible was the Dardanelles project, and how vital its effect would have been.

Captain Basil Liddell Hart

The First Grave Speaks to the Second Grave

Churchill planned this expedition to Gallipoli, where I was killed. He planned the expedition to Antwerp, where my brother was killed. Then he said that Labour is not fit to govern. Rolling his eyes for fresh worlds, he saw Egypt, and fearing that peace might be established there, he intervened and prevented it. Whatever he undertakes is a success. He is Churchill-the-Fortunate, ever in office, and clouds of dead heroes attend him.

E. M. Forster

I like to hear the news from the Dardanelles,
I like to hear the whistle of the Allyman's shells.
I like to hear the rifle-fire,
I like to see the blinking Allymans retire.
I like to hear the click-click of the pick and spade,
    (the French they are no bon.)
Look out, look out, the gas clouds are coming:
Go get your respirator on.

252,000 British and French, and 218,000 Turkish killed, wounded, or missing.

Gallipoli

There was no co-ordination of effort. There was no connected plan of action. There was no sense of the importance of time

David Lloyd George

MAY 26

At the Berliners' table (at Bad Kissingen) Italy is going to receive a bigger pounding than England as you will see from the following table. Punishment for the use of following words: for French: 5 pfennigs: for Russian: 10 pfennigs: for English: 15: Italian: 20. But if America once joins there will be a difficult problem for they have no language of their own. To my mind the English fine will have to be doubled.

Heinrich Mann, *to Mimi Mann*

JUNE 2

The Russian Front, Galicia

The dawn was beautiful. Soon after we went off to look for the battle. The cannon were booming now in the forest. We went off in our haycarts to look for them. We got right into the forests which were lovely in the early morning, the sky red and gold, the birds singing. Although the cannon sounded so near we found nothing there and went off to another part. Here we found plenty, and soon we were settled just behind a trench with a battery banging in our ear. The soldiers had settled into the trench as though they had been born in it and they looked at us with a kind of amiable indifference. Then came a long wait. I got a bad headache from the noise of the battery and felt lonely and miserable – not frightened, though shrapnel was singing over our heads. After five we moved down to another trench where I sat until dark. Nice old colonel here – fine old farm with a beautiful old tree – all very merry here, beautiful hot supper, soldiers sewing, laughing, waiting. Old Colonel tells stories about lovely women when the noise pauses. At dark set off to find dead. This really rather alarming, the hedges filled with silent soldiers, the moonlight making everything unreal and unsafe. We found our men then were met by an officer with a large silent company behind him who told us that we must hurry as they were going to begin an attack. We *did* hurry, and just as we got our carts out of the position and began to climb the hill, the whole landscape behind us, which had been dead still, cracked into sound. The cannon broke out on every side of us – fire and flashes and coloured lights and a noise as though the sky, made of china had broken into a million pieces and fallen – a magnificent unforgettable spectacle.

> Hugh Walpole

JUNE 5

Henri Gaudier-Brzeska killed in charge, at Neuville St Vaast.

JUNE 8

I am thinking of enlisting if they will have me, though it is against all my principles of justice – though I would be doing the most criminal thing a man can do – I am so sure my mother would not stand the shock that I don't know what to do.

> Isaac Rosenberg, *to Sydney Schiff*

Above the Battle

For the finer spirits of Europe there are two habitations: our earthly Fatherland, and that other, the City of God. Of the first we are the guests, and of the second we are the builders. To the one let us give our lives, our faithful hearts; but neither family, friend, nor Fatherland, nor anything that we love, has power over the soul, which is light. It is our responsibility to rise above the tempests, and thrust aside clouds that threaten to overshadow it; to build higher and stronger, dominating the injustice and hatred of the nations, the walks of that City wherein may gather the souls of all the world.

> Romain Rolland

JUNE 16

Eastern Front

Have been in the thick of things for nearly a month, under fire several times, and have decided that a dentist is much more alarming. The worst part of a battle is its invisibility and never knowing what it's going to do next. Waiting with a cart under shrapnel for wounded is depressing if it lasts long, but doing anything definite is highly inspiring, and amusing sometimes in most unexpected ways. I had the other night a race from the Austrians in a haycart that was Gilbertian, quite especially as I'd lost my braces and my glasses were crooked! Day before yesterday eight hundred wounded in twelve hours. I cut off fingers with a pair of scissors as easily as nothing.

Hugh Walpole, *to Henry James*

A battle is an amazing mixture of hell and a family picnic – not as frightening as the dentist but absorbing, sometimes thrilling like football, sometimes dull like church, and sometimes simply physically sickening, like bad fish. Burying dead afterwards is worst of all.

Hugh Walpole, *to Arnold Bennett*

JUNE 27

Be more autocratic, my very own sweetheart.

Tsarina, *to Tsar*

Greeting to the Sergeant

You've got a kind face, you old bastard,
You ought to be bloody well shot:
You ought to be tied to a gun-wheel,
And left there to bloody well rot.

JUNE 28

A German Poet Reflects

Those like ourselves, dear friend, who have remained out of the war, have much leisure for doubting: probably always, we declare, all suffering and misery have been present to the most extreme. Always, entire wretchedness has existed within humanity, as much as there is, a constant, just as there is a constant of happiness; only the distribution changes. He who was ignorant of so much misery may now be overwhelmed. But who, if he were really alive, was so ignorant? Wonderful, of course, is the evidence of such vast misery suffered, accepted and achieved everywhere, by everyone. Greatness is revealed, steadfastness, strength, confrontation with life *quand-même*, – but how much in such behaviour is obstinacy, despair and by now habit? And the fact that so much greatness is depicted and endured can scarcely diminish the pain of knowing that this chaos, this useless muddle, the entire human blundering of the trumped-up doom that is our fate, in one word this unmitigated disaster was actually *necessary* to extract proofs of fortitude, devotion and grandeur. Whereas *we*, the arts, the drama, stimulated nothing at all in these same people, brought nothing to the surface, could change no one. What other occupation have we than the proclaiming of causes for real change, so unconvinced and unconvincing? For almost a year this has been our question, our torment – and our task: to do it more vehemently, more inexorably. How are we to do it?

> Rainer Maria Rilke, *to Freiherr von Münchhausen*

JUNE 29

I am venturing to trouble you with the mention of my personal situation, but I shall do so as briefly and considerately as possible. I desire to offer myself for naturalization in this country, that is, to change my status from that of an American citizen to that of British subject. I wish to testify at this crisis to the force of my attachment and devotion to England and to the cause for which she is fighting . . . I can only testify by laying at her feet my explicit, my material and spiritual allegiance, and throwing into the scale of her fortune my all but imponderable moral weight – 'a poor thing but my own!' Hence this respectful appeal.

> Henry James, *to H. H. Asquith*

JUNE 30

Cossacks

Wonderful sight, Cossacks swimming their horses in the lake. Hundreds of horses, hundreds of the finest men in the world flashing naked in the sun – the blue water, the little pink village with the brown church, the green reeds. Such colour and peace and happiness, the Cossacks playing with one another like babies. How to reconcile all the different sides of this amazing affair.

> Hugh Walpole, *to his mother*

JULY

200,000 Welsh miners successfully strike against the Munitions of War Act in which strikes in key war industries were made illegal.

What will you lack, sonny, what will you lack
When the girls line up on the street,
Shouting their love to the lads come back
From the foe they rushed to beat?
Will you send a strangled cheer to the sky,
And grin till your cheeks are red?
But what will you lack when your mates go by
With a girl who cuts you dead?

JULY 5

If the War Loan is to have any chance with the 'working classes', at least in the Midlands, the compulsory closing of the picture palaces will become an absolute necessity. They are probably a more serious menace to the nation now than even drink.

A Black Country Vicar, *to 'The Times'*

There was not one film showing to give any idea of the work of the British Army or the British Navy. The whole audience looked forward to the antics of one Charlie Chaplin. I could not but compare a similar scene at a great picture theatre in Germany, where prices had lowered and parents are entitled to take their children free; where all soldiers enter free, and all wounded free, in order that the nation may obtain, from ocular demonstration, information on the one national topic – the war. If I may be permitted to say so, the impression created in my mind by the contrast was unpleasant. I am told that there are thousands of these picture-theatres in London and in the provinces, in Scotland and Ireland, and that Charlie Chaplin is the idol of millions of your people. The only sign of war was that some of your generals were thrown on the screen, but they received relatively small applause. An English friend of mine explained that the English are not enthusiastic in the matter of loud clapping, but I pointed out that Charlie Chaplin received a positive ovation.

A Neutral, *to 'The Times'*

JULY 10

German South West Africa surrenders to General Botha of South Africa.

Kitchener hints at Conscription, mentioning the excuses of the various orders of slackers, the men always waiting to be fetched, and the need to appeal first to young bachelors. 'Volunteers – so far.'

This is no case of petty right or wrong
That politicians or philosophers
Can judge. I hate not Germans, nor grow hot
With love of Englishmen, to please newspapers.
Beside my hate for one fat patriot
My hatred of the Kaiser is love true: –
A kind of god he is, banging a gong.
But I have not to choose between the two,
Or between justice and injustice. Dinned
With war and argument I read no more
Than in the storm smoking along the wind
Athwart the wood. Two witches' cauldrons roar.
From one the weather shall rise clear and gay;
Out of the other an England beautiful
And like her mother that died yesterday.
Little I know or care if, being dull,
I shall miss something that historians
Can rake out of the ashes when perchance
The phoenix broods serene above their ken.
But with the best and meanest Englishmen
I am one in crying, God save England, lest
We lose what never slaves and cattle blessed.
The ages made her that made us from the dust:
She is all we know and live by, and we trust
She is good and must endure, loving her so:
And as we love ourselves we hate her foe.

                    Edward Thomas, killed at Arras, April 9, 1917

German Atrocities

A Nurse Hume was said to have shot a German officer who had attacked a wounded Belgian, the Germans then cutting off her left breast. The story was in fact invented by her sister, later convicted for forgery, Nurse Hume herself never having left Huddersfield. The *Daily Mirror* of July 25, 1915, showed three Prussian officers 'loaded with golden and silver loot', though the photograph was actually taken July 9, 1914, during the Army Steeplechase at Grunewald.

(Derived from) Cate Haste

Whipped Cream

Early in the summer the first demonstration took place in Berlin. About 500 women collected in front of the Reichstag building. They were promptly suppressed by the police, and no newspaper printed an account of the occurrence. These women were rather vague in their demands. They called Von Bülow an old fathead for his failure in Italy and confirmed that the whipped cream was not so good as before the war. There was some talk of high prices for food and the women all said that they wanted their men back from the trenches.

James W. Gerard

AUGUST

A Wounded Man

The Russians had lured us into a trap. I had actually set eyes on the Russian machine-guns before I felt a dull blow on my temple. The sun and the moon were both shining at once and my head ached like mad. What on earth was I to do with this scent of flowers? Some flower – I couldn't remember its name however I racked my brains. And all that yelling round me and the moaning of the wounded, which seemed to fill the whole forest – that must have been what brought me round. Good Lord, they must be in agony! Then I became absorbed by the fact that I couldn't control the cavalry boot with the leg in it, which was moving about too far away, although it belonged to me . . . Over on the grass there were two captains in Russian uniform dancing a ballet, running up and kissing each other on the cheeks like two young girls. That would have been against regulations in our army. I had a tiny round hole in my head. My horse, lying on top of me, had lashed out one last time before dying, and that had brought me to my senses. I tried to say something, but my mouth was stiff with blood, which was beginning to congeal. The shadows all round me were growing huger and huger, and I wanted to ask how it was that the sun and moon were both shining simultaneously. I wanted to point at the sky, but my arm wouldn't move. Perhaps I lay there unconscious for several days.

> Oskar Kokoshka

AUGUST 20

POST CARD

I write to you beneath this tent
While summer day becomes a shade
And startling magnificent
Flowers of the cannonade
Stud the pale blue firmament
And before existing fade

> Apollinaire

The Envelope

The envelope was exposed, no doubt, to rain on the top of a packet, and the address is no longer legible among the violet mottlings on the dried and frayed paper. Alone there survives in a corner the address of the sender. I pull the letter out gently – 'My dear mother' – Ah, I remember! Biquet, now lying in the open air in the very trench where we are halted, wrote that letter not long ago in our quarters at Gauchin-l'Abbé, one flaming and splendid afternoon, in reply to a letter from his mother, whose fears for him had proved groundless and made him laugh – 'You think I'm in the cold and rain and danger. Not at all; on the contrary, all that's finished. It's hot, we're sweating, and we've nothing to do only to stroll about in the sunshine. I laughed to read your letter' – I return to the frail and damaged envelope the letter which, if chance had not averted this new irony, would have been read by the old peasant woman at the moment when the body of her son is a wet nothing in the cold and the storm, a nothing that trickles and flows like a dark spring on the wall of the trench.

> Henri Barbusse

'Sir Richard Hannay' Observes Wilhelm II

He gave his hand to Stumm and turned away. The last I saw of him was a figure moving like a sleep-walker, with no spring in his step, amid his tall suite. I felt that I was looking on at a far bigger tragedy than any I had seen in action. Here was one that had loosed Hell, and the furies of Hell had got hold of him. He was no common man, for in his presence I felt an attraction which was not merely the mastery of one used to command. That would not have impressed me, for I had never owned a master. But here was a human being who, unlike Stumm and his kind, had the power of laying himself alongside other men. That was the irony of it. Stumm would not have cared a tinker's cuss for all the massacres in history. But this man, the chief of a nation of Stumms, paid the price of war for the gifts that had made him successful in peace. He had imagination and nerves, and the one was white hot and the others were quivering. I would not have been in his shoes for the throne of the universe.

       John Buchan

British losses reach 252,000.

SEPTEMBER

John Kipling vanishes on the Western Front.

If any question why we died
Tell them – because our fathers lied.

       Rudyard Kipling

Private Life

Perhaps the largest of the 'black holes' in history is the inner story of the emotional, including the sexual, dependences of its principal actors. Sometimes they were acted out in the open, as by Charles VII of France or the Emperor Franz Joseph; more often, as with Asquith and Lloyd George, the outlines emerged into public view only after their death . . . Whatever disclosures of this kind are still to come, they are unlikely to surpass the astonishing figure of a British Prime Minister writing daily, often from the Cabinet itself, his inmost thoughts and secrets to this young woman. I would not dispute Roy Jenkins's belief that the shock of Miss Stanley's sudden engagement to Asquith's own friend and colleague Edwin Montague, coinciding with the Dardanelles fiasco and the storm of dissatisfaction with the conduct of the war in March/May 1915, was the cause of his strange passivity, amounting almost to indifference, over the formation of the Coalition. It was a curious repetition of the same kind of emotional shock, when eighteen months later the death of his son Raymond in Flanders marked the onset of the collapse of Asquith's authority which ended in his ejection in December 1916.

> Enoch Powell

OCTOBER 10

From Munich

I must leave these rooms tomorrow as the landlady is returning from the country, and with them the splendid large Picasso with which I have now lived for almost four months. Four months – what times have gone by and what with them? For me, they pass with increasingly sad insight into the universal misery and madness in which all drives relentlessly forward, human strength and existence (whose purpose cannot be put into words), being wasted on blatant and distorted slogans. What chaos there will be afterwards, when all our credulously accepted ideas are toppled from the pedestals upon which we displayed them, and the confused survivors want once more to resume the discarded laws of their inner being. Can no one prevent it and stop it? Why are there not two, three, five, ten people who would unite and cry out in the marketplaces: Enough! and be shot down and at least have surrendered their lives for it to be enough, whereas those out at the front die only that the horror shall go on and on and there be no end to the dying. Why is there not one person who will endure it no longer, who refuses to endure it, – if he cried but for a single night in the midst of the false beflagged city, cried and would refuse to be silenced, who would dare call him liar? How many of us hold this cry back with an effort, or don't they? If I am mistaken and there are not many who would cry so, then I do not understand humanity and am not myself part of it and have nothing in common with it.

> Rainer Maria Rilke, *to Ellen Delp*

A German revisits Germany from Switzerland

I found from the first hour that the stories told to me by so many have been confirmed: Germany has become different, Germany is more silent, more dignified, more serious, and more mature. And that does not seem oppressive, as one might fear, but beautiful, even noble.

Hermann Hesse, *to 'Neue Zürcher Zeitung'*

OCTOBER 11

Prison St. Gilles, Brussels

My dear Sister,

  Mr. Graham will give you twenty francs from me to pay my little debts. Miss J. owes me (she will remember) 100 francs. Take it to buy a clock for the entrance hall. It was given me by Mr. Mayor. At the end of the daily account book you will see the Red Cross accounts. Money spent out of school funds but not entered should have been covered by the two cheques I told you of and which are not entered either. I am asking you to take charge of my will and a few things for me. You have been very kind, my dear, and I thank you and all the nurses for all you have done for me in the last ten weeks. My love to you all. I am not afraid, but quite happy.

Yours,
E. Cavell

OCTOBER 12

Nurse Edith Cavell shot, 7 a.m.

The shootings of Nurse Cavell and Captain Fryatt had seemed to me acts the usefulness of which did not balance the moral obloquy incurred and were on that account unjustifiable.

Ex-Chancellor, Prince von Bülow

A French Liaison Officer

'We're in luck . . . this Scotch division is a picked troop. With it we'll see things.' And he confided in me as a great secret that the

British Army was preparing a gas attack in imitation of the one the Germans had launched at Ypres. This battle, the first I saw, was the Battle of Loos.

The spectacle of the troops on their way to take up combat posts with heads bent before the passage of shells like wheat bowed down by the wind, the fresh shell holes smelling of earth and powder, awaked in me a keen longing that I had not felt for a long time – the desire to write. The contrast between the calm of the khaki-clad soldiers, who stood at the cross-roads directing traffic with the calm gestures of policemen in Piccadilly Circus, and the danger of their position seemed to me beautiful and worthy of being recorded; sadder, but less beautiful, was the contrast later on between the appearance of the General on the morning of battle, very courteous and dignified, in a uniform resplendent with red and gold, and the return that same evening of his corpse stained with blood and mire.

André Maurois

Miles behind the lines
   behind the lines,
We've got a sergeant-major
Who's never seen a gun,
He's mentioned in despatches
For drinking the privates' rum,
And when he sees old Jerry
You should see the bugger run
   miles behind the lines.

Soldiers' Slang

JERRY – German, singular or plural, noun and adjective. A familiar expression almost of affection, obviously derived from *German*. Used constantly by private soldiers in such phrases 'Jerry's damn quiet, tonight': 'Poor old Jerry, he's not half getting it from them heavies of ours'; 'What should I see but a couple of Jerries.'

JERRY UP! – An exclamation of warning (or of faint interest), meaning that a German aeroplane was overhead and might drop bombs. If it was daylight and the 'plane was over, so as to threaten a machine-gun attack, the remarks were wilder and stronger. Sometimes *Jerry Over*.

John Brophy and Eric Partridge

OCTOBER 23

W. G. Grace, the Great Cricketer, Dies

The magnificent machine had run down at last, and his weakness was enhanced by the shock of an air raid in the neighbourhood. Probably the last of his cricketing friends to talk to him was Mr Leverson-Gower, who was stationed nearby and came over to see him. He said that the air raids worried him. 'You can't be frightened of aeroplanes, Old Man,' said his visitor. 'You, who had Jones bowling through your beard.' 'That was different,' he answered. 'I could see that Jones, and see what he was at. I can't see the aeroplanes.' He was obviously very ill, but he signed a photograph not only for Mr Leverson-Gower's driver, but for half a dozen other men in the battalion.

Bernard Darwin

NOVEMBER 2

War is a great and necessary disintegrating autumnal process. Love is the great creative process, like spring, the making of an integral unit out of many disintegrating processes. If it goes any further, we shall have so thoroughly destroyed the unifying force from among us, we shall have become each one of us so completely a separate entity, that the whole will be an amorphous heap, like sand, sterile, hopeless, useless, like a dead tree . . . Prussia is not evil through and through. Her mood is *now* evil. But we reap what we have sowed. It is as with a child: if with a sullen, evil soul one provokes an evil mood in the child, there is destruction. But no child is all evil. And Germany is the child of Europe: and senile Europe, with her conventions and arbitrary rules of conduct and life and very being, has provoked Germany into a purely destructive mood.

D. H. Lawrence, *to Lady Cynthia Asquith*

Dear Mr. Schiff,

I could not get the work I thought I might so I have joined this Bantam Battalion (as I was too short for any other) which seems to be the most rascally affair in the world. I have to eat out of a basin together with some horribly smelling scavenger who spits and sneezes into it etc. It is most revolting, at least up to now – I don't mind the hard sleeping, the stiff marches etc. but this is unbearable. Besides my being a jew makes it bad among these wretches. I am looking forward to having a bad time altogether.

Isaac Rosenberg

NOVEMBER 13

Final failure of British and Anzacs at the Dardanelles.

Mr. Churchill has resigned. This was the momentous news contained in letters exchanged between Mr. Winston Churchill and Mr. Asquith. The reasons that Mr. Churchill gives are such that anyone can understand. He is young and active, and he naturally does not desire to remain in 'well-paid inactivity.' Rumour, often cruel and baseless, credits him with the Antwerp and Dardanelles expeditions. History will prove that he was in no way responsible for those adventures.

Daily Mirror, London

I have a clear conscience, which enables me to bear my responsibility for past events with composure. Time will vindicate my administration at the Admiralty and assign me my due share in the vast series of preparations and operations which have secured us the command of the seas.

Winston Churchill, *to H. H. Asquith*

You had the conception of the Dardanelles, the only imaginative conception of the war.

Clement Attlee, *to Winston Churchill*, 1954

Public Life: George V on Industrial Relations

From the Clyde the king went to the Tyne . . . and spoke personally with a number of foremen and workers in the armament works and shipyards . . . He thanked the workmen in a speech for what had been done, but urged that more was still required. He voiced the hope that, 'all restrictive rules and regulations would be removed, and that all would work to one common end and purpose.' This was a courageous gesture on the king's part to help forward the solution of the very difficult problem of suspending the trade union restrictions which at the time were seriously hampering output.

David Lloyd George

NOVEMBER 25

Kultur

It is my unshakable conviction that the country to which God gave Luther, Goethe, Bach, Wagner, Moltke, Bismarck and my grandfather will yet be called upon to fulfil great tasks for the wellbeing of humanity.

> Kaiser Wilhelm II, *to Houston Stewart Chamberlain*

DECEMBER 4

Henry Ford leaves America on unofficial peace mission, returning December 24. 'I didn't get much peace but I heard in Norway that Russia might well become a huge market for tractors soon.'

While shepherds watched their flocks by night
    All seated on the ground,
A high-explosive shell came down
    And mutton rained around.
       Saki

The Breaking of Nations
1915

Only a man harrowing clods
    In a slow silent walk
With an old horse that stumbles and nods
    Half asleep as they stalk.

Only thin smoke without flame
    From the heaps of couch-grass;
Yet this will go onward the same
    Though Dynasties pass.

Yonder a maid and her wight
    Come whispering by:
War's annals will cloud into night
    Ere their story die.
       Thomas Hardy

By the end of 1915 Germany still had a good chance of winning the war . . . or achieving a good draw in a negotiated peace. Falkenhayn squandered it at Verdun.

> Alistair Horne

By the end of 1915 the French army had already suffered 1,961,687 casualties, of which 1,001,271 were killed or missing.

> Corelli Barnett

A DRIFTER AT TARENTUM

He from the wind-bitten North with ship and companions descended,
Searching for eggs of death spawned by invisible hulls,
Many he found and drew forth, of a sudden the fishing ended
In flame and a clamorous breath known to the eye-pecking gulls.

> Rudyard Kipling

In December butter became very scarce, and the women waiting in long lines before the shops often rushed the shops. In this month many copper roofs were removed from buildings in Berlin. I was told by a friend in the Foreign Office that the notorious Von Rintelen was sent to America to buy up the entire product of the Du Pont Powder Factories . . .

On the night of the peace interpolation in the Reichstag a call was issued by placards for a meeting on the Unter den Linden. I went out on the streets and found that the police had so carefully divided the city into districts that it was impossible for a crowd of any size to gather on the Unter den Linden. There was quite a row at the session in the Reichstag. Scheidemann, the Socialist, made a speech very moderate in tone, but he was answered by the Chancellor, and then an endeavour was made to close the debate. The Socialists made such a noise, however, that the majority gave way, and another prominent socialist, Landsberger, was allowed to speak. He also made a reasonable speech, in the course of which he said that even Socialists would not allow Alsace-Lorraine to go back to France. It made use of a rather good phrase, saying that the 'Disunited States of Europe were making war to make a place for the United States of America.'

> James W. Gerard

Until the end of 1915, the war had seemed a purely military affair: battles were won and lost, strong places fell or were defended, campaigns succeeded or ended in disaster. Suddenly, the initial impetus exhausted, events behind the front recovered their importance: policy overshadowed strategy, and the decision passed from generals to peoples. In every country new ministries were formed or new courses followed. Since the war had become too serious a matter to be left to the soldiers, every country was faced with the same question – whether to fight on at the risk of destroying the structure of society. Compromise or the knock-out blow was the issue which lay behind the events of the bitter winter of 1916–17 – behind the rise to power of Lloyd George as much as behind the fall of Bethmann Hollweg, behind the first Russian revolution and the French mutinies. So too behind the changes which followed the death of Francis Joseph in November 1916.

A. J. P. Taylor

In 1916, one Frenchman in every 25 became a casualty.

1916

JANUARY 1

It is hard to say anything about the war. There seems to be a calm
before the storm. No one knows what is coming next. What it will
lead to and how long it will last. The state of exhaustion here is
already very great, and even in Germany they are no longer un-
hesitatingly optimistic.

Sigmund Freud, *to Max Fitingen*

*In 1916 the Escadrille Americaine, a squad of American volunteer
airmen, begin fighting in France. Later, it became known as the
Lafayette Escadrille.*

We meet 'neath the sounding rafters,
    The walls around us are bare;
They echo the peals of laughter;
    It seems that the dead are there.

So stand by your glasses steady,
    This world is a world of lies.
Here's a toast to the dead already;
    Hurrah for the next man who dies.

Cut off from the land that bore us,
    Betrayed by the land that we find,
The good men have gone before us,
    And only the dull left behind.

So stand by your glasses steady,
    The world is a web of lies.
Then here's to the dead already,
    And hurrah for the next man who dies.

Lafayette Escadrille Mess Song

Elijah was reputed to be the patron saint of aviators, but as he went to Heaven in a chariot of fire, this was something we weren't too keen about.

> Kiffin Rockwell, an original member of the Escadrille Americaine (later Lafayette Escadrille), killed June 1916

The deeds of this squadron at Verdun thrilled America and did much to win her to the Allied cause.

A Fiancé's Death in France

In Sussex, by the end of January, the season was already on its upward grade; catkins hung bronze from the bare, black branches, and in the damp lanes between Hassocks and Keymer the birds sang loudly. How I hated them as I walked back to the station one late afternoon, when a red sunset turned the puddles on the road into gleaming pools of blood, and a new horror of mud and death darkened my mind with its dreadful obsession. Roland, I reflected bitterly, was now part of the corrupt clay in to which war had transformed the fertile soil of France; he would never again know the smell of a wet evening in early spring.

I had arrived at the cottage that morning to find his mother and sister standing in helpless distress in the midst of his returned kit, which was lying, just opened, all over the floor. The garments sent back included the outfit that he had been wearing when he was hit. I wondered, and I wonder still, why it was thought necessary to return such relics – the tunic torn back and front by the bullet, a khaki vest dark and stiff with blood, and a pair of blood-stained breeches slit open at the top by someone obviously in a violent hurry. Those gruesome rags made me realise, as I had never realised before, all that France really meant. Eighteen months afterwards the smell of Étaples village, though fainter and more diffused, brought back to me the memory of those poor remnants of patriotism.

> Vera Brittain

JANUARY 27

Conscription becomes law in Britain.

Protest in London

Conscription.
Why they want it, and why they say they want it.

They say they want it to punish the slackers,
They say they want it to punish the strikers,
They say they want it to crush Germany,
They say they want it to crush Labour,
They say they want it to free Europe,
They say they want it to enslave England.

Don't let them get what they want. Because they keep saying they
   want Something Different.

The Cat kept saying to the Mouse that she was a high minded
person, and if the Mouse would only come a little nearer they could
both get the cheese.
The Mouse said, 'Thank you, Pussy, it's not the cheese you want,
it's my skin.'

> Lytton Strachey, *in the 'No Conscription Pamphlet, No. 3'*

FEBRUARY 21

*Battle of Verdun begins, lasting ten months. Falkenhayn, Crown
Prince Wilhelm, Pétain, still remembered, presiding over one of the
most blood-drenched of all mass-slaughters. 281,100 German
casualties: 315,000 French.*

Shells disinter the bodies, then reinter them, chop them to pieces,
play with them as a cat plays with a mouse.

> French observer

Have so many ever died for so little gain? Between 1 April and
1 May, the casualty totals had mounted from 81,607 Germans and
89,000 French to 120,000 and 133,000 respectively; by the end of the
month, French losses alone had reached approximately 185,000
(roughly equal to the overall German losses in the Battle of
Stalingrad).

> Alistair Horne

Verdun

In command of this large [air] force was the Marquis de Rose, whose mission . . . was simply to 'sweep the skies'. A forty-year-old ex-cavalry officer described by Spears as a gay and gallant spirit appearing to design his own uniforms.

      Alistair Horne

The New Chivalry

In the combat tactics of the early days, however, the French shone, for this was a form of warfare ideally suited to their individualistic temperament (though, later, it was to be the cause of grievous losses). 'We are the refuge,' said a French airman, 'of all those who fear too close a confinement of the spirit, the discipline of the corps of troops' . . . Never since the Middle Ages and the invention of the long-bow had the battlefields of Europe seen this kind of single combat. When the champions of either side met to fight spectacular duels in and out of the clouds, the rest of the war seemed forgotten; even the men in the trenches paused to watch, as the hosts of Greece and Troy stood by when Hector and Achilles fought. Accompanying this personalised warfare, there returned a chivalry and a sporting instinct that had all but vanished with the advent of the army of the masses. A remarkable camaraderie grew between enemies. Once a German pilot dropped one of his expensive fur gloves during a raid over a French airfield. The next day he returned to drop the other; with a note begging the finder to keep it, as he had no use for only one glove. With medieval courtesy, the recipient dropped a thank-you note over the donor's base. Fewer flyers took after the cold killer, von Richthofen, than after Boelcke and Navarre, who both hated killing and aimed whenever possible for the engine instead of the pilot. The death of a renowned foe usually brought mourning rather than triumph to the victorious camp; when Boelcke himself was killed (in collision with his best friend), planes from every British airfield within range dropped wreaths on his base, regardless of the risk involved. But though this sense of chivalry endured throughout the war, Verdun was to spell the end of the solitary ace and single combat. It was at Verdun that the word 'Airforce' first began to have a meaning.

      Alistair Horne

The battered earth bore nothing but groaning wounded who couldn't be helped, distended bodies that your foot sank into, among broken guns, punctured helmets, scattered equipment. You advanced by leaping from shell hole to shell hole, their bottoms covered with muddy water and often dead men, half-buried by an explosion. Sometimes no one was in them, sometimes there were men, who welcomed you with muttered curses because you would get their previous shelter spotted. A spectral, semi-conscious life, interrupted only by the eruption of danger: sudden attacks, periodic bombardments, the insidious accumulation of gas in gullies and hollows, machine-guns discovered by surprise – everything over-whelmed the footsoldier. All this explains the eternal fame of Verdun – as hell, created as much by misery as by danger.

      Jacques Meyer

Charles de Gaulle, at Verdun, wounded for the third time.

1916, when the entire West European culture was severely shaken, if not nearly destroyed. Then the arch-villain was Marshal von Falkenhayn, the most 'scientific general' ever to ruin his country, as Liddell Hart remarked, who put into effect a 'calculated' method of winning the war for Germany. The arts of strategy were forgotten, the uncertainties of the battlefield dismissed. The French army was to be destroyed not by attempting a breakthrough, but by attacking a position which the French were obliged to defend at all costs and where they would 'bleed to death' whether the objective, Verdun, was captured or not. This was to be done simply by a concentration of weaponry which could not be matched within the narrow French salient. The result was the great ten-month battle of 1916, with its 700,000 dead or missing on a sixteen-kilometre front. It is true that the French army was never the same again, but nor was the German. The only net German gain in exchange for one-third of a million dead was 'the acquisition of a piece of raddled land a little larger in area than the combined Royal Parks in London.'

      Robert Conquest

And two things have altered not
    Since first the world began –
The beauty of the wild green earth
    and the bravery of man.

       T. P. Cameron Wilson

MARCH

I have been in this reg. about two months now and have been kept
going all the time. Except that the food is unspeakable, and perhaps
luckily, scanty, the rest is pretty tolerable. I have food sent up from
home and that keeps me alive, but as for the others, there is talk of
mutiny every day. One reg. close by did break out and some men
got bayoneted. I don't know when we are going out but the talk is
very shortly.

       Isaac Rosenberg, *to Sydney Schiff*

SHADOW

Here you are beside me again
Memories of my companions killed in the war
The olive-branch of time
Memories that make only a single memory
As a hundred skins make only a single coat
As these thousands of wounds make only a single newspaper article
Impalpable and dark presence who have assumed
The changing shape of my shadow
An Indian on the watch through all Eternity
Shadow you creep beside me
But you do not hear me any more
You will not know any more the divine poems I sing
But I hear you still and see you still
Destinies
Multiple shadow may the sun preserve you
You who love me so much that you will never leave me
And who dance in the sun without stirring the dust
Shadow ink of the sun
Signature of my light
Holder of sorrows
A god that condescends

       Apollinaire

Dr Weizmann, we need 30,000 tons of acetone. Can you make it?

Winston Churchill

The Dada Movement, Anti-War, Anti-political, Art, and Gestures, Protests from the Cabaret Voltaire, Zurich

No more painters, no more writers, no more musicians, no more sculptors, no more religions, no more republicans, no more royalists, no more imperialists, no more anarchists, no more socialists, no more bolsheviks, no more proletariat, no more democrats, no more bourgeois, no more aristocrats, no more weapons, no more police, no more countries, enough of all these imbecilities, no more of anything, *nothing, nothing, nothing*.

Tristan Tzara, *in the Manifesto of the Dada Movement*

Women

To the women of France, the war had brought an emancipatory revolution. Never had they been so great a power in the country. At the outbreak of war, to a woman they had rushed off to become nurses, fill the administrative gaps left by the men, work in the munitions factories. The soldiers grumbled on returning home to find their wives turned yellow by picric acid, but they had little redress. Initially, the women were doubtless drawn by the glamour of the nurse's uniform and by a sense of adventure; later, as the French women who had not lost a husband, lover, or brother became fewer and fewer, the more frivolous motives became replaced by a formidable dedication. Most of them had become marraines to one or more soldiers, according them benefits ranging merely from encouraging letters to parcels of food and woollies to the highest a woman can offer a man. All of them in their letters exhorted their adopted soldier to 'tenir coûte que coûte' and their influence was mighty. No other section of the French community was boosting the will to war more substantially than the women; and it was certainly no accident that, as a source of inspiration, La Madelon had almost replaced La Marseillaise. Perhaps symbolic of the whole spirit of 1916 was the divine Sarah Bernhardt, one leg amputated, but still stumping the boards with a wooden leg. Here was France herself, mutilated but undaunted.

Alistair Horne

Pacificism from Bloomsbury

The 'Bloomsburies' were all doing war-work of 'National Importance', down in some downy English county, under the wings of
powerful pacifist friends; pruning trees, planting gooseberry
bushes, and haymaking, doubtless in large sunbonnets.

P. Wyndham Lewis

Madame Curie, in the Military Hospitals of France, Belgium and Italy

Her new profession brought her into contact with the most varied
types of human being. Certain surgeons, understanding the usefulness of the X-ray, treated her as a great colleague and a precious
fellow-worker. Others, more ignorant, regarded her apparatus with
deep distrust. After a few conclusive radioscopic experiments, they
were astonished that 'it worked' and could hardly believe their eyes
when, at the spot indicated by the rays and pointed out by Marie,
their scalpel encountered the bit of shell which had been vainly
sought for in suffering flesh. Suddenly converted, they commented
upon the event as upon a miracle . . .

Fashionable women, the guardian angels of the hospitals, needed
only one glance to classify this grey-haired woman, so indifferently
dressed, who neglected to mention her name; and sometimes they
treated her like a subordinate. Marie was amused by their mis-
understandings. When such trivial manifestations of vanity had
annoyed her a little, she purified her soul by remembering a nurse
and a soldier who were her working comrades at the hospital in
Hoogstade: Queen Elizabeth and King Albert of Belgium.

Marie, often cold and distant, was charming to the wounded. She
had what could be sweetest to them: a pleasing tone of voice, light
hands, a great deal of patience, and an immense religious respect
for human life. To save a man's life or to spare him suffering, an
amputation or an infirmity, she was ready for the most exhausting
efforts. She gave up only when every chance had been tried in vain.

Eve Curie

Wartime European Royalty

While today all royalties and public men pose for the movies Tsar Ferdinand of Bulgaria and his family are probably the first royalties to act in a cinematograph. In 1916 there was released in Berlin a play in which Tsar Ferdinand, his wife, and two daughters by a former wife, appeared acting as Bulgarian royalties in the development of the plot.

James W. Gerard

CONCERT PARTY: BUSSEBOOM

The stage was set, the house was packed,
    The famous troop began;
Our laughter thundered, act by act;
    Time light as sunbeams ran.

Dance sprang and spun and neared and fled,
    Jest chirped at gayest pitch,
Rhythm dazzled, action sped
    Most comically rich.

With generals and lame privates both
    Such charms worked wonders, till
The show was over: lagging loth
    We faced the sunset chill;
And standing on the sandy way,
    With the cracked church, peering past,
We heard another Matinee,
    We heard the maniac blast.

Of barrage south by Saint Eloi
    And the red lights flaming there
Called madness: Come, my bonny boy,
    And dance to the latest air.

To this new concern, white we stood,
    Cold certainty held our breath;
While men in the tunnels below Larch Wood
    Were kicking men to death.

Edmund Blunden

THE VULTURE

Describing circle after circle
a wheeling vulture scans a field
lying desolate. In her hovel
a mother's wailing to her child:
'Come, take my breast, boy, feed on this,
grow, know your place, shoulder the cross.'

Centuries pass, villages flame,
are stunned by war and civil war.
My country, you are still the same,
tragic, beautiful as before.
How long must the mother wail?
How long must the vulture wheel?

                    Alexander Blok

MARCH 24

The Folkestone–Dieppe packet boat is sunk by U-Boats, without warning. Americans perish, and US indignation is voiced by Woodrow Wilson's threat to break off relations with Germany. Germany temporarily agrees to cease attacks on civilian shipping, a concession enduring only until February 1, 1917, when faltering Russian morale and strength encourages almost total German disregard of American opinion.

During the war, 203 German U-Boats sank 5,408 ships, excluding neutrals, amounting to some 11,000,000 tons.

Substitutes for Monkeys

Professor Z., the bacteriologist, once told me the following story.
    One day, talking to General B., I happened to mention that I was anxious to obtain some monkeys for my experiments. The General immediately said, quite seriously:
    'What about Jews – wouldn't they do? I've got some Jews here, spies that are going to be hanged anyway – you're quite welcome to them if they are any use to you.'
    And without waiting for an answer he sent his orderly to find out how many spies were awaiting execution.

I tried to explain to His Excellency that men would not be suitable for my experiments, but he was quite unable to understand me, and opening his eyes very wide he said:

'Yes, but men are cleverer than monkeys, aren't they? If you inoculate a man with poison he will be able to tell you what he feels, whereas a monkey won't.'

Just then the orderly came in and reported that there was not a single Jew among the men arrested for spying – only Romanians and Bohemians.

'What a pity!' said the General. 'I suppose Bohemians won't do either? . . . What a pity . . . !'

      Maxim Gorky

April 17

Then we advanced upon a Russian town that the Germans had already taken but had had to relinquish. Only the indispensable Jews were there again. Since the days of their forefather Joseph these strange people from the ghetto, who also have their uses as a scapegoat whenever a government has to massacre somebody in order to divert public attention from domestic difficulties, have regarded war as a typical Christian amusement – goyim naches. But since the days of the Pharaohs they have also maintained their special talent for dealing in grain.

Many soldiers who survived the world war and returned home might not have found their parents, wives, and children still there had it not been for the cunning of the Jews organizing food supplies behind the lines. Not merely in the two last winters of the war, but from the very beginning, everyone in Austria would have starved, while the men were playing at soldiers instead of working and the women were not only keeping house, bearing and looking after children, but working in armament factories. The army itself went to the Jews. In quiet sectors, however, they would be rounded up from the villages and forced to dig graves, which they did not like. They hid like fieldmice in subterranean storage places where they had stocks of corn, hay, bonds and other valuables.

      Oskar Kokoshka

APRIL 29

After a siege of 143 days, Major General Sir Charles Townshend surrenders Kut al Amara to the Turks. 65 per cent other ranks die; the entire force of Indians are ordered by the victors to march across the desert. All perished.

The Trenches

We arrive at a junction of trenches, and on the top of the maltreated hillock which is outlined on the cloudy greyness, a mournful signboard stands crookedly in the wind. The trench system becomes still more cramped and close, and the men who are flowing towards the clearing-station from all parts of the sector multiply and throng in the deep-dug ways.

These lamentable ways are staked out with corpses. At uneven intervals their walls are broken into by quite recent gaps, extending to their full depth, by funnel-holes beyond, where earthy bodies are squatting with their chins on their knees or leaning against the wall as straight and silent as the rifles which wait beside them. Some of these standing dead turn their blood bespattered faces towards the survivors; others exchange their looks with the sky's emptiness . . .

The sinister ramparts on this way of desolation contrast still more. They impel a feeling of suffocation, of a nightmare of falling which oppresses and strangles; and in these depths where the walls seem to be coming nearer and closing in, you are forced to halt, to wriggle a path for yourself, to vex and disturb the dead, to be pushed about by the endless disorder of the files that flow along these hinder trenches, files made up of messengers, of the maimed, of men who groan and who cry aloud, who hurry frantically, crimsoned by fever or pallid and visibly shaken by pain.

> Henri Barbusse

From the Austrian Front

By now it was time for the thighs. The pleasant burning slid into the hips. The masseur, too, seemed infected with the pleasure he himself was causing. Again a droning purr forced its way out of him, like the long, melodious rumblings of great tigers sunning their bodies behind the iron bars of a cage.

To avert these buzzing sonorities Ferdinand resumed the conversation.

'But out in the trenches I suppose you had to serve along with the others.'

The bath-superintendent grasped a brush.

'Beg to report, sir, I haven't ever been in the trenches.'

'What were you with, then? Commissariat?'

'No, sir, not the Commis either. I've always been attached to the Division Staff.'

The word 'attached', thus tenderly pronounced, tickled Ferdinand, it sounded so ambiguous. By now the superintendent stood behind him at the head of the couch. His hands on the recumbent shoulders beat out gracefully castigating roulades. He continued in the same gentle voice without interruption of this music.

'I'm attached as a freedman to the Division.'

This archaism, whose implications were beyond him, descended like an icy douche on Ferdinand. He repeated it with an effort, as a question – 'Freedman?'

But, as though he had swallowed insults enough, the bath-superintendent put an end to this little game of cross-examination.

'Surely, sir, you knew I was the hangman. The whole Division could tell you that, sir.'

Franz Werfel

Easter Rising in Ireland

The plan of rising in arms against the might of England seemed desperate, but there was the ghost of a chance that it would succeed. It was timed for Easter, 1916, and that spring England had her hands more than full on the Continent. Sir Roger Casement's job was to run arms in from Germany. At the last moment he was caught and his cargo captured. The official leader of the Nationalist Movement, Erin MacNeill, called the rising off, but Patrick Pearse was determined to go on with it. He and his six friends called themselves the Provisional Government of the Irish Republic. 'We declare the right of the people of Ireland to the ownership of Ireland . . .'

Dublin still bears the marks of that rising, physically in the bullet-scarred walls of her public buildings and morally in her mourning for the men who suffered in it. 58 Irishmen were killed in the fighting. The British held a court-martial and sentenced 97

others to death as rebels. The sentence was actually carried out in
the case of 16 men. Only one leader was reprieved, and that was
because he had been born in America and the English were anxious
not to offend the United States just when there was a chance that
they would come in to the World War on the English side. The name
of the reprieved man was Eamonn de Valera.

> J. Hampden Jackson

The old earth of the battlefields is thirsty for the wine of our blood.

> Padraic Pearse

APRIL 30

Dublin Revolt on Verge of Collapse,
    Rebel Leader Surrenders.
  Connolly Reported Killed.
    Post Office Destroyed by Fire

> *Sunday Times*, London

Ireland's Ordeal.
The Sinn Fein Rebellion.
    German Plots and Irish Dupes.
        The Fight for Dublin.
      A Masque of Anarchy.
        Hope and Tragedy.

> *Observer*, London

Ireland is a small country much afflicted by ballads, and by persons
shooting and bombing their way to a place in the ballads to be. I
have heard Yeats' line, 'a terrible beauty is born', used to glorify or
bedizen the sordid horrors which the Provisional IRA and their
competitors have brought to the streets of Belfast.

> Conor Cruise O'Brien, 1978

In Russia

Comrade and worker in a foreign army, I know you are no enemy of
mine, so, comrade, extend me your hand. You and I together suffer
beneath lies and violence. Our chief foe is in the rear. So let us train
our guns on him, our real common enemy. For my enemy is not, like
myself, robbed in his own country of all rights, not one whose life,

like mine is crushed by capitalism and a fight for bread. No, my enemy is at home, the enemy of the international working class, and that enemy is capitalism! For that enemy has enslaved the working class.

> Alexandra Kollontai

In Germany

The finest, the most intelligent, the best trained forces of international Socialism . . . the Workers of Great Britain, France, Germany and Russia, are being slaughtered in masses. That is a greater crime by far than the brutish sack of Louvain or the destruction of Rheims Cathedral. It is a deadly blow against the power which holds the whole future of humanity, the only power that can save the values of the past and carry them on into a newer and better human society.

> Rosa Luxemburg

MAY 1

Anti-War Agitation in Berlin

May Day 1916 was chosen for the first trial of strength . . . At eight o'clock in the morning a dense throng of workers – almost ten thousand – assembled in the square, which the police had already occupied well ahead of time. Karl Liebknecht, in uniform, and Rosa Luxemburg were in the midst of the demonstrators and greeted with cheers from all sides. Liebknecht's voice then rang out: 'Down with the War! Down with the Government!' The police immediately rushed at him . . . For the first time since the beginning of the war open resistance to it had appeared on the streets of the capital. The ice was broken.

> Paul Frölich

Anti-war demonstrations take place in Jena, Dresden and other German cities.

MAY 13

Perhaps the most extraordinary thing about a modern battlefield is the desolation and emptiness of it all . . . one cannot emphasise too much. Nothing is to be seen of war or soldiers – only the split and shattered trees and the burst of an occasional shell reveal anything of the truth. One can look for miles and see no human being. But in those miles of country lurk (like moles or rats, it seems) thousands, even hundreds of thousands of men, planning against each other perpetually some new device of death. Never showing themselves, they launch at each other bullet, bomb, aerial torpedo and shell. And somewhere too (on the German side we know of their existence opposite us) are the little cylinders of gas, waiting only for the moment to spit forth their nauseous and destroying fumes. And yet the landscape shows nothing of all this – nothing but a few shattered trees and three or four lines of earth and sandbags, these and the ruins of towns and villages are the only signs of war anywhere visible. The glamour of red coats – the martial tunes of flag and drum – aide-de-camps scurrying hither and thither on splendid chargers – lances glittering and swords flashing – how different the old wars must have been!

> Harold Macmillan, *to his mother*

Air Power

One sprightly morning in the early summer of 1916 ten or twenty small German bombers appeared over London, looking like gnats. We rushed up to the roof of the warehouse where I worked to watch this novelty, with excitement. They dropped a few bombs, killed some horses in Billingsgate and turned Cloth Fair, Cheapside, and Aldersgate into rivers of broken glass. Afterwards, outside a public house at the bottom of St Mary at Hill, a bedraggled woman singer celebrated the raid by singing an Edwardian ballad, 'City of Laughter, City of Tears,' in that howling, hiccupping manner which London singing usually has. On this morning Great Britain ceased to be an island.

> V. S. Pritchett

Moonrise Over Battlefield

After the fallen sun the wind was sad
like violins behind immense old walls.
Trees were musicians swaying round the bed
of a woman in gloomy halls.

In privacy of music she made ready
with comb and silver dust and fard;
under her silken vest her little belly
shone like a bladder of sweet lard.

She drifted with the grand air of a punk
on Heaven's streets soliciting white saints;
then lay in bright communion on a cloud-bank
as one who near extreme of pleasure faints.

Then I thought, standing in the ruined trench,
(all round, dead Boche white-shirted lay like sheep),
'Why does this damned entrancing bitch
seek lovers only among them that sleep?'

        Edgell Rickword

May 23

One fearful addition to the honours of War since I have been away is
the steel helmet which we all have to wear now, when in the shell
area. They are monstrously tiresome and heavy and I suppose if
idiots like Pemberton Billing had not asked questions in Parliament
about them we should have been allowed to go on with our comfortable caps.

        Raymond Asquith, *to K.A. 3rd Grenadier Guards, B.E.F.*

May 24

One thing we must get into our thick heads is that whenever the
German man or woman gets a suitable culture to thrive in, he or she
means death or loss to civilized people, precisely as germs of any
disease mean death or loss to mankind. There is no question of hate
or anger or excitement in the matter, any more than there is in
flushing out sinks.

        Rudyard Kipling, *to the 'Daily Express', London*

MAY 31

Battle of Jutland

There seems to be something wrong with our bloody ships today.

Admiral David Beatty

The British lost 111,980 tons of shipping, with 6,945 casualties. The Germans, 62,233 tons, and 2,921 casualties.

Linking these figures with the fact of their fleet's numerical inferiority, the Germans claimed a victory. Since the British had forced the Germans back into port, they too claimed a victory. It was the British claim that rang hollowly in the world's ears – including British ears. For the legend of British maritime supremacy demanded a crushing victory without ambiguity – a victory proved by a long list of ships sunk. British propaganda did its best for Jutland, but it was a curious 'victory' in that for forty years a controversy was to rage as to who was principally to blame for it. Admirers of Jellicoe blamed Beatty's rashness; admirers of Beatty blamed Jellicoe's caution. The sailors blamed the politicians' meanness over money for the weakness of British equipment . . . Astonishing manipulations of fact were made in order to prove that, except for bad luck, the British of the Jutland era were as brilliant at building and fighting ships as in Nelson's time. The apologies and the searches for scapegoats served as a substitute for vital analysis.

Corelli Barnett

At sea as well as in the trenches, strategy withered into attrition; and the last military chances of avoiding a long war and utter mutual exhaustion had gone.

Corelli Barnett

JUNE 4

Thrilling tales of the Great Naval Battle.
    Whole German High-Seas Fleet Out.
  Two Zeppelins Destroyed.

Sunday Times, London

The German High Seas Fleet ran away.

Sunday Times, London

Both the German personnel and material stood the test brilliantly.

   German Admiralty

At the commencement I was sitting on the top of a turret and had a very good view of the proceedings. I was up there during a lull, when a German ship started firing at us, and one salvo 'straddled us'. We at once returned the fire. I was distinctly startled and jumped down the hole in the top like a shot rabbit! I didn't try the experiment again. The ship was in fine state on the main deck. Inches of water sluicing about to prevent fires getting a hold on the deck. Most of the cabins were also flooded. The hands behaved splendidly, and all of them were in the best of spirits as their hearts' desire had at last been granted, which was to be in action with the Germans . . . It was certainly a great experience to have been through.

   Albert, Duke of York, afterwards King George VI

Jutland, a British Verdict

Jutland was in fact defeat for British technology. More than that, as with the French at Crécy and Sedan, a social system had been exposed by battle as decadent and uncreative. Jutland proves that already in 1914, when Britain and her empire had never seemed richer, more powerful, more technologically able, dry rot was crumbling the inner structure of the vast mansion. Jutland proves that the spectacular collapse of British power and British industrial vigour after 1945 was not a sudden disaster due, as comforting legend has it, to the sale of overseas investment in 1914–18, and 1939–45, but the final acute phase of seventy years of decline . . . Fundamentally it was the Victorian navy that fought at Jutland.

   Corelli Barnett

War is nothing to enthuse over, it does not civilize, it does not cleanse, it does not make anything true or just. And it does not make men more brotherly.

It does just the opposite – anyone today can confirm this, but all want to forget it, they don't even *wish* to recognize it. *Brotherliness*. Democratic. One million dead: very sad, says someone, as though waving away a flag. And the same man: 'I escaped military service through bribery.'

> Heinrich Mann

The Crisis of the War.
> Three Great Struggles.
France, Italy and Armenia.
> 'Verdun At All Costs'.
Higher Bids but no Bargain.
> The Battle in the Alps.
A Fight to Force Peace.

> *Observer*, London

The Eastern Front

A million Russians, under General Alexei Brusilov, counter-attack, taking some half a million Austro-Hungarian prisoners, encouraging Romanian entry into the war on the Allied side, and helping restore Franco-British morale, particularly on the eve of the Somme battles, which, once again, aimed to achieve the breakthrough. As in 1914, this great effort diverted German pressure on the allies in the west.

Before weakening in August through lack of equipment, the offensive captured 300,000 prisoners and 400 guns, but after the German counter-attack the Russian personnel losses had passed the million.

JUNE 5

You cannot imagine what torture it is for me to inhabit a 'patriotic household', and to be forced to submit to the talk they exchange. You hear nothing but madness and criminal statements. If the feeble Russians allow themselves to be defeated and the Italians don't speedily change their tempo, we will eventually be able to run through France with fearful ease. Miracles will then be superfluous, and our own world will assume an aspect absolutely intolerable.

> Heinrich Mann, *to his wife, Mimi*

Kill a good few for me.

> Ethel Munro, *to her brother, 'Saki'*

JUNE 6

Lord Kitchener drowned on his way to Russia, the Hampshire *sunk by a mine, with no survivors.*

JUNE 7

Meanwhile, Verdun Continues

Second-Lieutenant Herduin, seeing his company – now down to some thirty-five men – about to be encircled, gave the order to withdraw . . . His order appears to have released a chain reaction: elements in the 347th broke, and some of its men did not stop running until they reached Verdun . . . General Boyer ordered Herduin and another young ensign, Millaud, to be shot – without trial – for cowardice. The sentence was carried out by the officers' own platoons, with tears in their eyes.

> Alistair Horne

The first signs of mutiny appeared in the French army.

In the aftermath, too, Verdun was to become a sacred national legend, and universally a household word for fortitude, heroism and suffering; but it was also a modern synonym for a Pyrrhic victory. Long after the actual war was over, the effects of this one battle lingered on in France. Of the men to arise from the triumph of Verdun, one in particular [Pétain] will be forever associated with the appalling tragedy of a generation later, and today the marks of Verdun upon France and the French have not been eradicated.

> Alistair Horne

The Germans finally fail to take Verdun: they had lost 300,000 men, and won a few square miles of wreckage.

JUNE 28

Karl Liebknecht, German socialist politician, colleague of Rosa Luxemburg, sentenced to two and a half years' hard labour for anti-war agitation. 55,000 Munition Workers on sympathy strike.

Send for the boys of the old Brigade
To keep old England free!
Send for me father, me mother and me brother,
But for Gawd's sake don't send me!

JULY 1

*The battle of the Somme began in an effort to break the trench-war
deadlock. Commanded by Sir Douglas Haig, the British lost 57,470
on the first day. The Brusilov offensive in the East maintained full
momentum, and Verdun still repelled Falkenhayn and the Crown
Prince.*

But the men who left them thriftily to die in their own dung,
Shall they come with years and honour to the grave?

      Rudyard Kipling

With the battle of the Somme the stalemate on all fronts became so
complete that neither group of combatants appeared to have a
chance of forcing a decision in the field, and the question of peace
negotiations began to be considered in London, Berlin and Vienna.

      J. F. C. Fuller

The Somme Controversy

*This stupendous carnage remains controversial. Against such his-
torians as Hart and Barnett, and all literary men, John Terraine (The
Times, 13 November, 1976), regarding it as the 132nd day of the
Battle of Verdun, replied that the terrible first day was a freak, not
repeated in the remaining 141. Though he conceded that Allied
civilian morale has never recovered, he declared that military morale
did so at once. The battle was a watershed, extinguishing the myth of
German infallibility. Hindenburg became pessimistic, and Ludendorff admitted that the German army had been bled to a standstill.
German casualties were about 450,000, helped by an order 'soldierly
but not sane' (Liddell Hart) that every lost trench must be recaptured.
The British lost over 400,000, the French almost 200,000.*

I don't want to be a soldier,
I don't want to go to war.
I'd rather stay at home
Around the streets to roam
And live on the earnings of a fucking lady-typist.
I don't want a bayonet in my belly,
I don't want my bollocks shot away,
I'd rather stay in England,
In merry, merry England,
And fuck my bloody life away.

JULY 4

British Pacifists

Some of the early batches when nothing could be done with them,
were taken singly and run across the yard to special rooms – airy
enough but from which they could see nothing. They were fed on
bread and water and some of them presently came round. I had
them placed in special rooms, nude, but with their full army kit on
the floor for them to put on as soon as they were so minded. There
were no blankets or substitutes for clothing left in the rooms which
were quite bare. Several of the men held out naked for several hours
but they gradually accepted the inevitable. Forty of the conscientious objectors who passed through my hands are now quite
willing soldiers.

> Lieutenant-Colonel Reginald Brooke, Commander of
> Military Detention Barracks, Wandsworth, writing in the
> *Daily Express*, London

In the lime-white cellars of Arras he struck at a lean
descendant of that gigantic and albino generation:
    ("Rats white as ghosts but gross as a Q.M.S.,
    "Fattened on Hanoverians fat with Wurst.")

At a café table in the Grande Place de Montreuil he
arraigned the twill breeches of a murderous field-marshal:
At Le Cateau my brother drank to a wronged commander.
    ("A slug, red-tabbed and soft-arsed.")

Alone, with a fifty-pound pack, he marched southward
from Mons till he reached the sluggish and forgetful banks
of the green Marne:
   ("Angels of Mons? I saw that Gotha hover
   "To swoop on *our* poor devils like St Michael.")

"At Souchez – so Father said – nine corpses froze in the
"parapet, and a beckoning finger was used as a hook for
"billy-cans, webbing and tin-hats:
"Oh God, he was so *familiar* with the dead!
"Why will he never tell us what they told him?"

At Pilken the air was moist and vomiting with breath that
bubbled up from the green pits of the drowned Grenadiers:
   ("Even the R.S.M. was beady of brow;
   "But Capitaine de Rose, marquis and airman . . . ")

Who? Why? What blue-winged angel, in the elevation of his
birth and daring, climbing to the lonely contrast of a cold sky?
Did you climb, bloom, droop in the skies of Picardy,
High, high above the scarlet commonality of poppies?

"The adjutant," said Father, "Barney Rogers, chartered
"accountant, sprang full four feet towards heaven before
"hell sucked him down there:
"Ah, how I loved my comrades *when they fell*;
"Humped or flat, they were boys playing possum."
"By Idiot Farm, Mogg's Turn, Jerk House and Dead Dog
"Curve we came to Vampire Point, Trip Junction,
"Sergeant's End."
   "And then? And then? Beyond the arms of the Salient
   "When sergeants ended, splintered captains knelt?"

Lifting his face, which had long been sunk on the map-like and rusty
indentations of a café table, my brother frowned for the truth of
feeling:
"As if we'd missed the only true event
'And now must whistle in the wind that blows after it."

      Philip Toynbee

July 9

The Call Up

My Dear Catherine,

I never wrote to tell you that they gave me a complete exemption from all military service, thanks be to God. That was a week ago last Thursday. I had to join the Colours in Penzance, be conveyed to Bodmin (60 miles), spend a night in barracks with all the other men, and then be examined. It was experience enough for me, of soldiering. I am sure I should die in a week, if they kept me. It is the annulling of all one stands for, this militarism, the nipping of the very germ of one's being. I was very much upset. The sense of spiritual disaster everywhere was quite terrifying. One was not sure whether one survived or not. Things are very bad.

Yet I liked the men. They all seemed so decent. And yet they all seemed as if they had chosen wrong. It was the underlying sense of disaster that overwhelmed me. They are all so brave, to suffer, but none of them brave enough, to reject suffering. They are all so noble, to accept sorrow and hurt, but they can none of them demand happiness. Their manliness all lies in accepting calmly this death, this loss of their integrity. They must stand by their fellow man: that is the motto.

This is what Christ's weeping over Jerusalem has brought us to, a whole Jerusalem offering itself to the Cross. To me, this is infinitely more terrifying than Pharisees and Publicans and Sinners, taking *their* way to death. This is what the love of our neighbour has brought us to, that, because one man dies, we all die.

D. H. Lawrence, *to Catherine Carswell*

The Silent One

Who died on the wires, and hung there, one of two –
Who for his hours of life had chattered through
Infinite lovely chatter of Bucks accent:
Yet faced unbroken wires; stepped over, and went
A noble fool, faithful to his stripes – and ended.
But I weak, hungry, and willing only for the chance
Of line – to fight in the line, lay down under unbroken
Wires, and saw the flashes and kept unshaken,

Till the politest voice – a finicking accent, said:
'Do you think you might crawl through there: there's a hole'.
Darkness, shot at: I smiled, as politely replied –
'I'm afraid not, Sir.' There was no hole no way to be seen
Nothing but chance of death, after tearing of clothes.
Kept flat, and watched the darkness, hearing bullets whizzing –
And thought of music – and swore deep heart's deep oaths
(Polite to God) and retreated and came on again,
Again retreated – and a second time faced the screen.

      Ivor Gurney

The tragedy of the Somme battle was that the best soldiers, the stoutest-hearted men were lost; their numbers were replaceable, their spiritual worth never could be.

      German soldier

THE SCENE OF WAR: THE HAPPY WARRIOR

His wild heart beats with painful sobs,
His strained hands clench an ice-cold rifle,
His aching jaws grip a hot parched tongue,
And his wide eyes search unconsciously.

He cannot shriek.

Bloody saliva
Dribbles down his shapeless jacket.

I saw him stab
And stab again
A well-killed Boche.

This is the happy warrior,
This is he . . .

      Herbert Read

JULY 10

I agree with you about the utter senselessness of war, but I do not think about it even so often as one day in seven; one of its chief effects being to make one more callous, short-sighted and un-imaginative than one is by nature. It extends the circle of one's acquaintance, but beyond that I cannot see that it has a single redeeming feature. The suggestion that it elevates the character is hideous. Burglary, assassination, and picking oakum would do as much for anyone.

> Raymond Asquith, *to Lady Diana Manners*

The Refugees

Mute figures with bowed heads
They travel along the road:
Old women, incredibly old
and a hand-cart of chattels.

They do not weep:
their eyes are too raw for tears.

Past them have hastened
processions of retreating gunteams
baggage-wagons and swift horsemen.
Now they struggle along
with the rearguard of a broken army.

We shall hold the enemy towards nightfall
and they will move
mutely into the dark behind us,
only the creaking cart
disturbing their sorrowful serenity.

> Herbert Read

JULY 11

Trinity College
Cambridge

Dear Russell,

It is my duty to inform you that the following resolution was unanimously passed by the College Council today:

'That, since Mr. Russell has been convicted under the Defence of the Realm Act, and the conviction has been affirmed on appeal, he be removed from his Lectureship in the College.'

> H. McLeod Innes, *to Bertrand Russell*

A Neutral's View, from the Northern Mountains

Nothing but this vast highland expanse in all directions – and the valleys look like narrow fissures in the great mountain plain. Deep down below winds the river of human life, how far away it seems up here. A man can breathe more freely, there is rest for eye and mind.

But other, more distant pictures arise. There are fortifications, trenches – piles of mutilated human flesh.

The Europeans, 'torch bearers of civilization', are eating at each other, trampling down civilization, ruining Europe; and who will be the better? It is like an avalanche, growing ever more ravaging, as it falls sweeping away trees, woods, homesteads, farms. The catastrophe gets greater and greater. All know the avalanche will consume the valley but no force can stop it. It must run its course. And for what are they fighting? For Power – for nothing else.

It has to happen. European *civilization has failed* – it was rotten to the core. Like a diseased tree in the forest it fell as soon as the storm burst upon it. Civilization? What does it mean if it cannot tame the monster within us – if it does not lead us away from savagery? That should be its essence; without that it is merely husk. But the monster is raging with fury unrestrained. The greatest victory is the conquest of self. Surely this embraces not only the individual but also to nations, to all human society. We wage incessant war to master Nature's powers and make life safe; but we ourselves create the greater disasters, the deepest wretchedness. Nor have we advanced far enough to halt it. What a terrible, a humiliating admission!

Fridtjof Nansen

July 15

A Brother's Death in Italy

'Regret to inform you Captain E. H. Brittain M.C. killed in action Italy June 15th.'

'No answer,' I told the boy mechanically, and handed the telegram to my father, who had followed me into the hall. As we went back into the dining-room I saw, as though I had never seen them before, the bowl of blue delphiniums on the table; their intense colour, vivid, ethereal, seemed too radiant for earthly flowers.

Then I remembered that we should have to go down to Purley and tell the news to my mother.

Late that evening, my uncle brought us all back to an empty flat. Edward's death and our sudden departure had offered the maid – at that time the amateur prostitute – an agreeable opportunity for a few hours' freedom of which she had taken immediate advantage. She had not even finished the household handkerchiefs, which I had washed that morning and intended to iron after tea; when I went into the kitchen I found them still hanging, stiff as boards, over the clothes-horse near the fire where I had left them to dry.

Long after the family had gone to bed and the world had grown silent, I crept into the dining-room to be alone with Edward's portrait. Carefully closing the door, I turned on the light and looked at the pale, pictured face, so dignified, so steadfast, so tragically mature. He had been through so much – far, far more than those beloved friends who had died at an earlier stage of the interminable War, leaving him alone to mourn their loss. Fate might have allowed him the little, sorry compensation of survival, the chance to make his lovely music in honour of their memory. It seemed indeed the last irony that he should have been killed by the countrymen of Fritz Kreisler, the violinist whom of all others he had most greatly admired.

And suddenly, as I remembered all the dear afternoons and evenings when I had followed him on the piano as he played his violin, the sad, searching eyes of the portrait were more than I could bear, and falling on my knees before it I began to cry 'Edward! Oh, Edward!' in dazed repetition, as though my persistent crying and calling would somehow bring him back.

Vera Brittain

AUGUST
The Eastern Front

The Germans, under Mackensen and Falkenhayn successfully counter-attack, driving the Russians back with immense casualties.

The Western Front

The magpies in Picardy
Are more than I can tell.
They flicker down the dusty roads
And cast a magic spell
On the men who march through Picardy,
Through Picardy to hell.

T. P. Cameron Wilson, killed in action 1918

My Nelly's a goer
My Nelly's a goer!
She's got wonderful eyes of blue.
She uses such wonderful language too,
Her favourite expression is bugger to you.
My Nelly's a goer.

AUGUST 6

BREAK OF DAY IN THE TRENCHES

The darkness crumbles away –
It is the same old druid Time as ever.
Only a live thing leaps my hand –
A queer sardonic rat –
As I pull the parapet's poppy
To stick behind my ear.
Droll rat, they would shoot you if they knew
Your cosmopolitan sympathies.
(And God knows what antipathies).
Now you have touched this English hand
You will do the same to a German –
Soon, no doubt, if it be your pleasure
To cross the sleeping green between.
It seems you inwardly grin as you pass
Strong eyes, fine limbs, haughty athletes
Less chanced than you for life,
Bonds to the whims of murder,
Sprawled in the bowels of the earth,
The torn fields of France.

What do you see in our eyes
At the shrieking iron and flame
Hurled through still heavens?
What quaver – what heart aghast?
Poppies whose roots are in men's veins
Drop, and are ever dropping;
But mine in my ear is safe,
Just a little white with the dust.

> Isaac Rosenberg

AUGUST 20

Falkenhayn replaced by Hindenburg, now supreme commander of the German armies, with Ludendorff, as First Quartermaster General, soon assuming virtual dictatorial powers.

AUGUST 22

I have given you no facts as yet, of which for a wonder there is a certain supply to hand. But I cannot end I suppose without telling you that the day before yesterday Basil Hallam was killed before my eyes by falling 6,000 ft. or so from an escaped balloon. He came to earth in a village half a mile from where I stood, falling a few yards from Mark Tennant, shockingly foreshortened, but recognisable by his cigarette case.

> Raymond Asquith, *to Lady Diana Manners*

AUGUST 27

Romania declares war on Germany.

SEPTEMBER

The Tank on the Somme

The tank was designed to provide effective movement on a battlefield where firearms (big guns and machine guns) reigned supreme, and where the physical obstacles to mobility (trenches, barbed wire, mud) had accumulated in number and variety. By 1916 the aeroplane had taken from the cavalry the reconnaissance duties it was no longer able to fulfil. The other role of the *arme blanche*, as the shock weapon to exploit the initial breakthrough, was about to be exploited by the tank . . .

In September 1916 the new weapon received its baptism of fire. Haig decided to exploit its surprise value in order to force to a decision his disastrous Somme offensive. Conditions, however, militated against its successful use in this first operation. By the time they were ready for use the long offensive had already carved up the ground over which the tanks were expected to advance, and heavy rains were to turn it into little short of a bog; the tanks themselves had not been sufficiently tested and mechanical failures were heavy; and worst of all, their initial impact on the Germans was diluted by Haig's decision to use them in driblets across the full extent of his battle front. However, even this drastic misconception of their use failed to hide the potential of the machines.

> David Lance

It is always bad when an army tries, through technical innovation, to find a substitute for the spirit. That is irreplaceable.

> Field Marshal Paul von Hindenburg

The Pacifist

In September, one of the conscientious objectors at Dyce, Walter Roberts, died after a short illness. To some of the men Roberts' death was a direct result of the damp and unhygienic conditions in which he had been forced to live, but when Ramsay MacDonald referred to the severity of these conditions, he provoked an impatient response from Mr. C. B. Stanton:

'What about our sons and others who are at the Front? Do they cry about a little mud in their camps? What about the boys whom I saw at the Front, my own son among them, up to their eyebrows in mud – boys who are risking everything? Yet we can find time here to cry out about the woes of this poor creature who is a conscientious objector in his own country's greatest hour of trouble . . . We can ill afford in this country to coddle and canoodle around these people.'

To the conscientious objectors the death of Walter Roberts had a symbolic significance that would certainly have been lost on Mr Stanton. Although Roberts had died of natural causes he was regarded as the first victim of official persecution and elevated to the rank of martyr. It was an understandable but inaccurate interpretation of the facts: Roberts no more died of persecution than a soldier succumbing to the influenza epidemic could be said to have died of conscription . . . Fenner Brockway wrote a heroic valediction in the *Tribunal* that skilfully reconciled the ideals of international socialism with the claims of the Christian faith:

'And now the struggle of this brave bearer of the banner of Peace is over. His body rests beside those of many noble men at Hawarden; his spirit is free and united with the Life Universal in which Englishman and German, Austrian and Russian are one. He has followed faithfully the Vision of Universal Peace; he has won the Peace that is eternal. To all of us his life and death must be an inspiration . . . He was worthy to be the first to die in our struggle.'

John Rae

SEPTEMBER 4

I may tell you that we are giving very special attention to this question of body-shields, but, strange to say, our great difficulty is to get the soldiers at the Front to use them. Even with the steel helmet there was a considerable amount of grumbling when they were called upon to wear it, and it is only experience which has taught them the very great value and safety given by it, and now, as you know, they will not do without the steel helmet.

David Lloyd George, *to Sir Arthur Conan Doyle*

SEPTEMBER 19

Death of British Prime Minister's son, Raymond

Heartbreaking day. Came downstairs in high spirits, opened newspaper and saw in large print: LIEUTENANT ASQUITH KILLED IN ACTION. Darling, brilliant, magically charming Raymond – how much delight and laughter goes with him! It seems to take away one's last remains of courage. One might have known that nothing so brilliant and precious could escape, but after each blow one's hopes revive, and one reinvests one's hope and interest. Now I feel I have really relinquished all hope and expect no one to survive.

Lady Cynthia Asquith

OCTOBER 1

I am much obliged to you for your kindness in writing to me about the caterpillars. There are plenty of good ideas if only they can be backed with power and brought into relief. But think what a time it took – from February 1915 when I gave the original orders – to September 1916 when the first use was made of these machines! And even then I think it would have been better to wait and act on a much larger scale – having waited so long. The caterpillars are the land sisters of the monitors. Both were intended to restore to the stronger power an effective means of offensive. The Monitor was the beginning of the torpedo-proof fleet. The caterpillar, of the bullet-proof army. But *surprise* was the true setting for both.

Winston Churchill, *to Sir Arthur Conan Doyle*

A Calais Brothel

A queue of 150 men waiting outside the door, each to have his short turn with one of the three women of the house . . . Each woman served nearly a battalion of men each week for as long as she lasted. According to the assistant provost-marshal, three weeks was the usual limit: 'after which she retired on her earnings, pale but proud'.

John Ellis

A draft of seventeen officers came in October to fill the gap left in the companies by the Somme. The Boche had done his work with his usual thoroughness; we had to make a fresh start. 'Anyway they won't be with us long,' Hill had said when he inspected the draft. 'I give the best of them two months.'

Two months have gone and his verdict is in a fair way of proving true. The average subaltern, if he comes out now for the first time, does no more than sample war. A few, and these the more fortunate, were hit, happily before they showed signs of wear. And some went on leave and did not return, and some went sick, and some were discarded to trench mortars or in drafts to other Fusilier battalions.

Lord Moran

NOVEMBER 14

Lord Lansdowne, Minister without Portfolio, submits a memor-andum to the Cabinet, proposing that peace negotiations should be seriously considered.

Put out that bloody cigarette.

> Saki (H. H. Munro), last words before being killed by a German sniper

NOVEMBER 16

Allied Military Conference at Chantilly

The essential idea which governed me was that the battle of 1916 had so thoroughly disorganized the enemy's defences and the German reserves had been used up to such an extent that, if we now made a supreme effort, we could hardly fail to obtain decisive results.

> General Joffre

NOVEMBER 18

The Battle of the Somme Ends

Lloyd George considered that the Somme offensive had been a bloody and disastrous failure, he was not willing to remain in office, if it was to be repeated next year; he said that Thomas [French Minister of Munitions], Bissolati [Italian socialist leader] and others thought the same; they would all resign simultaneously and tell their respective fellow countrymen that the war was being run on the wrong lines, and that they had better make peace rather than repeat the experience of 1916.

> Lord Hankey

Does it matter? – losing your leg? . . .
For people will always be kind,
And you need not show that you mind
When the others come in after hunting
To gobble their muffins and eggs.

Does it matter? – losing your sight? . . .
There's such splendid work for the blind;
And people will always be kind,
As you sit on the terrace remembering
And turning your face to the light.

Do they matter? – those dreams from the pit? . . .
You can drink and forget and be glad,
And people won't say that you're mad;
For they'll know that you've fought for your country,
And no one will worry a bit.

        Siegfried Sassoon

Old Kaiser Bill
Went up the hill
To see the terrible slaughter.
He fell down
And broke his crown,
And so he bloody well oughter.

THE SCENE OF WAR: FEAR

Fear is a wave
beating through the air
And on taut nerves impingeing
Till there it wins
Vibrating chords.

All goes well
So long as you tune the instrument
To simulate composure.

(So you will become
A gallant gentleman.)

But when the strings are broken . . .
Then you will grovel on the earth
And your rabbit eyes
Will fill with the fragments of your shattered soul.

        Herbert Read

NOVEMBER 20

Kaiser Franz-Josef of Austria-Hungary dies, after a reign of sixty-six years. He had endured the first of his many tragedies, defeat by Napoleon III, in Italy in 1859. 'Call me at seven. I am behind with my work.'

DECEMBER 5

A Change of Premier?

The King is alleged to be very terribly distressed and to have said, 'I shall resign if Asquith does.' The prospective attitude of the Liberal ministers was discussed. Everyone was convinced that not one of them would take office under Lloyd George, with the possible exception of Montagu. Bluetooth had assured me that the latter would, but nearly all the Asquith family repudiated the idea. George had been a very wily, foxy cad, and the Government whips must have been very bad, as apparently the P.M. was very much taken by surprise.

It had been a well-managed plot. According to Margot and others, Northcliffe has been to Lloyd George's house every day since the beginning of the war, the imputation being that George feeds him with Cabinet information, telling him the next item of the Government programme, so that he is able to start a Press agitation, and thus gain the reputation of pushing the Government into their independently determined course of action. It was said that the F.O. was really Lloyd George's ambition, and during the last weeks he has been going to the Berlitz School and reading histories of the Balkans. I believe the French like him, but he is loathed in Russia and Italy. He has had to cart Winston – whose exclusion was, I believe, one of Bonar's conditions. Certainly one cannot imagine a crazier executive than George, Carson, and Bonar. Of course, it would virtually be only George.

Lady Cynthia Asquith

December 6

H. H. Asquith resigns, succeeded as Prime Minister by David Lloyd George and a Coalition Cabinet, dedicated to more ruthless conceptions of war.

Romania defeated. Germans enter Bucharest.

Winter has found its way into the trenches at last, but I will assure you, and leave to your imagination, the transport of delight with which we welcomed its coming. Winter is not the least of the horrors of war. I am determined that this war, with all its powers for devastation, shall not master my poeting; that is, if I am lucky enough to come through all right. I will not leave a corner of my consciousness covered up, but saturate myself with the strange and extraordinary new conditions of this life, and it will all refine itself into poetry later on.

Isaac Rosenberg, *to Lawrence Binyon*

Winter Warfare

Colonel Cold strode up the Line
   (tabs of rime and spurs of ice);
stiffened all that met his glare:
   horses, men, and lice.

Visited a forward post,
   left them burning, ear to foot;
fingers stuck to biting steel,
   toes to frozen boot.

Stalked on into No Man's Land,
   turned the wire to fleecy wool,
iron stakes to sugar sticks
   snapping at a pull.

Those who watched with hoary eyes
   saw two figures gleaming there;
Hauptman Kälte, Colonel Cold,
   gaunt in the grey air.

Stiffly, tinkling spurs they moved,
    glassy-eyed, with glinting heel
stabbing those who lingered there
    torn by screaming steel.

        Edgell Rickword

DECEMBER 12

A New Power in the West

General Joffre replaced by General Nivelle as French Commander-in-Chief. Central Powers, Bulgaria and Turkey issue declarations of willingness to discuss peace.

DECEMBER 18

President Wilson issues a Note inviting all belligerents to state their war aims and agree to a post-war League of Nations to maintain peace.

CHRISTMAS DAY

The Army has orders to shoot at sight should the Hun want to fraternize and come across. Sgt. Hepple says a Hun suddenly stood head and shoulders above the parapet, took a drink from a bottle, held it out towards the sergeant, and got down again.

        William St Leger

DECEMBER 29

The Yussopov Palace, St Petersburg

Rasputin poisoned with cyanide at a supper party, then shot twice, recovered, shot again, finally kicked to death and dropped into the Neva river through a hole in the ice.

'You will lose both your son and your crown within six months of my death.'

1917

The War that will end War

> H. G. Wells

The hard-faced men who did well out of the war.

> David Lloyd George

When a butcher tells you that his heart *bleeds for his country* he has in fact no uneasy feeling.

> Dr Johnson

In the last months of 1916 and the first of 1917, while America was still neutral, the Central Powers and the Allies each stated the outline terms upon which they were prepared to discuss peace. As Lord Hankey points out, those put forward by the Allies were essentially those which, after two more years of slaughter, were imposed by the Treaty of Versailles.

> Corelli Barnett

I think it better that in times like these
A poet keep his mouth shut, for in truth
We have no gift to set a statesman right;
He has had enough of meddling who can please
A young girl in the indolence of her youth,
Or an old man upon a winter's night.

> W. B. Yeats

Daddy, what did you do in the Great War?

> British Recruiting Poster

I tried to stop the bloody thing, my child.
> Bob Smillie, Scottish Miners' Leader

A man's brains spattered on
a stretcher-bearer's face;
His shook shoulders slipped their load,
But when they bent to look again
The drowning soul was sunk too deep
For human tenderness.
> Isaac Rosenberg

Maddening nomad hordes
of Asia
out of the vats the fire they've poured.
Razin's gallows they've avenged
and all the pangs of Pugachev
whose beard was wrenched from his face.
The hooves
have struck right through
the scruff of earth
frozen stiff for ages
and the blue eternal heaven's like a sock
holed in the heel
which from the washtub emerges
scrubbed clean of dirt.
> Anatoly Marienhof

The appearance of many women . . . has excited lively anger and
indignation in the population. This bitterness is directed particularly against certain women, frequently of ripe age, who do not
engage in sports, but nevertheless show themselves in public continually clad in knickerbockers. It has even happened during the
service. Such behaviour is a cruelty to the earnest minds of the
mountain population, and in consequence there are often many
disagreeable occurrences in the streets.
> *Generalkommando for Bavaria*

From America

DOOMSDAY

The end of everything approaches;
I hear it coming
Loud as the wheels of painted coaches
On turnpikes drumming;
Loud as the pomp of plumy hearses,
Or pennoned charges;
Loud as when every oar reverses
Venetian barges;
Loud as the caves of covered bridges
Fulfilled with rumble
Of hooves; and loud as cloudy ridges
When glaciers tumble;
Like creeping thunder this continues
Diffused and distant,
Loud in our ears and in our sinews,
Insane, insistent;
Loud as a lion scorning carrion
Further and further;
Loud as the ultimate loud clarion
Or the first murther.

          Elinor Wylie

Protest

Early in 1917, Sassoon returned to France, with a clear concept of his poetic purpose. Four months of combat, ended by a bullet wound which resulted in his removal again to England, convinced him that not only was Wells right but that for himself some decisive, dramatic act of protest was necessary. Here the confirmed angry prophet in him moved toward a desperate plan. He would refuse to fight again and issue an explanatory proclamation outlining his reasons. The late John Middleton Murry helped him draft the proclamation, and Bertrand Russell subsequently saw that the document found its way to Parliament about the same time as Sassoon's copy to his commanding officer. It read:

I am making this statement as an act of wilful defiance of military authority, because I believe that the War is being deliberately prolonged by those who have the power to end it. I am a soldier, convinced that I am acting on behalf of soldiers. I believe that this War, upon which I entered as a war of defense and liberation, has now become a war of aggression and conquest. I believe that the purpose for which I and my fellow soldiers entered upon this War should have been so clearly stated as to have made it impossible to change them, and that, had this been done, the objects which actuated us would now be attainable by negotiation. I have seen and endured the sufferings of the troops, and I can no longer be a party to prolong these sufferings for ends which I believe to be evil and unjust. I am not protesting against the conduct of the War, but against the political errors and insincerities for which the fighting men are being sacrificed. On behalf of those who are suffering now I make this protest against the deception which is being practiced on them; also I believe that I may help to destroy the callous complacency with which the majority of those at home regard the continuance of agonies which they do not share, and which they have not sufficient imagination to realize.

For this act of defiance the government decided to incarcerate Sassoon in a mental institution. He was ordered to the Craiglockhart War Hospital in Edinburgh, where his therapy was directed by the famed psychologist, W. H. R. Rivers. Much of it consisted of playing golf and writing verses. Sassoon subsequently returned to combat and distinguished himself in action, but he continued to belabor the home front for its lack of imagination, understanding, and sympathy.

      Joseph Cohen

Lloyd George agrees to the proposed Nivelle offensive, despite the misgivings of Field-Marshal Sir Douglas Haig, British Commander-in-Chief, and General Sir William Robertson, Chief of the Imperial General Staff.

You have come to the parting of the ways . . . One will lead you to victory and a glorious peace, the other to revolution and disaster.

      Sir George Buchanan, *to Tsar Nicholas II*

Do you mean that I am to regain the confidence of my people, Ambassador, or that they are to regain *my* confidence?

Tsar Nicholas II, *to Sir George Buchanan*

In the Middle East, the Turkish Empire, ally of Germany, is defending itself from Arab nationalism – and T. E. Lawrence.

There came a warning patter from the drums and the poet of the right wing burst in strident song, a single invented couplet, of Feisal and the pleasure he would afford us at Wejh. The right wing listened to the verse intently, took it up and sang it together once, twice and three times, with pride and self-satisfaction and derision. However, before they could brandish it a fourth time the poet of the left wing broke out in extempore reply, in the same metre, in answering rhyme, and capping the sentiment. The left wing cheered it in a roar of triumph, the drums tapped again, the standard-bearers threw out their great crimson banners, and the whole guard, right, left and centre, broke together into the rousing regimental chorus,

> I've lost Britain, and I've lost Gaul,
> I've lost Rome, and, worst of all,
> I've lost Lalage –

only it was Nejd they had lost, and the women of the Maabda, and their future lay from Jidda towards Suez. Yet it was a good song, with a rhythmical beat which the camels loved, so that they put down their heads, stretched their necks out far and with lengthened pace shuffled forward musingly while it lasted.

T. E. Lawrence

JANUARY 10

Allied Peace terms shown to President Wilson, but thought far too harsh, giving Ludendorff his chance for militaristic plans.

JANUARY 22

President Wilson makes further pleas for 'peace without victory', rebuffed by Germany.

Nobody knows how tired we are,
　　Tired we are,
　　Tired we are,
Nobody knows how tired we are –
　　And nobody seems to care.

FEBRUARY 1

Berlin

Kaiser orders unrestricted submarine warfare.

To all U-Boats – Sink on Sight.

FEBRUARY 3

America severs diplomatic relations with Germany.

LIEDHOLZ

When I captured Liedholz
I had a blacken'd face
like a nigger's
and my teeth like white mosaics shone.

We met in the night at half-past one
between the lines.
Liedholz shot at me
and I at him;
in the ensuing tumult he surrendered to me.

Before we reached our wire
he told me he had a wife and three children.
In the dug-out we gave him a whiskey.
Going to the Brigade with my prisoner at dawn
the early sun made the land delightful
and larks rose singing from the plain.

In broken French we discussed
Beethoven, Vietzsch and the International.

He was a professor
living at Spandau
and not too intelligible.

But my black face and nigger's teeth
amused him.

　　　　　Herbert Read

In 1917, I urged with all my might that spirits should not be allowed to be drunk in the army in France. These were forbidden in France to the French. With us, far from being forbidden, the drinking of spirits was made easy. Canteens and clubs behind the lines and at the bases were stocked with alcohol.

Profiteers made money out of it at the expense of the youth of the nation, which, had there been no war, would never have learnt the taste of strong drink, at least until years of discretion had been reached.

As it turned out, families and homes were broken up through this evil, habits being introduced into homes which, but for the war and the drink evil, would have remained unshackled and free.

The legacy we have with us now. I know of at least a dozen cases myself, where the habits of drink and the vices associated with it and the loss of control due to it, have reacted on men who today are only in their early thirties.

It was a lamentable failure on the part of responsible soldiers to realise their position. It had to do with profit and selfishness. To expel whisky, the one whisky and soda a day men in high places would have had to give it up altogether. But why not? Men were giving up their lives!

In 1917 a class of men were being granted commissions, who until then had had no idea of rising to the heights of social beverages – whisky, gin, cocktails and the like. The acquisition of a star does not itself alter a man's desires, if he is given a chance and is allowed to do as he would wish.

Half the cases of indiscipline on the part of officers which came through my hands (and there were a good many) were, directly or indirectly, attributable to drinking being made easy. And in addition, of course, the physique suffered.

I have heard it said that the British Empire was consolidated with the aid of 'baccy, beer and the Bible, plus the gallant efforts of the British soldier. I have no doubt about the latter; but the record of beer and the Bible in the war leaves me stone cold. Both sides suffered from alcoholic debauchery, while both used the Bible as propaganda for hate!

General F. P. Crozier

FEBRUARY 26

At the Calais Conference, Lloyd George, without informing the War Cabinet, the War Minister, the Imperial General Staff or the Army Council, agrees to place Haig at Nivelle's disposal, for the great and conclusive offensive.

U-Boats sink American ship, drowning eight American citizens.

MARCH 1

Sensational publication in America of a reckless telegram, intercepted by British Intelligence, containing a message from the German Foreign Secretary, Zimmermann, offering Mexico an alliance, should Germany and America go to war, and offering Texas, Arizona and New Mexico as a reward.

Petrograd

Along the streets, along the paths in the park, in the direction of the Narodni Dom, hundreds, thousands of soldiers in grey are moving slowly, some of them dragging machine-guns behind them like small iron pigs tied to a string. This is one of the innumerable machine-gun regiments that has just arrived from Oranienbaum. They say that there are more than ten thousand men in it. They do not know what to do with themselves, and ever since they arrived this morning they have been wandering about the town, looking for lodgings. The passers-by step aside when they meet them, for these men are war-weary, hungry and fierce. Some of them, I noticed, had squatted down by a large, round flower-bed and had scattered their rifles and haversacks over it.

Presently, not hurrying himself in the least, the gardener came up with his broom. He surveyed them angrily:

'What sort of a camping ground do you think you've got here? This is a flower-bed – flowers are going to grow here. You know what flowers are, don't you? Are you all blind? This is the children's playground. Come off it, I say. D'you hear me?'

And the fierce, armed men meekly crawled away from the flower-bed.

Maxim Gorky

MARCH 8

The Tsar leaves Petrograd for his military headquarters.

MARCH 9

Bread riots in Petrograd.

Petrograd – Nothing Serious

Some disorders occurred today, but nothing serious.

>   Sir George Buchanan

MARCH 10

I command that the disorders in the capital to be ended tomorrow; they are wholly impossible at this grave moment of war with Germany and Austria.

>   Nicholas II

MARCH 11

Rodzianko, President of the Duma, Telegraphs the Tsar

Position serious. Anarchy in the capital. Government paralysed. Arrangements for transport, supply and fuel in complete disorder. General discontent increasing. Disorderly street firing. Part of troops firing on each other. Essential to trust someone who holds confidence of the nation with formation of a new government. There must be no delay. I pray God that in this hour responsibility will not fall on the wearer of the Crown.

MARCH 12

Guards mutiny in Petrograd, revolutionaries capture the Winter Palace and the Fortress of Peter and Paul.

MARCH 13

Petrograd – The Attack on the Astoria Hotel

This hotel had been for a very considerable period allotted to officers for whom special terms were made. Officers of every kind stayed there, amongst them members of the Allied forces.

As a Russian remarked on Monday at dinner-time: 'I wonder they don't go for this place. A cabby goes to the public-house, has to pay two roubles, for an execrable meal. We have an admirable dinner for two roubles fifty, with wine if we want it.' When the soldiers did attack the Astoria, however, it was for better reason than a desire to pillage. At 8.45 on Tuesday morning a company of soldiers passed the hotel, the red flag flying, and a band playing. Shots were suddenly heard, quite unmistakably from the roof of the Astoria. The soldiers at once smashed the long windows that ran from ceiling to floor, and the hotel was at their mercy. A scene of great confusion followed. One lady was struck by a bullet in the neck; a general who had been caught shooting at the soldiers was killed. English officers coming downstairs protested. 'I beg your pardon,' said a soldier politely, 'but this is our affair.' Too much stress cannot be laid here on the perfect politeness with which all Allied officers were treated. The English officers in especial were allowed to do what they pleased, and when the women and the servants in the hotel saw this, they put themselves under English protection.

There was practically no looting, and the greatest consideration was shown to everyone by soldiers, to whom the richness and extravagances of the Astoria must have been most inhumanly tempting. A lady, when a soldier went into her room, came to him with her hands full of money. 'What's this for?' he asked. 'We're on quite a different job here.'

No Englishman who was an observer of the incidents at the Astoria Hotel on that Tuesday will forget the impression that the Russian soldiers made upon him. 'To men who can behave on such a day in such a fashion,' someone said, 'the conquest of the World is possible.'

> Hugh Walpole

MARCH 15

Petrograd

Comrades, I have been appointed Minister of Justice. No one is a more ardent republican than I; but we must bide our time. We shall have our Republic, but we must win the War; then we can do what we will.

> Alexander Kerensky

In the account book of the Great War, the page recording the Russian losses has been ripped out. The figures are unknown. Five millions, or eight? We ourselves know not. All we do know is that, at times, fighting the Russians, we had to remove the piles of enemy bodies from before our trenches, so as to get a clear field of fire against new waves of assault.

Field Marshal Paul von Hindenburg

MARCH 16

GERARD TELLS WILSON
KAISER IGNORES U.S.

Says Germany will not modify U-boat war – Failure would aid peace.

A personal report on conditions in Germany and the events leading up to the break between the country and the United States was made to President Wilson today by James W. Gerard, former American ambassador at Berlin . . .

The former ambassador expressed his belief that Germany is staking everything on the ruthless submarine campaign and that failure of this would brighten prospects for peace. He was with the President for more than an hour, repeating and amplifying the statement already made to Secretary Lansing, in which he said Germany was determined to put no restrictions upon the relentless operations of submarines, despite the prospect of war with the United States.

New York Tribune

CZAR OF RUSSIA ABANDONS THRONE;
ARMY REVOLTS AND JOINS PEOPLE.

DUMA LEADERS IN COMPLETE CONTROL
AFTER FIERCE BATTLES; OLD CABINET
ARRESTED AND MINISTER PROTOPOPOFF REPORTED KILLED.

NEW CABINET IS FORMED;
PRINCE LVOFF NOW PREMIER.
GRAND DUKE MICHAEL CHOSEN REGENT; –
PRO-GERMAN FORCES CRUSHED – 'PUSH
THE WAR' PARTY IS TRIUMPHANT.

REVOLT WILL HELP
ALLIES, BONAR LAW
TELLS COMMONS.

New York Tribune

CZAR NICHOLAS II
WAS DOMINATED
BY DARK FORCES

Grand Dukes swayed him
by threats; Rasputin ruled
through mysticism.

Reigned for 22 years

Whole period filled with
Revolutions, War and
Bloodshed.

New York Tribune

MARCH 16

Tsar Abdicates. The Duma Heads a Revolution in Petrograd.

Troops side with the People.

Reactionaries Arrested: People's Revenge on Police.

The two days' silence from Petrograd was broken last night. News comes that the Duma has placed itself at the head of a revolutionary movement and that, supported by the troops in Petrograd, it has declared a Provisional Government.

The Tsar has abdicated, and his brother, the Grand Duke Michael Alexandrovitch, has been appointed Regent. This was announced in the House of Commons last night.

The first duty of a British correspondent in these days of national upheaval is to assure his compatriots that 'Russia is alright' as a friend, ally, and fighter. The fiery trials she is undergoing will only steel her heart and arms.

I have been day and night in the streets for the last three days; I have seen long queues of hungry men, women, and children at the bakers', seen wanton firing with rifles and machine-guns, seen civil war in the main thoroughfares; but I have not heard a single word against the war.

The shortage of food, the lack of organisation, and the neglect of the most elementary precautions are popularly ascribed to German influences. The word 'provocation' was on all lips. These influences the Russians are resolved to exterminate. The killing of Rasputin was the match which set fire to a vast heap of patriotic determination. Russia would deserve well of her Allies. She would give herself a chance.

Manchester Guardian

The great point of the present upheaval lies in the fact that it is in no wise anti-monarchical.

The Times, London

MARCH 17

The programme outlined by the Provisional Government yesterday would appear to be progressive enough to satisfy even the most advanced believer in ordered freedom. In addition to all the ordinary rights of citizenship in the freest and the most experienced democracies of Europe and of America, to a comprehensive amnesty – which, however, does not seem to extend to the principal Reactionaries – and to the abolition of all social, religious, and national restrictions, it proposes to extend the right of striking to the troops, 'so far as military conditions permit', and to substitute for the police a national Militia with elected officers. A Constituent Assembly, chosen by universal suffrage, is to determine the future Constitution, and these measures are to be put in execution forthwith, notwithstanding the existence of the war.

The best testimony to the bearing of the Revolution upon the great world-struggle is that borne by the American and by a portion of the German Press. In both countries its true character is recognized as clearly as in the message of congratulation which the leaders of the British Labour Party have addressed to their Russian comrades. The Americans treat it like the Englishmen, with the deepest sympathy, as an effort against the reactionary elements which have so long striven to shut Russia off from the free West and to throw her into the arms of the German 'militarists'. No single incident in the war, our Washington Correspondent states, except, perhaps, the Jutland battle, has caused such profound sensation in the United States. It is recognized as a great victory for Liberalism and for the Allies, and as a heavy blow to the evil cause embodied in Prussian despotism.

The Times, London

Williamsburg, America

The overthrow of the Czar filled us with joy. What had been a dream for years was now a reality. The prison of the peoples had collapsed. We sang the *Marseillaise* and the *International* in the streets, cut classes for the day, and rushed to tell our families the great news. Almost the entire American Press, from the extreme right to the extreme left, applauded the Revolution.

Joseph Freeman

A Future British Prime Minister Greets the Russian Revolution

A sort of springtide of joy has broken out all over Europe.

J. Ramsay Macdonald

A white snowy shroud brightened the murkiness of polar swamps. But there was such delight in our jingling sledges as we crossed the frontier river into Torneo. In front of us lay the New Russia. It was not yet our own, for it remained only bourgeois, but had not the workers' and peasants' yearning for peace, and for a fundamental clean sweep of the Old Russia, been shown in the creation of the Soviets? Ahead was struggle and work, work and struggle. Then, March 1917, my soul felt as bracingly bright and fresh as the snow and frosty air about me.

Alexandra Kollontai

Great Changes Approach

The Revolution grew directly out of the war, and the latter became the touchstone for all parties and forces of the Revolution.

Trotsky

The buds will swell with sap again,
And shoots of green will sprout,
But that spine of yours is cracked,
O age of beauty and of anguish,
A fatuous grin upon your face,
You glare behind you, weak and rapacious,
Like a beast that once was lithe,
at the tracks your paws have made.

Osip Mandelshtam

Approaching the conclusion of an extremely important speech
the great statesman stumbling
on a beautiful, empty phrase
trips over it
And undone, mouth agape,
displays his teeth
And the molar decay of his peaceful logic
exposes the nerve of war
the delicate question of hard cash.

Jacques Prévert

It was natural that the Allies, burning with indignation against
Germany, breathless and bleeding in the struggle, face to face with
mortal dangers, should stand amazed at the cool, critical, detached
attitude of the great Power across the Atlantic. In England particularly, where laws and language seemed to make a bridge of mutual
comprehension between the two nations, the American abstention
was hard to understand.

Winston Churchill

A German Intrigue

Telegram 15

The State Secretary to the Foreign Ministry Liaison Officer
at General Headquarters
Telegram No. 461
AS 1125   Berlin, 23 March 1917
The Imperial Minister in Bern has sent the following telegram:
'Federal Counsellor [Bundesrat] Hoffmann has been told that lead-

ing Russian revolutionaries here wish to return to Russia via Germany as they are afraid to travel via France because of the danger from submarines. Please send instructions in case applications to this effect should be made to me. Romberg.'

Since it is in our interests that the influence of the radical wing of the Russian revolutionaries should prevail, it would seem to me advisable to allow transit to the revolutionaries there. I would therefore support the granting of permission. Would Your Excellency please inform the High Command of the Army and ask for their opinion in this matter?

ZIMMERMANN

Telegram 16

The Liaison Officer at General Headquarters at the Foreign Ministry
Telegram No. 371
AS 1148   25 March 1917, 12.15 a.m.
In reply to telegram No. 461
High Command of the Army instructs me to telegraph as follows: 'No objections to transit of Russian revolutionaries if effected in special train with reliable escort. Organization can be worked out between representatives of IIIb [Military Passport Office] in Berlin and Foreign Ministry.'

LERSNER

Our tactics – total mistrust, no support for the Provisional Government. Above all, distrust Kerensky. No alliance with other parties.
        Lenin

RECRUITED-POPLAR

March, 1917

    They say – They say
(And that's the bugles going all the day
Past Cooper's Arms and round by Stepney way
Till you'll be mad for hearing of them play)
    They say – They say
You were the finest stuff men ever had
To make into a soldier. And they say

They put the needed strength and spirit in you,
Straightened your shoulders, made you clean and true,
And fit for England's service – I can say
They clothed you warm, and fed and worked you fair
The first time in your life, on Derby Day;
Maybe that did a little – Anyway
They made a man out of you this year, the sort
That England's rich and proud to own, they say
    They say – They say
And so they went and killed you. That's their way.

      Margaret Postgate

The war on the Western Front has meanwhile continued.

They stopped post a day before we left, and it was impossible to write again till we got back to our old haunts. We are all sad to leave the quiet of that untroubled country, where such pleasant days have been spent. We could not have hit upon a better time for we saw all the change of trees and fields and hills from bleakness to fresh green and warm lovely lights. I must return to these landscapes above the hills. Just before I left I came upon a bank where real French violets grew, you know those dark ones that have such an intoxicating smell. Alas I was with the Company at the time, and though I meant to hunt out the bank after and send some flowers to you I never had time. Flowers bloom everywhere and we have just come up to the trenches for a time and where I sit now in the reserve line the place is just joyous, the dandelions are bright gold over the parapet and nearby a lilac bush is breaking into bloom; in a wood passed through on our way up, a place with an evil name, pitted and pocked with shells the trees torn to shreds, often reeking with poison gas – a most desolate ruinous place two months back, today it was a vivid green; the most broken trees even had sprouted somewhere and in the midst, from the depth of the wood's bruised heart poured out the throbbing song of a nightingale. Ridiculous mad incongruity! One can't think which is the more absurd, the War or Nature; the former has become a habit so confirmed, inevitable, it has its grip on the world just as surely as spring or summer. Thus we poor beings are double enthralled. At the mercy of the old elements which we take pains to study, avoid, build and dress for we are now in the

power of something far more pitiless, cruel and malignant, and so
we must study further, build ten times as strong, dress cunningly
and creep about like rats always overshadowed by this new terror.
Of course we shall get used to it just as we are almost accustomed to
the damnable climate of England. Already man has assumed an
indifference quite extraordinary to shells, fire, mines and other
horrors. It's just as well because it is going to be our daily bread for
months and months to come.

    Paul Nash

MARCH 24

Emperor Karl of Austro-Hungary initiates secret Peace proposals,
including an acknowledgment of French rights to Alsace-Lorraine.

Civilians

Yacht Club, London, Saturday, 24 March – Dined with Sir W.
Weir [Director of Air Supply], Major Weir [Flying Staff, W.O.] and
Richmond, at Savoy, after spending half an hour in the Angelica
Kauffman room at Weir's flat.

    They began to try to startle me right off. Weir and Richmond said
that the labour situation was acutely bad. Tyne strike not better.
Men out at Barrow, and men out at three or four small factories that
worked for Weir. The strikes were not officially countenanced by
Trades Unions; the organization alien [U.S.A.] working through
shop stewards, etc.

    Talking about the Labour question they all agreed that the
margin of labour was sufficient. That is, that the Government could
draw all the men it needed for the Army out of essential occupations
and that the men left in the essential occupations could do all the
work provided they would produce their maximum output, which
they don't and won't. All three were enthusiastic about the effort of
France.

    Arnold Bennett

German-American relations at flashpoint. Woodrow Wilson, in his
loneliness, decides for War.

MARCH 27

Washington

[Colonel House] arrived in the afternoon, just after the
Cabinet meeting was over, and Wilson and he went together into
the study. Wilson was not feeling well and complained of a
headache. House was the first man to learn from his lips that the
decision was taken. He had fought with himself night after night, he
said, in the hope of seeing some other way out. 'What else can I
do?', he asked, 'Is there anything else I can do?' But he could not
have hoped for an answer.

> Patrick Devlin

*For several days more, Wilson and House kept their momentous
secret.*

MARCH 30

The King has been thinking much about the Government's proposal
that the Emperor Nicholas and his family should come to England.
As you are doubtless aware, the King has a strong personal friendship for the Emperor and therefore would be glad to do anything to
help him in this crisis. But His Majesty cannot help doubting not
only on account of the dangers of the voyage, but on general
grounds of expediency, whether it is advisable that the Imperial
Family should take up their residence in this country.

> Lord Stamfordham, the King's Private Secretary, *to the
> Foreign Secretary*

If Germany is not absolutely crushed and a peace declared on any
reasonable terms, even if these should happen to leave her defeated, she will shut down the war as soon as she can for about a
generation. Then, unless vision fails me or God intervenes in some
strange way, she will employ this period in exploiting her vast
annexed territories filled with her slaves, and in extracting there-
from enormous wealth as she knows well how to do. She will recruit
their endless manpower into her armies; also during this time she
will breed up her own on stud farm principles, choosing the finest
fighting stock. Then at the end of thirty years from the end of the
forthcoming peace she will attack and lay all Europe beneath her

feet, since a number of disunited nations, soaked, under the guidance of Democracy, with disintegrating revolutionary principles, can never resist her concentrated and instructed might, whatever they have suffered from the burdens of armaments in the intervening years, which will be much. I believe that in this event Britain will go with the rest. Then there will be but one hope for the inhabitants – to flee to America – if they can – to make new homes in Canada or the States; since in such a case America alone will be able to hold her own against the Germans, and this only by ceaseless watching and the creation of vast armed forces on sea and land. Such are some of the dangers and mischiefs that this talk of peace with Germany may breed. People do not like to believe in the possibility still less in the probability of another war. I shall never forget how angry I made a considerable section of Canadian opinion by inculcation of this very truth, namely that unless Germany was crushed, Germany would most certainly re-arise and crush us, who from our nature, our party political system, and the power of labour in the community, cannot long remain prepared for war. Another war, they declared, was impossible. Germany would change her heart. But what says Germany – 'There is no international Law – treaties are but scraps of paper'. These are some of the things which would result unless God intervenes as He alone can do. I pray, too that I may be mistaken. But I do not feel as though I were. The rise of the British Empire in the teeth of the hamperings and opposition of British Statesmen and the elephantine obstinacy and stupidity of permanent officials, is and always must remain one of the marvels of the world. Truly the Anglo-Saxon race is great. The folly and self-seeking of such creatures lost us America, but the genius of our blood, even when mixed, is going to bring it back into a closer and more enduring union.

> H. Rider Haggard

APRIL 1

U-Boats sink the Aztec. *Twenty-eight Americans drowned.*

APRIL–MAY

British metal workers strike.

U-Boat sinkings reach a peak of 834,549 tons.

Had Germany been aware of the straits to which Britain had been reduced by the 1917 U-Boat campaign there can be little doubt that the entire country would have rallied to the support of the Navy in giving the hated enemy the death blow.

Edwyn A. Gray

Can the Army win the war before the Navy loses it?

Admiral Lord Fisher.

I couldn't forget my crew, my friends going down out there, drowned like rats in a trap, with some perhaps left to die of slow suffocation. I could imagine how some might even now be alive in the strong, torpedo compartments, lying in the darkness, hopeless, waiting for the air to thicken and finally smother them.

Kapitänleutnant Baron von und zu Peckelshaim

300,000 workers strike in Berlin.

APRIL 2

The Fateful Alliance

On a bright April morning, Londoners beheld with deep emotion the Stars and Stripes floating in the air from the Victoria Tower at Westminster, side by side with the Union Jack.

H. A. L. Fisher

On the Western Front an English Poet Writes to an American Poet

I have seen some new things since I wrote last and had mud and worse things to endure which do not become less terrible in anticipation but are less terrible once I am in the midst of them. Jagged gables at dawn when you are cold and tired out look a thousand times worse from their connection with a certain kind of enemy shell that has made them look like that, so that every time I see them I half hear the moan of the approaching and hovering shell and the black grisly flap that it seems to make as it bursts. I see and hear more than I did because changed conditions compel me to go up to the very front among the infantry to do an observation and we spend nights without shells in the mud chiefly in waiting for morning and the arrival of the relief. It is a twenty-four-hour job and takes more to recover from. But it is far as yet from being unendurable . . . I think I get surer of some primitive things that one has got to get sure of about oneself and other people, and I think this is not due simply to being older. In short, I am glad I came out and I think less about return than I thought I should – partly no doubt I inhibit the idea of return. I only think by flashes of the things at home that I used to enjoy and should again . . . I doubt if anybody here thinks less of home than I do and yet I doubt if anybody loves it more.

. . . We expect soon to have to live in damp dug-outs for safety. There are some random shots but as a rule we know where to expect trouble and you can feel quite safe close to a place that is deadly dangerous. We work or make others work practically all day with no rest or holidays, but often we have a quiet evening and can talk or write letters or listen to the gramophone playing 'John Peel' and worse things far. People are mostly friendly and warm, however uncongenial. I am more than ten years older than four of the other five officers. They are nineteen, twenty, twenty-five, twenty-six and thirty-three years old. Those of twenty-five and twenty-six regard me as very old. I don't know if the two boys do – I get on better with them: in a sort of way we are fond of one another – I like to see them come in of a night back from some job and I believe they like to see me. What more should anyone want? I revert for ten minutes every night by reading Shakespeare's Tragedies in bed with a pipe before I blow the candle out. Otherwise I do nothing that I used to do except eat and sleep: I mean when I am not alone. Funny world. What a thing it is. And I hear nothing of you. Yet you are no more like an American in a book than you were two-and-a-half years ago. You are among the unchanged things that I can not or dare not think of except in flashes. I don't have memories except such as are involved in my impressions as I see or hear things about me. But if I went on writing like this I should make you think I was as damnably introspective as ever and practised the art too. Good-night to you and Elinor and all. Remember I am in 244 Siege Battery, B.E.F. France, and am and shall remain 2nd Lieut. Edward Thomas, Yours ever.

to Robert Frost

Outside Russia

The wonderful and heartening things have been happening in the last few weeks in Russia.

President Woodrow Wilson

Inside Russia

A hush that evening in the organ forest,
then singing for us: Schubert, cradle songs,
the noise of a mill, and the voice of a storm
where the music had blue eyes and was drunk and laughing.

Brown and green is the world of the song,
and young forever. There the maddened king
of the forest shakes the whispering crowns
of the nightingale lindens.

With darkness he returns, and his terrible strength
is wild in that song, like a black wine.
He is the Double, an empty ghost
peering mindlessly through a cold window.

Osip Mandelshtam

Washington

Congress had convened at noon and all the afternoon the slow crowds swarmed about the streets of Washington. Many carried little Stars and Stripes. It rained; and as night came on and the sky blackened, the Capitol, floodlit for the first time, stood out in white. The usual police protection was not thought to be enough for the President and, as if it were a symbol of the civil power giving place to the military, a cavalry squadron surrounded the President's automobile and clattered beside it to the Capitol. The corridors of the building were packed. At the door of Senator Lodge's room blows were exchanged. 'You are a damned coward,' a pacifist cried. The Senator, sixty-seven years old, walked up to him and hit him, saying: 'You are a damned liar.' The pacifist failed to turn the other cheek. The senator was rescued and the pacifist beaten up. 'I am glad I hit him,' the senator said.

The auditorium of the House was crammed. The Cabinet sat to the left of the Speaker, behind them the ambassadors and in front of the Speaker the justices of the Supreme Court. Every representative was in his place. The steps and the doorways were thronged with distinguished visitors. Shortly before half past eight the senators entered and marched solemnly down the centre aisle to their places behind the justices; the Vice-President took his chair beside the Speaker. A minute or two later the Clerk of the House announced: 'The President of the United States.' There was a tremendous ovation and then an intense stillness. The President walked to the rostrum, rested his arm on the high desk and began to read:

'Gentlemen of the Congress: I have called the Congress into extraordinary session . . .'

> Patrick Devlin

April 3

PRESIDENT CALLS FOR WAR DECLARATION
STRONGER NAVY, NEW ARMY OF 500,000 MEN,
FULL CO-OPERATION WITH GERMANY'S FOES

THE WAR RESOLUTION NOW BEFORE CONGRESS

JOINT RESOLUTION, Declaring that a state of war exists between the Imperial German Government and the Government and People of the United States and making Provision for the same.

Whereas, the recent acts of the Imperial German Government are acts of war against the Government and people of the United States:

Resolved, By the Senate and House of Representatives of America in Congress assembled, that the State of War between the United States and the Imperial German Government which has thus been thrust upon the United States is hereby formally declared and

That the President be, and he is hearby, authorized and directed to take immediate steps not only to put the country in a thorough state of defense but also to exert all of its power and employ all of its resources to carry on war against the Imperial German Government and to bring the conflict to a successful termination.

> *New York Times*

America grants huge dollar credit to Russian Provisional Government.

APRIL 4

U.S. TO JOIN THE ALLIES

MR WILSON'S CALL TO ARMS

BIG FRENCH ATTACK. GAINS ON BRITISH FRONT

President Wilson told the United States on Monday that war was necessary, and asked Congress to declare that a state of war with Germany exists.

The effect of his speech was electrical. It was received by Congress with great enthusiasm. The nation is at one with him, 'Yesterday,' says our Washington Correspondent, 'the United States was distracted by cross-currents of opinion, prejudice, and tradition. Today the tide of national thought sets in a steady stream of patriotism.'

The Times, London

The most serious question which Americans faced during the first half of the 20th century concerned their roles in Europe and in those large areas of the globe where Englishmen and Europeans owned colonies or spheres of influence.

This question presented itself as a result of World War I. In the first place, that war so wasted the resources of the Old World as to make the United States no longer merely a great power but the greatest of all powers. In the second place, the intervention of the United States, provoked by Germany's challenge to American maritime interests, had led to the dispatch of a huge American army to Europe, more than 250,000 American casualties, and, inevitably, American participation in the framing of peace terms for all of Central and Southern Europe.

President Wilson himself believed devoutly in the American mission. When he concluded that the United States had no choice other than war with Germany, he immediately sought to make the impending sacrifices serve ends nobler than mere punishment of the enemy. His war message of 1917 spoke of 'a World safe for democracy'.

His later statements about war aims emphasized ensuring a right of self-determination for Poles and nationality groups subject to Austro-Hungarian and Ottoman rule. When negotiating for an armistice in 1918, he made a virtual condition that Germany cease to be a monarchy and become a republic. In some respects, Wilson converted the war into a crusade for self-determination and democracy.

Ernest R. May

Propaganda

Fired by such notions [that German soldiers cut the hands off Belgian children] about the behaviour of the enemy and by others equally absurd, the American people launched themselves into the war with an emotional hysteria that can only be understood by realizing the power of propaganda in generating common action by a nation under belligerent conditions. Those who did not accept the war ideology were usually few in number and always quite impotent. The almost primitive ecstasy that could sometimes grip the American people has recently been summarized in unforgettable fashion.

We hated with a common hate that was exhilarating. The writer of this review remembers attending a great meeting in New England, held under the auspices of a Christian Church – God save the mark! A speaker demanded that the Kaiser, when captured, be boiled in oil, and the entire audience stood on chairs to scream its hysterical approval. This was the mood we were in. This was the kind of madness that had seized us.

James Duane Squires

Amsterdam

The Vossische Zeitung says that the German Empress has given very valuable jewels in her private possession for sale in a neutral country.

The Times, London

Petrograd

During the first days after the Revolution there was a noticeable tendency among the older men in the Army to return to their villages. I recorded a similar phenomenon in Petrograd. Wild rumours had gone forth that there was to be a division of lands. Stupid people believed them. Cases of desertion were not infrequent but the men are now returning of their own accord.

The Times, London

Barrow

The men on strike at Barrow have agreed to resume work today on the conditions upon which they left . . . the result of the ballot was announced at an open air mass meeting yesterday afternoon, the figures being:

For Local Conference and resumption, 1,623.

Against Local Conference and resumption, 1,250.

The Times, London

APRIL 7

Windsor Castle, Six degrees of frost in the night. The United States declared war against Germany yesterday by a large majority in the Congress: 373 to 50.

George V

We are in this war because we were forced into it; because Germany not only murdered our citizens on the high seas, but also filled our country with spies and sought to incite our people to civil war. We were given no opportunity to discuss or negotiate. The forty-eight hour Ultimatum given by Austria to Serbia was not, as Bernard Shaw said, 'a decent time in which to ask a man to pay his hotel bill.' What of the six-hour Ultimatum given to me in Berlin on the evening of January 31st, 1917, when I was notified at six that ruthless warfare would commence at twelve? . . . I believe that we are not only justly in this war, but prudently in this war. If we had stayed out and the war had been drawn or won by Germany we should have been attacked, and that while Europe stood grinning by: not directly at first, but through an attack on some Central or South American State to which it would be at least as difficult for us to send troops as for Germany. And what if this powerful nation, vowed to war, were once firmly established in South or Central America? What of our boasted isolation then?

James W. Gerard

Further Considerations

The wisdom of America's entry into the war was questioned by Mr. Ramsay Macdonald, leader of the British Labour Party. On August 17 he addressed a statement to Colonel House and the President, in which he wrote: 'The majority of our people welcomed America's entry into the war, but a minority, much larger than newspapers or vociferous opinion indicates, regards it not with any hostile feelings but with regret. They come to that view because (a) they do not think that American military help was required in order to compel any of the Powers to make a reasonable peace; and (b) they think that America, out of the war, would have done more for peace and good feeling than in the war, and would also have had a better influence on the peace settlement.' Further he wrote: ' . . . whilst you can have peace without victory, history shows that as a rule nations have had victory without peace . . . It would also compel them to welcome political activities parallel with military activities.'

Years later – in August, 1936 – Mr. Churchill in a statement to William Griffen, editor of the New York Enquirer, is reported by the latter to have said that 'America should have minded her own business and stayed out of the World War. If you hadn't entered the war the Allies would have made peace with Germany in the Spring of 1917. Had we made peace then there would have been no collapse in Russia followed by Communism, no breakdown in Italy followed by Fascism, and Germany would not have signed the Versailles Treaty, which has enthroned Nazism in Germany. If America had stayed out of the war, all these "isms" wouldn't today be sweeping the continent of Europe and breaking down parliamentary government, and if England had made peace early in 1917, it would have saved over one million British, French, American, and other lives.'

J. F. C. Fuller

The war had lasted nearly three years; all the original combatants were at extreme tension; on both sides the dangers of the front were matched by other dangers far behind the throbbing lines of contact. Russia has succumbed to these new dangers; Austria is breaking up; Turkey and Bulgaria are wearing thin; Germany herself is forced even in full battle to concede far-reaching Constitutional rights and franchise to her people; France is desperate; Italy is about to pass within an ace of destruction; and even in stolid Britain there is a different light in the eyes of men. Suddenly a nation of one hundred and twenty millions unfurls her standard on what is already the stronger side; suddenly the most numerous democracy in the world, long posing as a judge, is hurled, nay, hurls itself into the conflict. The loss of Russia was forgotten in this new reinforcement. Defeatist movements were strangled on the one side and on the other inflamed. Far and wide through every warring nation spread these two opposite impressions – 'The whole world is against us' – 'The whole world is on our side'.

> Winston Churchill

APRIL 9

Easter Monday

Offensive resumes on the Western Front at Arras. Canadians storm Vimy Ridge, as a preliminary to the Nivelle Offensive. 1½ miles captured, 21,000 prisoners taken. 158,000 British and Canadian casualties.

There's a little wet home in the trench,
That the rain storms continually drench,
A dead cow close by, with her hooves in the sky,
And she gives off a beautiful stench.
Underneath us, in place of a floor
Is a mess of cold mud and some straw,
And the Jack Johnsons roar as they speed through the air
O'er my little wet home in the trench.

> Canadian Song

In the middle of April 1917 the Germans took a sombre decision. Ludendorff refers to it with bated breath. Full allowance must be

made for the desperate stakes to which the German leaders were
already committed. They were in the mood which had opened
unlimited submarine warfare with the certainty of bringing the
United States into the war against them. Upon the Western Front
they had from the beginning used the most terrible means of offence
at their disposal. They had employed poison gas on the largest scale
and had invented the 'Flammenwerfer'. Nevertheless it was with a
sense of awe that they turned upon Russia the most grisly of all
weapons. They transported Lenin in a sealed truck like a plague
bacillus into Russia.

> Winston Churchill

It was a mistake I do not care to recall.

> Ludendorff, 1920

APRIL 16

In the East
Lenin arrives in Petrograd

The Revolution must not mean that the new class rules, governs,
through the *old* state machinery, but that this class *smashes* that
machinery, and rules, governs, through *new* machinery.

> Lenin

'Lenin plainly knew exactly how to behave. He stood there as
though nothing taking place had the slightest connection with him
– looking about him, examining the persons round him and even
the ceiling of the imperial waiting-room, adjusting his bouquet
(rather out of tune with his whole appearance) and then, turning
away from the Ex-Com delegation altogether he made his "reply".

'"Dear comrades, soldiers, sailors and workers. I am happy to
greet in your persons the victorious Russian revolution, and greet
you as the vanguard of the world-wide proletarian army . . . the
piratical imperialist war is the beginning of civil war throughout
Europe . . . world-wide socialism has already dawned . . . Germany is seething . . . any day now the whole of European capita-

lism may crash. The Russian revolution accomplished by you has prepared the way and opened a new epoch. Long live the world-wide socialist revolution."

'Suddenly,' Sukhanov goes on, 'before the eyes of all of us, completely swallowed up by the routine drudgery of the revolution, there was presented a bright, blinding exotic beacon . . . Lenin's voice, heard straight from the train, was a "voice from outside". There had broken in upon us in the revolution a note that was . . . novel, harsh and somewhat deafening.'

> Alan Moorehead

Start of the Nivelle Offensive, on the Aisne

To avoid repeating the bloodbaths of Verdun and the Somme, General Nivelle persuades the Allied leaders to agree to another attack but with his own novel plans. He, himself already ill from consumption and with only another year to live, was much influenced by the very sick and reckless Colonel d'Alenson.

After ten days, following 34,000 dead, 90,000 wounded, 20,000 missing, French mutinies were hatching.

APRIL – AUGUST

187,000 French casualties in Nivelle's offensive, the second battle of the Aisne, against the Hindenburg line. 244,897 Allied casualties. Hindenburg and Ludendorff command the Germans.

If you want to find the old battalion,
I know where they are, I know where they are,
      I know where they are –
They're hanging on the old barbed wire.
      I've seen 'em, I've *seen* 'em,
Hanging on the old barbed wire.

This war, with all its ugliness, is great and wonderful.

> Max Weber

Sit on the bed. I'm blind, and three parts shell.
Be careful; can't shake hands now; never shall.
Both arms have mutinied against me, – brutes.
My fingers fidget like ten idle brats.

I tried to peg out soldierly, – no use!
One dies of war like any old disease.
This bandage feels like pennies on my eyes.
I have my medals? – Discs to make eyes close.
My glorious ribbons? – Ripped from my own back
In scarlet shreds. (That's for your poetry book.)

        Wilfred Owen

The Price of Glory

Unfortunately Nivelle's assurances had also reached German ears. Security had been even worse neglected than before the Douaumont fiasco the previous May, and some six weeks ahead of the offensive the defenders knew exactly what to expect. The huge weight of Nivelle's artillery preparation came down like a haymaker swung into thin air. The Germans had simply pulled back from their forward positions. On April 16, 1917, the French infantry – exhilarated by all they had been promised – left their trenches with an élan unsurpassed in all their glorious history. They advanced half-a-mile into a vacuum, and then came up against thousands of intact machine-guns. Angry, demoralised, bitterly disillusioned men flooded back from the scene of the butchery. By the following day, there had been something like 120,000 casualties. Niville had predicted 10,000 wounded; the medical services had added another 5,000 to this estimate, but in the event the offensive required over 90,000 evacuations. In the rear areas, some two hundred wounded literally assaulted a hospital train. [In one hospital, 4 thermometers were allocated to 3,500 beds.] Still Nivelle, as his ambitions collapsed in fragments around him, tried to persist with the hopeless offensive. But he had broken the French Army.

Details of the slaughter on the Chemin-des-Dames – appalling though the truth itself was – became fiercely exaggerated. With them the kind of incidents that had occurred sporadically at Verdun multiplied throughout the army. Again the macabre, sheep-like bleating was heard among regiments sent up to the line; this time mingled with cries of 'Down with the war!' and 'Down with the incapable leaders!' Men on leave waved red flags and sang revolutionary songs. They beat up military police and railwaymen, and uncoupled or derailed engines to prevent trains leaving for the front. Interceding officers – including at least one general – were set upon.

On May 3rd the mutiny proper broke out. The Nivelle Offensive was still continuing, broken-backed and the 21st Division (which significantly enough, had experienced some of the worst fighting at Verdun in June of the previous year) was ordered into battle. To a man it refused. The ringleaders were weeded out, summarily shot or sent to Devil's Island. Two days later the division went back into action, and was decimated. That touched off the powder-keg. Next the 120th Regiment refused to move into the line; the 128th ordered to show it an example, followed suit. Unit after unit refused duty, some of them the finest in the French Army, and over twenty thousand men deserted outright. Regiments elected councils to speak for them, ominously like the Soviets that had already seized power in the Russian Army, and set off to Paris en masse. The 119th Regiment mounted machine-guns on its trucks, and attempted to reach the Schneider-Creusot works, with the apparent intention of blowing it up. By June these acts of 'collective indiscipline', as the French Official War History euphemistically termed them, spread to fifty-four divisions – or half the French Army.

Alistair Horne

CORNFLOWER

Young man
of twenty
Who have seen such terrible things
What do you think of the grown men of your childhood
you
    have
        seen
            death
                face
                    to
                        face
                            more
                                than
                                    a
                                  hundred
                                    times
Communicate your fearlessness   you
   to those who will come   do
     after you   not
                                  know
                                      what
                                        life
                                          is

                Young man
        You are full of joy your memory is full of blood
           Your soul is also red
                With joy
    You have absorbed the life of those who died close to you
       You have the quality of decision
      It is 1700 hrs. and you would know how to
                Die
        If no better than your elders
          At least more piously
      For you know death better than life
        O sweetness of other times
          Immemorial slowness

    Apollinaire

On the Eastern Front

Ludendorff's successor, General Hoffmann, privately informs the Catholic political leader, Erzberger, himself now working for peace, that Germany has lost the war.

The people
            have broken
                        tsarist fetters.
Russia's boiling,
                        Russia's ablaze!
Lenin read
            in newspapers and letters
in Switzerland
                        where he lived in those days.
But what could one fish
                        out of newspaper tatters.
O
  for an airplane
                        skyward to speed –
home,
      to the aid
                  of the workers in battle –
that
    was his only longing and need.
But at last
            at the Party's bidding
                              he's on wheels.
If only
      the murderous Hohenzollern knew
that the German goods waggon
                              under German seals
carried
      a bomb
            for his monarchy, too.

            Vladimir Mayakovsky

The Army Corps Commander
    Had 100,000 men,
The Army Corps Commander
    Had 100,000 men,
But the Red Tabs frittered them away.
    Glory! Glory! Alleluia!
The Red Tabs frittered them away.

                British Marching song

It was during the war that I first came across Mr Eliot's work . . .
some poems which had come out in a sort of paperish volume from
England: *Prufrock*, *The Portrait of a Lady*, and a few more.

   The poems were not epicurean; still they were innocent of public-
spiritedness: they sang of private disgust and diffidence, and of
people who seemed genuine because they were unattractive or
weak . . .

   'I should have been a pair of ragged claws,
   Scuttling across the floors of silent seas.'

Here was a protest, and a feeble one, and the more congenial for
being feeble. For what, in that world of gigantic horror, was tolerable except the slighter gestures of dissent? He who measured
himself against the war, who drew himself to his full height, as it
were, and said to Armadillo – Armageddon 'Avaunt!' collapsed at
once into a heap of dust. But he who could turn aside to complain of
ladies and drawing-rooms preserved a tiny drop of our self-respect,
he carried on the human heritage.

                E. M. Forster

APRIL 21

A British Republic?
The moment has come to rid ourselves of the ancient trappings of
throne and sceptre . . . Republican societies should be formed
immediately.

                H. G. Wells

MAY

Dreams and Rhubarb

My sticks of rhubarb were wrapped up in a copy of the Star containing Lloyd George's last, more than eloquent speech. As I snipped
up the rhubarb my eye fell, was fixed and fastened on that sentence
wherein he tells us that we have grasped our niblick and struck out
for the open course. Pray Heaven there is some faithful soul ever
present with a basket to catch these tender blossoms as they fall.
Ah, God! it is a dreadful thought that these immortal words should
go down into the dreamless dust uncherished. I loved to think, as I
put the rhubarb into the saucepan, that years hence – P.G. many,
many years hence – when in the fullness of time, full of ripeness and
wisdom, the Almighty sees fit to gather him into His bosom, some
gentle stone-cutter living his quiet life in the little village that had
known great David as a child would take a piece of fair white marble
and engrave upon it two niblicks crossed and underneath:

In the hour of England's most imminent peril he grasped his
Niblick and struck out for the Open Course.

Katherine Mansfield.

MAY 1

250,000 engineers strike throughout Britain.

*Continual slaughter on the Western Front, Verdun remains untaken.
Casualties nearing 700,000. Allies finally failing on the Aisne.*

Why did we join the Army, boys?
Why did we join the Army?
Why did we come to France to fight?
We must have been bloody well barmy.

MAY 2

A German Revolutionary in Prison

You ask what I am reading. Natural science for the most part; I am
studying the distribution of plants and animals.

Yesterday I was reading about the reasons for the disappearance of song birds in Germany. The spread of scientific forestry, horticulture, and agriculture, has cut them off from their nesting places and their food supply. More and more, with modern methods, we are doing away with hollow trees, waste lands, brush-wood, fallen leaves. I felt sore at heart. I was not thinking so much about the loss of pleasure for human beings, but I was so much distressed at the idea of the stealth and inexorable destruction of these defenceless little creatures, that the tears came into my eyes. I was reminded of a book I read in Zurich, in which Professor Sieber describes the dying-out of the Redskins in North America. Just like the birds, they have been gradually driven from their hunting-grounds by civilised men.

I suppose I must be out of sorts to feel everything so deeply. Sometimes, however, it seems to me that I am not really a human being at all but like a bird or a beast in human form. I feel so much more at home even in a scrap of garden like the one here, and still more in the meadows when the grass is humming with bees than at one of our party congresses. I can say that to you, for you will not promptly suspect me of treason to socialism! You know that I really hope to die at my post, in a street fight or in prison.

But my innermost personality belongs more to my tomtits than to my comrades. This is not because, like so many spiritually bankrupt politicians, I seek refuge and find repose in nature. Far from it, in nature at every turn I see so much cruelty that I suffer greatly.

Take the following episode, which I shall never forget. Last spring I was returning from a country walk when, in the quiet, empty road, I noticed a small dark patch on the ground. Leaning forward I witnessed a voiceless tragedy. A large beetle was lying on its back, and waving its legs helplessly, while a crowd of little ants were swarming round it and eating it alive! I was horror-stricken, so I took my pocket handkerchief and began to flick the little brutes away. They were so bold and stubborn that it took me some time, and when at length I had freed the poor wretch of a beetle and had carried it to a safe distance on the grass, two of its legs had already been gnawed off . . .

I fled from the scene feeling that in the end I had conferred a very doubtful boon.

          Rosa Luxemburg

May 6

Dodges

Thorpe-le-Soken, Sunday, 6 May – Returned here on Friday and met Bertie Sullivan in the train. Carrying F.O. mails over to Holland in the Copenhagen, he had been torpedoed by a submarine. He said 6 subms. waited for the boat, in 3 pairs. He was shaving. He seems to have kept pretty calm, but he said he couldn't get his boots on. 'I was flurried,' he said. Of 17 bags, he saved 16, and sank one. Result, after several days, a sort of lack of feeling in fingers. (It was March and he was not in rowboat for long.)

Yesterday, for the first time, and at my suggestion, we had no bread on the table at dinner. People who want it must ask for it from the sideboard. Wells gave me this tip. The value of these dodges is chiefly disciplinary. If the whole of the well-to-do classes practised them, the wheat problem would be trifling.

> Arnold Bennett

May 17

Final failure of the Western offensive. Nivelle replaced by Pétain, 'the Hero of Verdun'.

May 19

French mutinies begin. Defused by Pétain.

The memory of his soldiers' faces at Verdun never ceased to haunt him. He could never pass an ambulance without a tightening of the throat.

> Corelli Barnett

22,385 found guilty of mutiny. Mass deportations. 55 officially shot.

MAY 20

PROFITEERS

There are certain brisk people among us today
Whose patriotism makes quite a display.
But on closer inspection I fancy you'll find
The tools that they work with are axes to grind.

Apparently guiltless of personal greed,
They hasten to succour their country in need;
But private returns in their little top shelves
Show it's one for the country and two for themselves.

Unselfish devotion this struggle demands,
All helping each other whole heart and clean hands.
No quarter for humbugs; we want to be quit
Of men who are making, not doing their bit.

Jones challenges Brown, and Brown implicates Jones,
To the slur of self-interest nobody owns;
But each one must know at the back of his mind,
If his patriotism spells axes to grind.

>   Jessie Pope

The Profiteer

Metevsky said to the one side . . .
>   Don't buy until you can get ours.
>   And he went over the border
>   And he said to the other side
The *other* side has more munitions. Don't buy
>   until you can get ours.
And Ackers made a large profit and imported gold into England.

>   Ezra Pound

During the years 1914 to 1918 the Vickers company delivered:

- 4 battleships
- 3 armed cruisers
- 53 submarines
- 62 light ships
- 3 auxiliary cruisers
- 2,328 heavy naval guns, field guns, and howitzers up to a calibre of 45cm.; further, more than
- 100,000 machine-guns of the well-known type invented by Sir Hiram Maxim

an unknown quantity of smaller guns

an unknown number of tons of armour plates, and

- 5,500 – let us put it into words – five thousand five hundred aeroplanes.

Even on the basis of peace-time prices that represents a prime cost of several hundred millions of pounds. The stated net profits of the company alone amounted to thirty-four million pounds, or three times its capital, and of that 67 per cent. went to Mr. Basil Zaharoff.

Robert Neumann

All through the war the great armament firms were supplied from the enemy countries. The French and the British sold war materials to the Germans through Switzerland, Holland and the Baltic neutrals, and the Germans supplied optical sights, it is said, for the British Admiralty. The armament industry, which had helped stimulate the war, made millions out of it. In England the sixpenny shares of a cellulose firm with political interests rose to £14. 10s; and condite profiteers could show dividends of 105.7 per cent. In America copper magnates increased profits up to 300 per cent. The factories of interlocking firms behind the enemy's lines were not bombed. Civilians starved and soldiers died, but armaments shares soared gratefully. During the 'Turnip Winter' in Germany, Krupps declared a dividend of 12 per cent. As in Russia before the revolution, so in Germany and Austria in 1917 and 1918, starvation became the real enemy to the gaunt, exhausted millions behind the lines.

C. J. Pennethorne Hughes

London

I dine at Pobos, a fashionable night club, with a friend, a legal man, whose son is with us, and ring up Madge at eight. 'All is well,' she tells me. The two war widows, the one with a child, the other expecting one, are to be great friends, united by a common bond which unites as no other can. 'Go and enjoy yourself,' she adds, 'you need it. God grants strength on these occasions! Night, night!' She rings off. 'Wonderful woman,' I muse. We sit on talking until two a.m. I drink strong coffee while my friend keeps a bottle of brandy busy after champagne. 'I thought,' I say, 'these places had to shut early, and not sell liquor after ten?' 'You thought wrong, old man, you come from the backwoods, "the mug line" the fellows in there call it,' he says, pointing to a private room. 'There are probably ten men in there now, at least, who are making huge fortunes out of your war; pretend to go in by mistake and look at them; and in there,' he says, pointing to another door, 'I will also show you something else which will interest you.' I open the door and behold a dozen or so fat profiteers 'doing themselves well'. They seem to be having a very good war!

> General F. P. Crozier

Mr Bottomley's War

I rejoice to know that the engineers' strike has at last been settled, but all the same I want today to have a very solemn talk with the men who have been 'out' – a talk of man to man, brother to brother – aye, and may not I say, worker to worker? I really don't think anyone works harder than I do. I am *always* working, even at my play. And although I am not a duly accredited Labour Leader, the man for whom I work hardest, and love to work for, is the Man in the Street – a phrase which connotes all the toilers of the nation, and all the sailors and the soldiers – God bless them. I am 'with them' all the time.

And today I have something to say to them – as I had to the Clyde workers two years ago, when, with the approval of the present Prime Minister, I called them together and had a heart-to-heart chat with them. Later I spoke to the Miners and the Railwaymen – and in each case was accorded that sympathetic attention which only mutual trust could engender. For I do not mince my words . . . So come, boys, let us have a confab . . . Well, I am going to start by saying something that will offend most of you – but I shall say it just the same. It is this; in the present condition of affairs *no* strike is in any circumstances justifiable. A strike today is an affront to the patriotism of the Empire – a blasphemy against our holy cause. It can have no 'merits' – its evil is rank beyond forgiveness; it stinks to Heaven and in the nostrils of all honest men. The man who in this crisis 'downs tools' is an enemy to King and Country. Deserting in face of friends is no less a crime than desertion in face of the foe . . . On the other hand, however, do not, for a moment, think that I attach less blame to employers – be they Government Departments or private firms – who, by any harsh regulations, or breach of faith, impose intolerable conditions upon workers and, above all who endeavour to line their filthy pockets with bloodstained gold. Speaking of such people two years ago I said: 'May their souls writhe in hell for their villainy;' and I repeat that aspiration . . .

Just ask yourself these questions: – Have our gallant sailors no just complaints? Was complete justice ever done to those who scaled the Vimy Ridge and pierced the Hindenburg Line? Was the debt of honour paid in full to the valour of Jutland Bank? Yet to these dauntless warriors no choice is offered between obedience or death – *and their pay is sixpence a day!* – with an altogether inadequate allowance to their dependents! You see that the demands of patriotism are absolute. In the name of God, I ask you not to be less self-sacrificing and enduring than your brothers on sea and land. We must have no more strikes while the war lasts.

There is already clear evidence that the supply of necessary munitions has been seriously hampered by the recent deplorable stoppage. You must do your utmost to make up for lost time. I imagine the thoughts of your son or pal out in the trenches had he been suddenly informed that guns and ammunition were running out. Can you see him falling, mortally wounded, writhing in agony – with a curse for the strikers on his lips? By Heaven! Were I a munition worker, I wouldn't sleep at night with that thought on my conscience! Come, lads, can't you trust at least *some* of us to see that the debt due to you by a grateful State shall be paid in full? Believe me, some of us are in grim earnest and are determined to see justice done. But henceforth you must play the Great Game until the war is over.

Yes, you must play the game, as the boys out there have played it – the game in which the stakes are the future of the British Empire, the fate of free peoples – the destiny of mankind. At present, I know, the war goes in our favour – but at what a cost ! . . . Meanwhile you must do nothing to hold Haig back.

Familiar voices from the distant trenches in Artois and Picardy are urging you to work your hardest to replenish the supply of shells and guns. It is the call of the blood. Answer it, brother. Stick henceforth to your work; play the man – the big, brave man on whose back our Empire rests.

Horatio Bottomley, in 'John Bull', London

Horatio Bottomley, M.P., was imprisoned in 1922 for fraud connected with Victory Bonds.

MAY 23

At 3.00 the Prime Minister brought Prince Sixte of Bourbon [brother of Empress of Austria] who is serving in the Belgium Army. He came to inform me that the Emperor of Austria had written to him to try and arrange for a separate peace with the Entente. The difficulty will be Italy. It is of course very secret: only M. Poincaré and M. Ribot know. It would be a great thing if it could be brought about.

George V

MAY 30

On the Middle Eastern Front

In ordinary times, so the Arabs said, snakes were little worse here than elsewhere by water in the desert: but this year the valley seemed creeping with horned vipers and puff-adders, cobras and black snakes. By night movement was dangerous: and at last we found it necessary to walk with sticks, beating the bushes each side while we stepped warily through on bare feet.

We could not lightly draw water after dark, for there were snakes swimming in the pools or clustering in knots around their brinks. Twice puff-adders came twisting into the alert ring of our debating coffee-circle. Three of our men died of bites; four recovered after great fear and pain, and a swelling of the poisoned limb. Howeitat treatment was to bind up the part with snake-skin plaster, and read chapters of the Koran to the sufferer until he died. They also pulled thick Damascene ankle-boots, red, with blue tassels and horse-shoe heels, over their horny feet when they went late abroad.

A strange thing was the snakes' habit, at night, of lying beside us, probably for warmth, under or on the blanket. When we learned this our rising was with infinite care, and the first up would search round his fellows with a stick till he could pronounce them unencumbered. Our party of fifty men killed perhaps twenty snakes daily; at last they got so on our nerves that the boldest of us feared to touch ground; while those who, like myself, had a shuddering horror of all reptiles longed that our stay in Sirhan might end.

> T. E. Lawrence

June 3

ANARCHISTS PARADE PETROGRAD STREETS
Reds call for the Commune.
Demand on Black Banners an end of Authority and Capitalists.
Incite crowd to Robbery.
Armed band of Agitators is left unmolested by the Government.
Rumored Royalist riots.

> *New York Times*

TREASON TO ADVISE
MEN AGAINST DRAFT.
Marshall says those who urge Eligibles not to register are liable to Death Penalty.
Declares Law is Plain.
Oscar S. Strauss predicts Jews will join the colors in large numbers.

> *New York Times*

MORE ANTI-DRAFT
AGITATORS IN JAIL.
ANARCHISTS HELD.

Federal Authorities firm in dealing with Campaign against Registration
2 women arrested here.
Wished President Dead.

> *New York Times*

STOCKHOLM — AND LEEDS.

1,500 PEACE CRANKS FOR TODAY'S MEETING.

WHO PAID THE BILL?

Leeds and Stockholm are today the centres for self-appointed amateur peace-makers. Both conventions are likely to be useful as safety-valves for blowing away crank views.

The Stockholm Conference began with an invitation by Dutch Socialists, and there was more than a suspicion that pro-German wire-pulling was its inspiration. Consequently no Labour or Socialist representatives of any of the Allied Countries would consent to take part in the convention.

Following on this came an invitation from the Russian Socialists.

Weekly Dispatch, London

JUNE 9

Siegfried Sassoon lunched with me at the Reform yesterday. He expected some decoration for admittedly fine bombing work. Colonel had applied for it three times, but was finally told that as that particular push was a failure it could not be granted. Sassoon was uncertain about accepting a home billet if he got the offer of one. I advised him to accept it. He is evidently one of the reckless ones. He said his pals said he always gave the Germans every chance to pot him. He said he would like to go out once more and give them another chance to get him, and come home unscathed. He seemed jealous for the military reputation of poets. He said most of war was a tedious nuisance, but there were great moments and he would like them again.

Arnold Bennett

London

It has always been my dream that the two English-speaking nations should some day be united in a great cause, and today my dream is realised. Together we are fighting for the greatest cause that peoples can fight. The Anglo-Saxon race must save civilization.

George V, *to General Pershing and staff*

*American Espionage Act. Bitterly opposed by radicals, pacifists and
dissidents as an exercise of political tyranny, the opposite of the allied
democratic war aims.*

JUNE 12

*Abdication of pro-German King Constantine under Allied pressure,
as a preliminary to forcing Greece into war.*

JUNE 28

FIRST AMERICAN TROOPS REACH FRANCE,
   SETTING RECORD FOR QUICK MOVEMENT;
      FRANTIC CROWDS CHEER THEIR LANDING.
SEAPORT DECKED IN FLAGS

All troops in excellent shape and enthusiastic over the successful
trip.

CONVOYED IN DANGER ZONE
PERSHING WILL JOIN EXPEDITION TODAY
COMMITTEE VOTES
WAR BAN ON BOTH
BEER AND WHISKY

Compromise rejected and drastic nation-wide Prohibition written
into Food Bill.

PERMITS MAKING OF WINES

But only to Prevent Waste of Fruits and by Authorisation of the
President.

       New York Times

On the Western Front

FRAGMENT: THE ABYSS OF WAR

As bronze may be much beautified
By lying in the dark damp soil,
So men who fade in dust of warfare fade
Fairer, and sorrow blooms their soul.

Like pearls which noble women wear
And, tarnishing, awhile confide
Unto the old salt sea to feed,
Many return more lustrous than they were.

   Wilfred Owen

Burnt black by strange decay
their sinister faces lie,
the lid over each eye;
the grass and coloured clay
more motion have than they,
joined to the great sunk silences.

   Isaac Rosenberg

The Dead in the Middle East

The dead men looked wonderfully beautiful. The night was shining gently down, softening them into new ivory. Turks were white-skinned on their clothed parts, much whiter than the Arabs; and these soldiers had been very young. Close round them lapped the dark wormwood, now heavy with dew, in which the ends of the moon-beams sparkled like sea-spray. The corpses seemed flung so pitifully on the ground, huddled anyhow in low heaps. Surely if straightened they would be comfortable at last. So I put them all in order, one by one, very wearied myself, and longing to be of these quiet ones, not of the restless, noisy, aching mob up the valley, quarrelling over the plunder, boasting of their speed and strength to endure God knew how many toils and pains of this sort; with death, whether we won or lost, waiting to end the history.

   T. E. Lawrence

Embarking at Night

Amory moved forward on the deck until he found a stool under an electric light. He searched in his pocket for notebook and pencil and then began to write, slowly, laboriously:

We leave tonight . . .
    Silent, we filled the still, deserted street,
        A column of dim grey,
And ghosts rose startled at the muffled beat
    Along the moonless way;
The shadowy shipyards echoed in the feet
    That turned from night and day.

And so we linger on the windless decks,
    See on the spectre shore
Shades of a thousand days, poor grey-ribbed wrecks . . .
    Oh, shall we then deplore
Those futile years!
        See how the sea is white!
The clouds have broken and the heavens burn
To hollow highways, paved with gravelled light
The churning of the waves about the stern
    Rising to one voluminous nocturne,
       . . . We leave tonight.

        F. Scott Fitzgerald

An American Poet

CLOCKS

Here is a face that says half-past seven the same way whether a
    murder or a wedding goes on, whether a funeral or a picnic
    crowd passes.
A tall one I know at the end of a hallway broods in shadows and is
    watching booze eat out the insides of the man of the house; it
    has seen five hopes go in five years: one woman, one child, and
    three dreams.
A little one carried in a leather box by an actress rides with her to
    hotels and is under her pillow in a sleeping-car between one-
    night stands.
One hoists a phiz over a railroad station; it points numbers to people
    a quarter-mile away who believe it when other clocks fail.
And of course . . . there are wrist watches over the pulses of
    airmen eager to go to France . . .

      Carl Sandburg

JULY 6

Technique on the Middle Eastern Front

We had a third try to communicate with the Turks, by means of a
little conscript, who said that he understood how to do it. He
undressed and went down the valley in little more than boots. An
hour later he proudly brought us a reply, very polite, saying that in
two days, if help did not come from Maan, they would surrender.

Such folly (for we could not hold our men indefinitely) might
mean the massacre of every Turk. I held no great brief for them, but
it was better they be not killed, if only to spare us the pain of seeing
it. Besides we might have suffered loss. Night operations in the
staring moon would be nearly as exposed as day. Nor was this, like
Aba el Lissan, an imperative battle.

We gave our little man a sovereign as earnest of reward, walked
down close to the trenches with him, and sent in for an officer to
speak with us. After some hesitation this was achieved, and we
explained the situation on the road behind us; our growing forces;
and our short control over their tempers. The upshot was that they
promised to surrender at daylight. So we had another sleep (an
event rare enough to chronicle) in spite of our thirst.

      T. E. Lawrence

Petrograd

Soldiers in steel helmets, just recalled from the front, are surrounding the Peter and Paul fortress. They are marching leisurely along the pavements and through the park, dragging their machine-guns behind them, their rifles carelessly dangling from their shoulders. Occasionally one of them calls out good-naturedly to a passer-by:

'Hurry up; there's going to be some shooting!'

The inhabitants are all agog to see the battle and are following the soldiers silently, with fox-like movements, dodging from tree to tree and straining their necks, looking eagerly ahead.

In the Alexander Park flowers are growing at the sides of the paths; the gardener is busying himself among them. He has a clean apron on and carries a spade in his hand. As he walks along he scolds both onlookers and soldiers as though they are a flock of sheep.

'Where are you walking, there? Is that grass made for you to trample on? Isn't there enough room for you on the path?'

A bearded, iron-headed peasant in soldier's uniform, his rifle under his arm, says to the gardener:

'You look out yourself, old boy, or we'll shoot you straight away.'

'Oh, will you? You just try! Fine shot, you are . . . '

'Don't you know there's a war on? There's going to be some fighting.'

'Oh, is there? Well, get on with your fighting, and I'll get on with my job.' Then, taking a pair of clippers from his pocket, he grumbled: 'Trampling about where you're not allowed to . . .'

'It's war.'

'What's that got to do with me? Fighting's all very well for them that likes it, and you've got plenty of others to help you; but I'm all alone in this job. You'd better clean that rifle of yours a bit; it's all rusty . . . '

There is a whistle, and the soldier, unable to light the cigarette in his lips, puts it hastily in his pocket and runs off between the trees.

The gardener spits after him in disgust and shouts angrily:

'What the devil are you running over the grass for? Isn't there any other road you can go by?'

Maxim Gorky

JULY 14

Berlin

German Chancellor, Bethmann-Hollweg, resigns. Ludendorff, the First Quartermaster General, nominally under Hindenburg and the Kaiser, becomes virtual dictator.

Mutinies in the German Fleet during July.

JULY 17

King George V renounces his Guelphic names together with all German titles and formal associations with the House of Saxe-Coburg-Gotha, and renames his dynasty 'the House of Windsor'.

JULY 18

Kerensky defeats attempted Bolshevik coup in Petrograd.

JULY 19

Berlin

Peace Resolution in the Reichstag carried by 212 votes to 126.

JULY 21–NOVEMBER 10

Passchendaele

Under Haig, the British and the Canadians attempt another breakthrough with the start of the Passchendaele offensive (the Third Battle of Ypres). Preliminary bombardment of 4,500,000 shells.

From far and near the ceaseless hammer-strike of great guns making the sky red and restless with tongues of leaping fire and bringing unseen, unimaginable destruction to the masses of men hidden in the dark woods and trenches.

> *The Times*, London

My dearest Papa.

What the ground must be like I shudder to think and we have completely obliterated the roads W. of Pilkem by shell fire . . . I'm writing this in the office as I'm on watch or night-duty as they call it and it's very cold and damp and still pouring in sheets the rain making a depressing pattering noise on the tin roof of the hut!! The telephone is ringing fairly often so I don't suppose I shall get much sleep tonight . . . But how thankful I am to think I am not living forward tonight and am sitting back here in comfort, one does appreciate this comfort when one has been forward and seen what it's like in the line now!! The nearest thing possible to hell whatever that is!!!

Edward, Prince of Wales, later King Edward VIII

400,000 British killed or wounded, lost in the mud for five hundred yards of swamped earth. 250,000 German casualties.

They died in Hell, they called it Passchendaele.

Siegfried Sassoon

GERMAN DEFENCE BROKEN

The Times, London

An advance of a thousand yards over Flemish mud so churned and battered that even the oldest denizen would not have recognised it, and won with a loss of British life heavier than that which had cost a century and a half earlier to conquer India and Canada together, was hailed in *The Times* with headlines of 'German Defence broken!' 'We have broken, the Special Correspondent of that paper wrote, and broken at a single blow in the course of some three or four hours, the German system of defence.' Next day it was broken again, and the next, and the next.

Arthur Bryant

Far from the bloodstained swamp, in the Olympian calm of GHQ, Haig, with his handsome head thrown back and his quiet, confident smile, would make a dramatic sweep with his hands over his maps to show visiting politicians how he was driving the Germans back to their frontiers. Mr F. S. Oliver, the historian, contemplating the deluge that poured continually from the skies, admired the serene way the commander-in-chief ignored the elements and persisted in his attacks. Presently the distant ridge would be captured and the plain of Belgium would open up before his victorious troops. Or so it seemed, looking out through the tall, rain-spattered windows of the château at Montreuil. The German generals pursued similar visions of early victory; that autumn Russia, rent by revolution and early anarchy, collapsed before their advancing armies, and in October the Austrians, believed to be at the last gasp, struck back with German aid at their Italian assailants and sent them in headlong rout with a loss of more than half a million men towards the Piave. These disasters, like those which had befallen Belgium, Serbia and Romania in the earlier years of the war, were attended by a mass flight of non-combatants – of whole nations on the trek leaving behind a vast, untidy trail of dying women, old men and children and the skeletons of starved animals . . . German civilians sang specially composed hymns of hate against England and, in the most civilised country in the world, quiet inoffensive English gentlemen and ladies who had never seen a blow struck in anger scorned the very mention of peace and spoke of the whole German race as they would of a pack of wild beasts. Only in the battle line itself was there no hatred: only suffering and endurance and infinite waste.

> Arthur Bryant

A Hymn of Hate Against England

French and Russian they matter not,
A blow for a blow, a shot for a shot,
We fight the battle with bronze and steel,
And the time that is coming Peace will seal,
You will we hate with a lasting hate,
We will never forgo our hate,
Hate by water and hate by land,
Hate of the hammer and hate of the crown,
Hate of seventy millions, choking down,
We love as one, we hate as one,
We have one foe and one alone – England!

> Ernst Lissauer

AUGUST 16

LONDON'S GREAT WELCOME TO OUR
AMERICAN ALLIES

HAIG STRIKES BIG BLOW NORTH OF LENS

> *Daily Mirror*, London

AUGUST 18

London

Frances told us a good Queen Mary story at breakfast. Going round a hospital, she was struck by a fair-haired mother with a very dark baby. She commented on this and returned to the woman's bedside again after completing her round, saying: 'His father must have been very dark – wasn't he?' To which the woman breezily replied: 'Sure Ma'am, I don't know – he never took his hat off.'

> Lady Cynthia Asquith

AUGUST 31

On the Italian Front

I saw at a moving picture theatre an impressive series of views representing the activities of the Italian troops in the mountains fighting on the Northern frontier. This suggested the remarkable resourcefulness of the Italians and the extraordinary difficulties under which they fought. Here were seen the picket posts, at which sometimes a soldier could remain but for five minutes without danger of freezing to death, before he was relieved; the telifers, by which guns and supplies were transported from peak to peak; the perfect mountain roads, improvised by the greatest roadbuilders in the world. Much as I had read of the skill and hardihood of the Italians, I had not before realised the uniqueness of the conflict of that front. Between the scenes an American soldier in khaki announced that ambulances were greatly needed by the Italian army . . . I went again the next night, having meanwhile 'had an idea', which, on conversation with the soldier, met with his approval. It was to organise a committee of American poets to furnish the needed ambulances . . . our committee was called 'The American Poets' Ambulances in Italy'.

> Robert Underwood Johnson

On the French Front

When Clemenceau came to the Somme Front we went with him. Later, President Poincaré and King George V were to meet at Abbeville and I was instructed to go to the station and accompany the President. 'You will detain him for a quarter of an hour,' General Asser said, 'because the King wants to talk to some Kaffir chieftains and this will delay our schedule for a bit.' This curious mission earned me the imprecations of the French general accompanying the President and my first highly embarrassed conversation with M. Poincaré. 'What's the meaning of this?' the General demanded, 'the King keeps the President waiting because he wants to talk to Negroes? It's unbelievable!'

'But sir,' I said, 'there is a reason . . . these are the head men of the Kaffir workers who made an agreement for just one year and who now want to go home. These workmen, however, are urgently needed to dig trenches, and it is hoped the King's prestige will make them stay.'

'Then all right,' M. Poincaré said resignedly. 'But it's ridiculous for me to wait in this station. Can't the itinerary be extended a little?'

'Alas, no.'

André Maurois

Cuff the Kaiser,
Cuff the cat,
King George never did a thing like that.

Eton Song

SEPTEMBER 2

On the Middle Eastern Front

The Hejaz show is a quaint one, the like of which has hardly been on earth before, and no one not of it can approximate how difficult it is to run. However, it has gone forward, and history will call it a success.

T. E. Lawrence

SEPTEMBER 11

Berlin: Able Seaman Köbes, a Leader of the Mutineers in the German Fleet writes:

My Dear Parents

I have been sentenced to death today, September 11th, 1917. Only myself and another comrade; the others have been let off with fifteen years' imprisonment. You will have heard why this has happened to me. I am a sacrifice of the longing for peace, others are going to follow. I cannot stop it now, it is six o'clock in the morning, I am being taken to Cologne at 6.30, and on Wednesday September 12th at 9 o'clock in the morning I am going to be sacrificed to military justice. I would have liked to press your hands once more to say goodbye, but I will do it silently. Console Paula and my little Fritz. I don't like dying so young, but I die with a curse on the German-militarist state. These are my last words. I hope that some day you and mother will be able to read them.

> Always
>   Your Son.
> Albin Köbes

Subconsciously we are yearning for a man, a powerful man.

> Gerhart Hauptmann

OCTOBER

American Espionage Act in use against Anarchist leaders and suspected war saboteurs.

With a hideous apathy this country has acquiesced in a regime of judicial tyranny, bureaucratic suppression and industrial barbarism.

> John Reed

OCTOBER 11

Paris

At the end of the party there was an air raid warning. I shan't tell you whether the planes flew to the right or left of Cassiopeia, I only know that I caught cold because I went out on the balcony and stayed there over an hour to see this wonderful Apocalypse with the soaring and descending aeroplanes seeming to complement or eclipse the constellations. Even if we had only had a view of the sky there would have been more than enough Beauty, it was so marvellous. But the fantastic thing was that like the Greco painting in which there is the celestial scene above and the terrestrial below, we were watching this sublime 'Plein Ciel' from the balcony high up; underneath the Ritz Hotel (where all this happened) appeared to have become a sort of 'Liberty Hall'. Ladies in nightgowns or even in bathrobes roamed the 'vaulted' hall, as they clutched their pearl necklaces to their bosoms.

Marcel Proust, *to Madame Straus*

OCTOBER 15

Gradually the evidence accumulated. Mata Hari tried to save herself by offering her services to French espionage and suggesting that she should go and live in Brussels and there act as a spy for the French. Her offer was accepted, and she was allowed to leave the country in the certainty that definite proofs of her duplicity would be forthcoming. Upon her return from Belgium on February 13, 1917, she was arrested at the Elysée Palace Hotel, 103 Avenue des Champs Elysées.

On July 24, she appeared before a court-martial, very soignée in a décolleté blue dress. Appealing glances from her almond-shaped eyes failed to make the questions she had to answer less deadly. Coolly she defended herself, but proof after proof from her H21 correspondence was brought forward in accusation. Nevertheless she proclaimed her innocence until the end.

A few months later Mata Hari was executed: on October 15, in the dry moat of Vincennes Castle in the wonted manner. She was dressed in a beige suit. Refusing to be blindfolded, she died at the hands of the firing squad at six-fifteen in the morning. One soldier fainted, the others marched away in a state of profound dejection.

After a mock funeral to ascertain whether anyone wished to claim her mortal remains, the body was handed over to the Paris medical faculty for purposes of anatomical dissection.

P. J. Bouman

OCTOBER 16

London

D. H. Lawrence came to see me at five, looking very gaunt. Last Friday the police searched their house, took letters to Frieda, and told them they must leave at once. It is hard for him. In Cornwall he lived so cheaply and healthily, and he will have to go on paying for the house there. His health doesn't allow of his living in London and all the money he has in the world is the prospect of eighteen pounds for the publication of some poems all about bellies and breasts which he gave me to read. People should either be left in peace or interned at the country's expense. I promised to do what I could in the matter, but doubt whether it will be much – after all, the woman is a German and it doesn't seem unreasonable.

Lady Cynthia Asquith

OCTOBER 21

First American Division established on Western Front. Some two million Americans reached Europe, in U.S. and British ships, another two million training at home, and, by April 1918, 300,000 arriving monthly.

OCTOBER 25

Petrograd

And here
            no token
                        of greatness
                                    or grandeur
                                                Lenin
                                                            came.
Already
        led
            by Lenin
                    into battle,
They didn't know him
                    from portraits yet:
        bustled,
                hollered,
                        exchanged banter.
With a quickfire of oaths,
                        hail-fellow-well-met.
And there,
        in that long-wished-for
                            iron storm
Lenin,
        drowsy with fatigue,
                        it would seem,

pacing,
          stopping,
                    hands clasped behind back,
dug his eyes
               into the motley scene.
Once I saw him
                 stabbing them
                               into a chap in puttees
dead-aiming
              sharp-edged
                            as razors,
seizing the gist
                  as pincers would seize,
dragging the soul
                   from under words and phrases.
And I knew
             everything
                          was disclosed
                                         and understood,
everything
            those eyes
                        were raking for:
where
      the shipwright
                       and miner stood,
what
     the peasant and soldier were aching for.
He kept all races
                   within his sight,
all continents
                where the sun goes setting
                                            or dawning;
weighed the whole globe
                         in his brain
                                       by night
And in the morning:
                     "To all,
                              every
                                    and each,

Slaves of the rich
One another
        hacking and carving:
to you we appeal
            this hour;
let the Soviets
      take over
              government-power!
       Vladimir Mayakovsky

NOVEMBER

*Haig suffers 400,000 British casualties, advancing five miles around
Ypres, shortly retaken by the Germans. 250,000 German casualties.
Passchendaele Ridge captured by the Canadians.*

More often in the latter stages of the war the regiments marched in
silence under their medieval steel-rimmed helmets with a certain
monotonous, almost brute-like grimness. But the humour and
cheerfulness found expression in an undertone of individual face-
tiousness; the 'Ave a 'eart, Fritz, we broke our bloody gun!' which
accompanied an intensive German bombardment unreplied to; the
time-honoured, 'there goes the fuckin' receipt!' when the British
response came at last . . .

   'What's the use of worrying?' ran the refrain of a music-hall song
much used for marching and barn-concerts at the end of the war.
'Eh, corporal, w'a's this?' asked the soldier of his exiguous bread
ration. 'That, m'lad, is your bread ration.' 'Blimey! A thowt it were
'Oly Communion!'

       Arthur Bryant

Washington

Is it not a shame that the world should have been so disturbed; that
peaceful men are compelled to lie out in the mud and filth in the
depth of a raw winter, shot at and stormed at and shelled. Waiting
for a chance to murder some other inoffensive fellow-creature?
Why must the people in Old Poland die of hunger, not finding dogs
enough to eat in the streets of Lemberg? The long lines of broken
peasants in Serbia and Romania; the population of Belgium and

Northern France torn from their homes to work as slaves for the Germans; the poor prisoners of war starving in their huts or working in factories and mines; the cries of the old and the children wounded by bombs from Zeppelins; the wails of the mothers for their sons; the very rustling of the air as the souls of ten million dead sweep to another world – why must all these horrors come upon a fair green world where we believed that love and help and friendship, genius and science and commerce, religion and civilization once ruled?

James W. Gerard

Here is one not long dead;
His dark hearing caught our far wheels,
And the choked soul stretched weak hands
To reach the living word the far wheels said,
The blood-dazed intelligence beating for light,
Crying through the suspense of the far torturing wheels
Swift for the end to break
Or the wheels to break,
Cried as the tide of the world broke over his sight.

Isaac Rosenberg

NOVEMBER 2

The Balfour Declaration, London

Dear Lord Rothschild,

I have much pleasure in conveying to you, on behalf of His Majesty's Government, the following declaration of sympathy with the Jewish Zionist aspiration which has been submitted to, and approved by, the Cabinet.

His Majesty's Government view with favour the establishment in Palestine of a national home for the Jewish people, and will use their best endeavours to facilitate the achievement of this object, it being clearly understood that nothing shall be done which may prejudice the civil rights of existing non-Jewish communities in Palestine, or the rights and political status enjoyed by Jews in any other country.

I should be grateful if you would bring this declaration to the knowledge of the Zionist Federation.

Yours sincerely,
Arthur Balfour

Through these pale cold days
What dark faces burn
Out of three thousand years,
And their wild eyes yearn,

While underneath their brows
Like waifs their spirits grope
For the pools of Hebron again –
For Lebanon's summer slope.

They leave these blond still days
In dust behind their tread
They see with living eyes
How long they have been dead.

       Isaac Rosenberg

Germany

I am restless. I hate the kitchen table at which I am writing. I lose patience over a book. I should like to push the landscape aside as if it irritated me. I must get [back] to the Front. I must again hear the shells roaring up into the sky and the desolate valley echoing the sound. I must return to my Company – live again in the realm of death.

       Helmut Zschulte

Politics

When we were delivered at Garaison, and the N.C.O. on guard inspected our baggage, he stumbled on a French translation of the Politics of Aristotle, which, with a view to the work on the Philosophy of Civilization I had brought with me: 'Why, it's incredible!' he stormed 'they're actually bringing political books into a Prisoners of War Camp!' I shyly remarked to him, that the book was written long before the birth of Christ. 'Is that true, you scholar there?' he asked of a soldier who was standing near. The latter corroborated my statement. 'What! People talked politics as long ago as that, did they?' he questioned back. On our answering in the affirmative, he gave his decision: 'Anyhow, we talk them differently today from what they did then, and, so far as I am concerned, you can keep your book.'

       Albert Schweitzer

NOVEMBER 5

Supreme Allied War Council established, largely by Lloyd George.

It was part of his devious manoeuvres against Haig whom he wished to dismiss but because of his own insecure parliamentary support . . . and of the King's friendship with Haig, could not.

      Corelli Barnett

NOVEMBER 7

Petrograd
Bolshevik revolution.

Lenin in Power, an American View

The Bolshevik Revolution seemed to revive and justify the most ardent socialist faith. The world's first working-class republic was established, and around it rallied all those Americans who were bitter against industrial oppression and war.

At first my friends and I had only the vaguest ideas as to what bolshevism was. The signing of the Brest-Litovsk Treaty early in 1918 seemed to us a victory of German autocracy over the workers' revolution. Many radicals now talked of volunteering in the American army to fight the Germans. The defeat of Germany seemed essential for the defence of the workers' republic. Writing about this period years later, Floyd Dell recorded both the universal enthusiasm of the radicals for Bolshevik Russia and the bitterness against Germany which it evolved.

This was a Socialism which meant what it said! The mind was incredulous at first – could this really be happening? Could it last? And then there was Brest-Litovsk, and Germany seemed to some of us, to me certainly, an enemy, because German militarism threatened the existence of Soviet Russia.

      Joseph Freeman

Russia

When in the throes of suicide
our people awaited the German guests
and the stern Byzantine spirit
abandoned our Russian Church,
I heard a voice – oh it was soothing!
that cried: 'Come here,
leave your wild and sinful country,
leave Russia forever.
I will wash the blood from your hands,
I will pluck the shame from your heart,
I will hide, with a different name,
Your insults and your hurts.'

But indifferently and calmly
I blocked my ears, like a child,
not to be tempted by dirty talk,
not, in my mourning, to be defiled.

> Anna Akhmatova

NOVEMBER 8

The question of peace is the burning question, the question most urgent at the present moment.

> Lenin

NOVEMBER 11

German Conference at Mons

Four able military minds evolved basic plans for a military absurdity, an absurdity to be prepared and carried out with a technical, tactical and organizational finesse never equalled on such a scale by France and Britain.

> Corelli Barnett

NOVEMBER 13

Paris

Clemenceau, the most formidable, implacable and inflexible of French politicians, who, as Mayor of Montmartre, had witnessed Commune and civil war in 1871, assumes almost dictatorial powers.

Clemenceau the Tiger

Deep in the jungle of French politics, this formidable septuagen-
arian had stalked his quarry for a generation. His claws had mauled
every administration of the last thirty years except his own; and his
passion for his country was only equalled by his distaste for practically all its public men. In his fierce simplicity he was not unlike a
character from Victor Hugo; in his principles he was undeniably the
last of the Jacobins; and in his ability to animate a fainting nation he
showed that democracy, unlike dictatorship, can rally from defeat.
Forty years before his vote had been cast against the surrender of
Alsace-Lorraine; and the lost provinces were always in his mind.
His single aim was now to win the war; and he believed in victory
because, as he said afterwards, there had to be a victory. Ruling
without noticeable colleagues, he dragged his country out of the
uncertainties of 1917. French defeatism was grasped with an un-
gentle hand. Malvy and Caillaux were arrested; Bolo was shot; and
as the *poilus* met their new Prime Minister, the front line learned to
know a muddy figure with a large moustache, fierce eyebrows, and a
battered hat.

Philip Guedalla

I will fight before Paris, I will fight in Paris, I will fight behind Paris.

Georges Clemenceau

*M. Malvy, French Minister of the Interior, with many dissidents,
pacifists, political extremists, and pro-Germans, tried for defeatism.*

NOVEMBER 15

The Migration of Birds, seen from Prison

What I have just written reminds me of an incident I wish to tell you
of, for it seems to me so poetical and so touching, I was recently
reading a scientific work upon the migrations of birds, a phenomenon which has hitherto seemed rather enigmatic. From this I learnt
certain species, which at ordinary times live at enmity one with
another (because some are birds of prey, while others are victims),
will keep the peace during their great southward flight across the
sea. Among the birds that come to winter in Egypt – come in such
numbers that the sky is darkened by their flight – are, besides

hawks, eagles, falcons and owls, thousands of little song birds such as larks, golden-crested wrens, and nightingales, mingling fearlessly with the great birds of prey. A 'truce of God' seems to have been declared for the journey. All are striving towards the common goal, to drop, half dead from fatigue, in the land of the Nile, and subsequently to assort themselves by species and localities. Nay more, during the long flight the larger birds have been seen to carry smaller birds on their backs, for instance, cranes have passed in great numbers with a twittering freight of small birds of passage. Is not that charming?

> Rosa Luxemburg

NOVEMBER 18

German and Austro-Hungarian armies finally rout the Italians at Caporetto. A sick man, General Luigi Capello was blamed for confusion, disobedience and panic retreat. 270,000 Italians captured.

NOVEMBER 19

A German in Berlin Hears of a Great Frenchman's Death
My dear Clara,
               Yesterday I wanted to write you a little birthday letter when the news of Rodin's death arrived; as you can imagine, this made all else forgotten. Now my greetings are set against this, which is, however, common to both of us, endlessly so, – like me, you will be remembering and mourning him, and will have to endure this all too final bereavement along with Paris and all that has been lost. I do not know the significance of Rodin's death to me in normal circumstances, – perhaps something manageable after all, – but now confusion prevails in me all the more because such an intimate affair as this has to fulfil itself, it cannot be softened, it is limitless, against the contemporary chaos and behind the unnatural and direful ramparts of the war these familiar figures drop from us, who can tell where? – Verhaeren, Rodin, – the great wise friends; their death becomes misty, unrecognisable . . . I feel only this: they will no longer be present when the dreadful stench evaporates, and will be impotent to relieve those who have to restore and care for the world once more. Yesterday and today I received two good loving letters about Rodin, – if only I could really believe in the

strength of human feeling amid this prevailing inhumanity . . .

Rainer Maria Rilke, *to Clara Rilke*

NOVEMBER 20

Russia to Abandon the War

We communicated over the wireless our proposals for the conclusion of a general peace both to our allies and our enemies. By way of
reply the Allied Governments addressed . . . remonstrances . . .
stating that all further steps on our part would lead to the most
serious results. We, on our part, replied on November 24 to this
protest by a manifesto to all workers, soldiers, and peasants, declaring that under no circumstances should we allow our army to shed
its blood by order of any foreign bourgeoisie. We brushed aside the
threats of the Western Imperialists and assumed full responsibility
for our peace policy before the international working class. First of
all, by way of discharging our previous pledges, we published the
secret treaties and declared that we repudiated all that was opposed
in them to the interests of the popular masses everywhere.

Trotsky

*November 1917 marked the end of a thousand years of cavalry
power, which had begun in A.D. 378 with the defeat and death of
Emperor Valens at Adrianople by mailed Gothic horsemen.*

At Cambrai in November 1917 a tank force of over three hundred
vehicles punched a hole four miles deep into the German lines in the
space of a single morning, an advance comparable in size to that
made at Passchendaele in four months . . . the tank was militarily
the major tactical innovation of the First World War.

David Lance

An Incident on the Middle Eastern Front

They kicked me to the head of the stairs, and stretched me over a
guard-bench, pommelling me. Two knelt on my ankles, bearing
down on the back of my knees, while two more twisted my wrists till
they cracked, and then crushed them and my neck against the wood.
The corporal had run downstairs; and now came back with a whip of

the Circassian sort, a thong of supple black hide, rounded, and tapering from the thickness of a thumb to the grip (which was wrapped in silver) down to a hard point finer than a pencil.

He saw me shivering, partly I think, with cold, and made it whistle over my ear, taunting me that before his tenth cut I would howl for mercy, and at the twentieth beg for the caresses of the Bey; and then he began to lash me madly across and across with all his might, while I locked my teeth to endure this thing which lapped itself like flaming wire about my body.

To keep my mind in control I numbered the blows, but after twenty lost count, and could feel only the shapeless weight of pain, not tearing claws, for which I had prepared, but a gradual cracking apart of my whole being by some too-great force whose waves rolled up my spine till they were pent within my brain, to clash terribly together. Somewhere in the place a cheap clock ticked loudly, and it distressed me that their beating was not in its time. I writhed and twisted, but was held so tightly that my struggles were useless. After the corporal ceased, the men took up, very deliberately, giving me so many, and then an interval during which they would squabble for the next turn, ease themselves, and play unspeakably with me. This was repeated often, for what may have been no more than ten minutes. Always for the first of every new series, my head would be pulled round, to see how a hard white ridge, like a railway, darkening slowly into crimson, leaped over my skin at the instant of each stroke, with a bead of blood where two ridges crossed. As the punishment proceeded the whip fell more and more upon existing weals, biting blacker or more wet, till my flesh quivered with accumulated pain, and with terror of the next blow coming. They soon conquered my determination not to cry, but while my will ruled my lips I used only Arabic, and before the end a merciful sickness choked my utterance.

> T. E. Lawrence

NOVEMBER 24

Breslau Prison

Sonichka, dear, I had such a pang recently. In the courtyard where I walk, army lorries often arrive, laden with haversacks or old tunics and shirts from the front; sometimes they are stained with blood. They are sent to the women's cells to be mended, and then go back for use in the army. The other day one of these lorries was drawn by a team of buffaloes instead of horses. I had never seen the creatures close at hand before. They are much more powerfully built than our oxen, with flattened heads, and horns strongly recurved, so that their skulls are shaped something like a sheep's skull. They are black, and have huge, soft eyes. The buffaloes are war trophies from Rumania. The soldier-drivers said that it was very difficult to catch these animals, which had always run wild, and still more difficult to break them to harness. They had been mercilessly flogged – on the principle of 'vae victis'. There are about a hundred head in Breslau alone. They have been accustomed to the luxuriant Rumanian pastures and have here to put up with lean and scanty fodder. Unsparingly exploited, yoked to heavy loads, they are soon worked to death. The other day a lorry came laden with sacks, so overladen indeed that the buffaloes were unable to drag it across the threshold of the gate. The soldier-driver, a brute of a fellow, belaboured the poor beasts so savagely with the butt end of his whip that the wardress at the gate, indignant at the sight, asked him if he had no compassion for animals. 'No more than anyone has compassion for us men,' he answered with an evil smile, and redoubled his blows. At length the buffaloes succeeded in drawing the load over the obstacle, but one of them was bleeding. You know their hide is proverbial for its thickness and toughness, but it had been torn. While the lorry was being unloaded, the beasts, which were utterly exhausted, stood perfectly still. The one that was bleeding had an expression on its face and in its soft black eyes like that of a weeping child – one that has been severely thrashed and does not know why, nor how to escape from the torment of ill-treatment. I stood in front of the team; the beast looked at me; the tears welled from my own eyes. The suffering of a dearly loved brother could hardly have moved me more profoundly, than I was moved by my impotence in face of this mute agony. Far distant, lost for ever, were the green, lush meadows of Rumania. How different there the light of the sun, the breath of the wind; how different there the song of the birds and the melodious call of the herdsman. Instead, the hideous street, the foetid stable, the rank hay mingled with mouldy straw, the strange and terrible men – blow upon blow, and blood running from gaping wounds. Poor wretch, I am as powerless, as dumb, as yourself; I am at one with you in my pain, my weakness and my longing.

Meanwhile the women prisoners were jostling one another as

they busily unloaded the dray and carried the heavy sacks into the building. The driver, hands in pockets, was striding up and down the courtyard, smiling to himself as he whistled a popular air. I had a vision of all the splendour of war!

      Rosa Luxemburg

NOVEMBER 25

Petrograd

Voting takes place for the Russian Constituent Assembly, the last free election ever held in Russia.
Social Revolutionaries 20.75 million
Bolsheviks 9.8 million

NOVEMBER 29

London

Lord Lansdowne, in a letter to the Daily Telegraph, *advocates a negotiated peace.*

DECEMBER 5
Armistice on the Eastern Front

On December 5 we signed the agreement for the suspension of hostilities along the whole front, from the Baltic to the Black Sea. We again appealed to the Allies to join us and to conduct the peace negotiations together with us. We received no answer although this time our allies did not try to intimidate us by threats.

      Trotsky

Despite tanks, Haig loses Battle of Cambrai. 45,000 casualties.

The Allowance

I never joined the army from patriotic reasons. Nothing can justify war. I suppose we must all fight to get the trouble over. Anyhow before the war I helped at home when I could and I did other things which helped to keep things going. I thought if I'd join there would be the separation allowance for my mother.

      Isaac Rosenberg, *to Edward Marsh*

Petrograd

At the height of the Revolution, (the poet) Mandelshtam, having by
some miracle got a room in the Astoria (the most elegant hotel in St
Petersburg) took a tub bath several times each day, drank the milk
that had been left at his door by mistake, and lunched at the Donon,
where the proprietor, out of his mind, extended credit to everyone.

          Arthur Sergevitch Lourie

Breslau Prison

Through the window the light of the lantern which burns all night
outside the prison falls on my blanket. From time to time one hears
the dull rattle of a distant train, or the sentry under the windows
clearing his throat as he takes a few paces in his heavy boots to
limber up his stiff legs. The sand grates so hopelessly under his
footfalls, expressive of the utter emptiness and despair of existence
in the dank night. I lie still and alone, immured in these manifold
layers of darkness, boredom, bondage, winter – and for all that my
heart beats with an inconceivable, unknown inner joy as if I were
walking in a flowery meadow in brilliant sunshine. And in the
darkness, I smile at life as if I knew some magic secret which gives
the lie to all that is evil and sad and transforms it into sheer radiance
and happiness. And then I seek to find a reason for this joy and fail
to find it and then I must smile again at myself. I believe the secret is
nothing but life itself; the deep nocturnal darkness is as beautiful
and soft as velvet, provided one looks at it the right way. And in the
harsh grinding of the wet sand under the heavy tread of the sentry
there is the small, lovely song of life – if one knows how to hear it.

          Rosa Luxemburg

December 11

*The British army under General Allenby captures Jerusalem from
the Turks, the first 'Christian' army to do so since the Crusaders'
victory of 1099, when they waded through the bloody city awash from
the massacre of its Islamic inhabitants and their children.*

When Allenby came to El Arish,
>   Down where the water melons grow,
He asked for water, but we said *Majeesh*
>   Down where the water melons grow.
So down he sat beneath a palm
Singing to himself this solitary psalm,
'Another little drink won't do us any harm',
>   Down where the water melons grow.

General Allenby

He was a big man in every way – physically, mentally and morally. He was universally nicknamed 'the Bull', and had many of that animal's external characteristics. There is a certain irony in the qualities of this gallant but low-brow animal being attached in the military mind to one who was in fact, of very high intelligence, if not actually scholarly.

In speech he resembled the bull most of all, and he was given to violent outbursts of temper; his explosive utterances and crushing rudeness to senior officers delighted all those who were fortunate enough to be listening. He rarely lowered his voice at any time, and certainly not when administering rebukes. To one brigadier-general who had incurred his displeasure, he said: 'There are fools, damned fools – and you, sir.'

Yet at bottom he was kindly and tolerant, and he had a sympathetic understanding of soldiers' problems. Although a strict disciplinarian, if not a martinet, he hated to punish a man; indeed, some officers thought him too easy by the standard of those days. When he was in command of the 5th Lancers, a trooper stood in front of him in the orderly room, quivering with nervous anticipation. The erring trooper fully expected at least fourteen days' field punishment, which he probably richly deserved. Colonel Allenby's face, as was habitual with him when he was about to deliver a blistering rebuke, was the colour of a ripe damson plum; his veins stood out on his forehead and he gripped his desk as if it might run away from him.

The Colonel seemed to be fighting for breath; the Adjutant and the Regimental Sergeant-Major gazed at the ceiling, while the prisoner and his escorts stared fixedly at a portrait of the King behind the Colonel's chair.

Then the blast came: 'Go away!' roared the Bull in a voice clearly audible at two hundred paces: 'I am far too angry with you to trust myself to punish you.' So yet another malefactor of the 5th Lancers stamped from the orderly room, dismissed with no punishment save a painful tongue-lashing. This was typical of the man; the fear of Allenby's wrath was a greater deterrent to many soldiers than a sojourn in the cells; a dressing-down from him was not an experience that the hardiest cared to repeat.

Nor did he spare his officers the rough side of his tongue. The story is told of a senior captain – a squadron commander of lengthy service – who collapsed altogether while being reproved by Allenby. 'The Bull' was genuinely surprised. 'What affected him like that?' he asked. 'I wasn't even really angry with him.'

Tim Carew

THE HERO

'Jack fell as he'd have wished,' the mother said,
And folded up the letter that she'd read.
'The Colonel writes so nicely.' Something broke
In the tired voice that quivered to a choke.
She half looked up. 'We mothers are so proud
Of our dead soldiers.' Then her face was bowed.

Quietly the Brother Officer went out.
He'd told the poor old dear some gallant lies
That she would nourish all her days, no doubt.
For while he coughed and mumbled, her weak eyes
Had shone with gentle triumph, brimmed with joy,
Because he'd been so brave, her glorious boy.

He thought how 'Jack', cold-footed, useless swine,
Had panicked down the trench that night the mine
Went up at Wicked Corner; how he'd tried
To get sent home, and how, at last, he died,
Blown to small bits. And no one seemed to care
Except that lonely woman with white hair.

Siegfried Sassoon

DECEMBER 16

London. General Freyberg V.C.

Freyberg inveighed against the Georgian Poets and reproached me for holding a brief for Siegfried Sassoon. I maintained that, having fully demonstrated his personal physical courage, he had earned the right to exhibit moral courage as a pacifist without laying himself open to the charge of cloaking physical cowardice under the claim of moral courage.

Freyberg is very uncompromising in his condemnation and, with some justice, says it is offensive to come back and say, 'I can't lead men to their death any more' – it implies a monopoly of virtue, as if other officers liked doing it because they acquiesced in their duty. He thought the poem called 'The Hero' caddish, as it might destroy every mother's faith in the report of her son's death. Certainly Siegfried Sassoon breaks the conspiracy of silence, but sometimes I strongly feel that those at home should be made to realise the full horror, even to the incidental ugliness, as much as possible.

He told us of an extraordinary case of a man who got his wife to forge letters saying he was the only survivor of eight sons. On the strength of this, he was taken out of the line, but subsequently he slightly wounded himself in order to get home and the whole fra ⅃ was discovered.

Lady Cynthia Asquith

A German Poet Writes

BATTLEFIELD

Yielding clod lulls iron off to sleep
bloods clot the patches where they oozed
rusts crumble
fleshes slime
sucking lusts around decay.
Murder on murder
blinks
in childish eyes.

August Stramm

Across the entry to Trench 97 a felled oak twists his great body, and a corpse stops up the trench. Its head and legs are buried in the ground. The dirty water glazes, and through the moist deposit the chest and belly bulge forth, clad in a shirt. We stride over the frigid remains, slimy and pale, that suggest the belly of a stranded crocodile; and it is difficult to do so, by reason of the soft and slippery ground. We have to plunge our hands up to the wrists in the mud of the wall.

At this moment an infernal whistle falls on us and we bend like bushes. The shell bursts in the air in front of us, deafening and blinding, and buries us under a horribly sibilant mountain of dark smoke. A climbing soldier has churned the air with his arms and disappeared, hurled into some hole. Shouts have gone up and fallen again like rubbish. While we are looking, through the great black veil that the wind tears from the ground and dismisses into the sky, at the bearers who are putting down a stretcher, running to the place of the explosion and picking up something inert – I recall the unforgettable scene when my brother-in-arms, Poterloo, whose heart was so full of hope, vanished with his arms outstretched in the flame of a shell.

We arrive at last on the summit, which is marked as with a signal by a wounded and frightful man. He is upright in the wind, shaken but upright, enrooted there. In his uplifted and wind-tossed cape we see a yelling and convulsive face. We pass by him, and he is a sort of screaming tree.

Henri Barbusse

DECEMBER 22

Trotsky signs draft Treaty of Brest-Litovsk.

We can face the people of France, Italy and Great Britain with a clear conscience. We did all we could to prevail upon the belligerent nations to join us in the peace negotiations.

Trotsky

General Hoffmann many times banged his soldier's boot on the table, at which the most intricate legal debates were carried on. For our part, we had not a moment's doubt at these negotiations General Hoffmann's boot was the only serious reality.

Trotsky

It would be difficult to over-emphasize the importance of the Treaty
. . . the high-water mark of stupidity on the part of German
military-political diplomacy . . . ensuring the whole-hearted support of America for the Allied cause; it saved the Bolshevik revolution from almost certain destruction; it robbed the German offensive of March, 1918, of the last ounce of strength . . . it set the
ultimate pattern for Stalin's foreign policy, and greatly influenced
the *ostpolitik* of Adolf Hitler.

> John Wheeler-Bennett

Greater forces were needed in 1918 to collect the plunder of Brest-
Litovsk than had been needed in 1917 to destroy the Russian
armies, and a million German soldiers, scattered from Finland to
the Caucasus, were the price paid for Greater Germany – a million
soldiers who might have turned the scale of the war in the west.

> A. J. P. Taylor

The Treaty of Brest-Litovsk

The greatest of all Lenin's difficulties was the war. Somehow the
mad loss of life on the German front must be stopped. An armistice
was signed on December 15 and Trotsky was sent to Brest-Litovsk
to negotiate a treaty. The delegates of Imperial Germany knew that
the Bolsheviks' surrender was unconditional. Trotsky had no bar-
gaining power, he had only his own superb effrontery and rhetorical
talent. He kept the Conference alive, arguing and procrastinating
while the Press of the world was filled week after week with reports
of his speeches. After Brest-Litovsk the world was no longer able to
ignore the aims and achievements of the Bolsheviks.

At last the evil hour could be postponed no longer: the German
terms must be accepted or Russia would be further invaded. The
terms were terrible: the surrender of Armenia, of the Ukraine and
of all the Baltic States – in other words Russia was to be deprived of
a quarter of her population and of her rich farm lands, a third of her
factories and three-quarters of her iron industry and coalfields. The
Bolsheviks wanted to refuse to sign but Lenin knew that no price
was too high to pay for peace; he also knew that Germany would not
be strong enough to enforce her terms. By a great effort he secured
a majority of one for acceptance. A few months later Imperial
Germany collapsed and the treaty was a dead letter.

> J. Hampden Jackson

In historical irony, Stalin, 1941, at the request of his allies, Hitler,
Ribbentrop and Himmler, surrendered to the Nazis, on the bridge of
Brest-Litovsk, many German communists who had fled to Russia
from the Gestapo.

Dey vus a bolcheviki dere, und dey dease him:
Looka vat youah Trotzsk is done, e iss
  madeh deh zhamefull beace!!
'He iss madeh deh zhamefull beace, iss he?
  'He is madeh de zhamevul beace?
'A Brest-Litovsk, yess? Aint yuh herd?
  'He vinneh de vore.
'De droobs iss released vrom de eastern vront, yess?
'Un venn dey getts to deh vestern vront, iss it
  'How many getts dere?
'And dose doat getts dere iss so full off revolutions
'Venn deh vrench is come dhru, yess,
'Dey say, 'Vot?' Un de posch say:
  'Aint yeh heard? Say, ve got a rheffolution.'

That's the trick with a crowd,
  Get 'em into the street and get 'em moving.
And all the time, there were people going
Down there, over the river.

  There was a man there talking,
To a thousand, just a short speech, and
Then move 'em on. And he said:
Yes, these people, they are all right, they
Can do everything, everything except act;
And go an' hear 'em, but when they are through,
Come to the bolsheviki . . .

And when it broke, there was the crowd there,
And the cossacks, just as always before,
But one thing, the cossacks said:
  'Pojalouista.'
And that got round in the crowd,
And then a lieutenant of infantry
Ordered 'em to fire into the crowd,
  in the square at the end of the Nevsky,

In front of the Moscow station,
And they wouldn't,
And he pulled his sword on a student for laughing,
And killed him,
And a cossack rode out of his squad
On the other side of the square
And cut down the lieutenant of infantry
And that was the revolution . . .
          as soon as they named it.

And you can't make 'em,
Nobody knew it was coming. They were all ready, the old gang,
Guns on the top of the post-office and the palace,
But none of the leaders knew it was coming.

And there were some killed at the barracks,
But that was between the troops.

          Ezra Pound

DECEMBER 27

World peace . . . Not even in deepest national bitterness have I
ever ceased believing that the hate and enmity between the Europeans is, finally, a deception, a mistake – that the sides tearing at
each other's throats are really no sides but working together, under
God's will, in fraternal torment, for universal resurrection.

          Thomas Mann, *to the 'Berliner Tageblatt'*

DECEMBER 29

*Romania admits defeat. More strikes all over Germany. 'Profiteer-
ing, criminal and glaring, in our German Fatherland.'*

The wind's out walking, flakes are whirling.
Twelve men go marching down the street.

Their rifle straps are of black leather.
Around them – lights and lights and lights . . .

A crumpled cap, a butt between his teeth,
A convict's diamond patch might fit his back!

Freedom, freedom,
Ah, you freedom without the Cross!

Tra-ta-ta!

'It's cold, comrades, bloody cold!
But Vanka's in a tavern with his Katya . . .
She's got some bills stuffed in her stocking!'

'Vanka damn him is well off, . . .
He was one of us but joined the army! . . .

'Vanka, you son of a bitch, you bourgeois,
Just you try to paw or kiss my girl!'

Freedom, freedom,
Ah, ah, without the Cross!
Katya's busy with her Vanka –
Very busy doing what?

Tra-ta-ta!

Around them – lights and lights and lights . . .
Sling your rifles on your shoulders . . .

Keep the revolutionary step!
Tireless enemies are not asleep!

Don't be yellow, comrade, grip your rifle!
Let us fire at our Holy Russia!

At Russia the stolid,
The wooden-hutted,
Fat-rumped and stolid!
Ah, ah, without the Cross!

Alexander Blok

DECEMBER 31

21,174 French desertions during the past year.
3½ million tons of British shipping lost in the Atlantic.
Britain lost 5,766,000 working days in 588 strikes.
French strikes involved 393,810 workers.

Whereas on the French home front in 1914–15 strikes had been negligible, in 1916 there were 314 . . . and in 1917, the year of the Army Mutinies, 696.

Alistair Horne

The Support of Numbers

When the name shell-shock was coined the number of men leaving the trenches with no bodily wound leapt up. The pressure of opinion in the battalion – the idea stronger than fear – was eased by giving fear a respectable name. When the social slur was removed and the military risks were abolished the weaklings may have decided in cold blood to malinger, or perhaps when an alternative was held out the suggestion of safety was too much for their feeble will. The resolve to stay with the battalion had been weakened, the conscience was relaxed, the path out of danger was made easy. The hospitals at the base were said to be choked with these people though the doctors could find nothing wrong with them. Men in France were weary. Unable or unwilling? It was no longer a private anxiety, it had become a public menace.

Soldiers in France in 1917 and 1918 had more need for the support of the corporate opinion of their units in the face of danger – the support of numbers – than those who had fought up to the battle of the Somme. The history of the use of mustard gas by the Germans brings out that need by warning us – with the emphasis of figures – what may befall an army which has forgotten that a soldier's conduct is shaped by what is expected of him. First used in July, 1917, there were one hundred and thirteen thousand casualties from this gas; it was a bid for a decision. At one time it appeared that it might come to play on land the part the submarines filled at sea.

Late in 1917 I was sent to Bologne to find some means of checking the backward stream. In a quarter of these men we found a nervous disorder – frequently hysteria – implanted on the physical harm caused by the gas, which in itself was often trivial. When after a few days the bodily hurt was gone, there was left an emotional disturbance like a mild attack of shell shock. The physical effects were often absent or of no moment; it was the mind that had suffered hurt. Mustard gas, after July, 1917, partly usurped the role of high explosive in bringing to a head a natural unfitness for war, or less commonly in undermining a fitness sapped by exceptional stress in the field.

In making a point that has been overlooked it would be easy to stretch the truth. Mustard gas was the cause of grave physical injury: of every hundred gassed men, thirteen had to be sent to England. But the majority were more frightened than hurt.

A soldier of judgment wrote to me: 'during a gas attack a hundred and fifty men drifted away from the battalion on our right while only ten left the Fusiliers, though the conditions were the same.' Could those fellows have stayed if they had wished? Was it the presence of gas or the absence of discipline?

     Lord Moran

Who are these? Why sit they here in twilight?
Wherefore rock they, purgatorial shadows,
Drooping tongues from jaws that slob their relish,
Baring teeth that leer like skulls' teeth wicked?
Stroke on stroke of pain, – but what slow panic,
Gouged these chasms round their fretted sockets?
Ever from their hair and through their hands' palms
Misery swelters. Surely we have perished
Sleeping, and walk in hell; but who these hellish?

     Wilfred Owen

These apparently rude and brutal natures comforted, encouraged and reconciled each other to fate, with a tenderness and tact which was more moving than anything in life. They had nothing, not even their own bodies, which had become mere implements of warfare. They turned from the wreckage and misery of life to an empty heaven, and from an empty heaven to the silence of their own hearts. They had been brought to the last extremity of hope, and yet they put their hands on each other's shoulders and said with a passionate conviction that it would be all right, though they had faith in nothing, but in themselves and in each other.

     Frederick Manning

For the last time, reflect, O ancient world!
    To a feast of work and peace in brotherhood,
For the last time, to a gay feast of brothers
    The lyre of the barbarian summons you.

     Alexander Blok

1918

*In the West Austria, Turkey and Bulgaria were beginning to falter.
The Germans knew that victory must be won before the full onslaught
of American power. Yet the US–British Convoy system was steadily
overcoming the U-Boats, and by March 179,703 American 'raw-
necks' had reached France. Two near mutinies would occur in the
German fleet, kept in port since Jutland. German reserves of men,
oil, petrol, rubber, horses and food were dwindling. Death rate
among children soared in Austria and Germany. Wholesale tubercu-
losis and rickets devastated Vienna. Germany was enduring 'the
Turnip Winter' with strikes, protests and defeatism. Should the renewed, and surely final German effort fail in the West, revolution on
the Russian scale must occur. No compromise could be expected
from the implacable old 'Tiger', Clemenceau, from Lloyd George,
and the resolutely anti-monarchical Woodrow Wilson. Already,
Ludendorff and Hindenburg were disregarding their 'Supreme
Warlord', while the French and British were feeling their way, re-
luctantly but inevitably, towards a unified command.*

*Silently, slowly, inexorably, the British blockade of the Central
Powers was tightening, inducing shortages, near-famine, disease and
gloom throughout the civilian populations. Some were now wearing
paper garments, chalk and sawdust were detected in loaves, vermin
was added to a mass diet of turnips, during Germany's 'Turnip
Winter'. Vital food supplies had to be diverted from the Front to the
cities, where unrest was seething. Few were soothed by news of
Krupps' 12% dividend. Ersatz became common.*

*One and a half million strike in Germany for 'Peace, Freedom,
Bread'. Six killed, scores wounded. Many workers now conscripted,
in an effort to prevent further protests.*

*From ex-Empress Eugénie, her old enemy Clemenceau acquired
Bismarck's letter in which he wrote that the defeated have no rights.*

Other Ranks

Ah, you are right, poor countless workmen of the battles, you who have made with your hands all of the Great War, you whose omnipotence is not yet used for well-doing, you human host whose every face is a world of sorrows, you who dream bowed under the yoke of a thought beneath that sky where long black clouds rend themselves and expand in dishevelled lengths like evil angels – yes, you are right. There are all those things against you. Against you and your great common interests, which are precisely and with sacred logic blended, there are not only the sword-wavers, the profiteers, and the intriguers.

There is not only the prodigious opposition of interested parties – financiers, speculators great and small, armour-plated in their banks and houses, who live on war and live in peace during war, with their brows stubbornly set upon a secret doctrine and their faces shut up like safes.

There are those who admire the exchange of flashing blows, who hail like women the bright colours of uniforms; those whom military music and the martial ballads poured upon the public intoxicate as with brandy; the dizzy-brained, the feeble-minded, the superstitious, the savages.

There are those who bury themselves in the past, on whose lips are the sayings only of bygone days, the traditionalists for whom an injustice has legal force because it is perpetuated, who aspire to be guided by the dead, who strive to subordinate progress and the future and all their palpitating passion to the realm of ghosts and nursery-tales.

With them are all the parsons, who seek to excite you and to lull you to sleep with the morphine of their Paradise, so that nothing may change.

They pervert the most admirable of moral principles. How many are the crimes of which they have made virtues merely by dowering them with the word 'national'? They distort even truth itself. For the truth which is eternally the same they substitute each their national truth. So many nations, so many truths; and thus they falsify and twist the truth. All those people are your enemies.

They are your enemies as much as those German soldiers are today who are prostrate here between you in the mud, who are only poor dupes hatefully deceived and brutalised, domestic beasts. They are your enemies wherever they were born, however they pronounce their names, whatever the language in which they lie. Look at them, in the heaven and on the earth. Look at them, everywhere! Identify them once for all, and be mindful for ever!

Henri Barbusse

Sentries

A sentry is faced suddenly by a large body of the enemy, his lowest instinct of self-preservation acts, but before any movement of flight can take place the instinct for the preservation of the race has intervened and barred the way to self-indulgence. The voice of duty tells him that his own safety must be subordinated to that of the army of which he is a member. And this voice of the herd is backed by threats of physical and moral penalties.

Lord Moran

In 1916, in desperation, the English had abandoned liberalism and invoked all the resources of State Management in a bid for sheer survival. The experiment was rewarded: the war-economy Lloyd George created sustained Britain during those crucial months of effort in 1918 which finally broke the will and discipline even of the people and armed forces of Germany.

Paul Johnson

JANUARY 8

A Chance of Peace?

President Wilson's terms to Germany. The Fourteen Points, include independence for Poland, restoration of Belgian independence, the return of Alsace-Lorraine to France (lost in 1871), an end to secret diplomacy, autonomous development of subject nationalities, the formation of a League of Nations.

JANUARY 19

The New Freedom

Lenin dissolves the Constituent Assembly, in which the Bolsheviks were in a minority. No alternative political parties were ever again permitted.

Without general elections, without total freedom of the Press and assembly, without free conflict of opinion, life evaporates from every public institution, becomes a mere pretence of life in which the bureaucracy alone remains as the new, living constituent. Gradually, public life becomes drowsy, a few dozen political leaders of tireless energy and unlimited experience command and govern.

      Rosa Luxemburg

Rosa Luxemburg and Karl Liebknecht were murdered by army officers on January 15, 1919.

I hope our Russian cousins are happy now. Trotsky I imagine will look after the interests of his co-religionists. Russia is like an amputated limb to our cause and America the cork substitute – I doubt whether she is more.

      Isaac Rosenberg

An American War Effort: George Creel, Chairman of the Committee on Public Information

Within a year, Creel's organisation counted 150,000 assistants. 75,000 of them acted as 'four minute men' who gave four minute addresses in the streets, in trains, cinemas and schools. With the American predilection for statistics, it was calculated that these 'four minute men' made 7,555,190 speeches and thereby addressed a probable aggregate of 314,454,000 listeners. Sixty million pamphlets and leaflets rained upon the American people. The aid of film and theatre was invoked – the film on a scale which proved that this youngest medium of mass communication was likely to have an impressive future.

      P. J. Bouman

A wandering fire at a terrible height –
can it be a star shining like that?
Transparent star, wandering fire,
your brother, Petropolis, is dying.

The dreams of earth blaze at a terrible height,
a green star is burning,
Or if you are a star, this brother of water and sky,
your brother, Petropolis, is dying.

A giant ship at a terrible height
is rushing on, spreading its wings.
Green star, in splendid poverty
your brother, Petropolis, is dying.

Above the black Neva transparent spring
has broken, the wax of immortality is melting.
O if you are a star, Petropolis, your city,
your brother, Petropolis, is dying.

       Osip Mandelshtam

JANUARY 24

250,000 on strike in Berlin, reported throughout Germany.

JANUARY 26

What is happening to me now is more tragic than the 'passion play'.
Christ never endured what I endure. It is breaking me completely.

       Isaac Rosenberg, *to Edward Marsh*

GETHSEMANE (1914–18)

The Garden called Gethsemane
  In Picardy it was,
And there the people came to see
  The English soldiers pass.

We used to pass – we used to pass
  Or halt, as it might be,
And ship our masks in case of gas
  Beyond Gethsemane.

The Garden called Gethsemane,
  It held a pretty lass,
But all the time she talked to me
  I prayed my cup might pass.
The officer sat on the chair,
  The men lay on the grass,
And all the time we halted there
  I prayed my cup might pass.

It didn't pass – it didn't pass –
  It didn't pass from me.
I drank it when we met the gas
  Beyond Gethsemane!

     Rudyard Kipling

FEBRUARY 5

First loss of American soldiers at sea. US Transport Tuscania *sunk.
210 lives lost, out of 2,397.*

FEBRUARY 12

Voices

Four Basic Principles Laid Down by Wilson. German Junkers
Only Obstacle; Austria's Tone Friendly; Russia
Demobilises Her Armies and Gets Out Of The War.

    The World, New York

The Lord pointed out to us by a hard school the path by which we
should go. The world, however, at the same time, has not been on

the right path. We Germans, who still have ideals, should work to bring about better times. We should fight for right and morality . . . We desire to live in friendship with neighbouring peoples, but the victory of German arms must first be recognised. Our troops under the great Hindenburg will continue to win it. Then peace will come.

> Kaiser Wilhelm II

FEBRUARY 23

The Treaty of Brest-Litovsk Finally Signed

Never had the Bolsheviks been under such a strain in the choices open to them as in those forty-eight hours in which they had to decide whether or not to accept this ultimatum. Having lost 2,500,000 people in the three and a half years of war, Russia was now to repay her aggressors with 34% of her population, 32% of her farming land, 89% of her coalfields and 54% of her industrial centres. For, as well as vast indemnities and the demobilisation of her army, she was to cede Latvia and Estonia and evacuate the Ukraine and Finland.

> Cathy Porter

MARCH

I suppose we have to wish for a German victory, and this is 1) a displeasing idea, and 2) still improbable.

> Sigmund Freud, *to Ferenczi*

MARCH 20

Do you know what it says for tomorrow in the *Brüdergemeinde*? It is the day of the Chosen People. Now, cannot we regard the offensive that begins tomorrow with confidence?

> Ludendorff, *to General von Tieschowitz*

'*The Brüdergemeinde' were the sacred texts of the Lay Brothers of the eighteenth-century Moravian Brethren, which reputedly had magical powers.*

It will be an immense struggle that will begin at one point, continue at another and take a long time. It is difficult but it will be successful.

> Ludendorff, *to Wilhelm II*

On the Eve

In the evening the Major rang me up and asked me why the hell his ammunition hadn't arrived. He was a certain Major 'the Honourable something' Anson, a nice enough fellow but rather conscious of his aristocratic connection. By that time my temper was getting a little short and I didn't like the way he spoke to me, so I told him that if his ammunition hadn't arrived it was because he was a damned fool and I refused to speak with him further. Later on his Colonel rang up and twenty minutes of wordy warfare ensued in the course of which I told him that what his battery commander required was a wet nurse and that I refused to act in that capacity. It was one of those rare occasions when differences of rank are forgotten and two persons of very different standing speak to one another as man to man. I cannot remember all I said to him but I know that I said things to him that I wouldn't have said to the most junior subaltern in the brigade. In due course we recovered ourselves and parted on excellent terms. His name was Colonel Eley, a territorial and an excellent soldier of the get-on-with-it type and quite unhampered by the more devastating of the old army traditions. But he was rather highly-strung and he reached his breaking point a few days later.

                    Captain F. N. Broome

MARCH 21–JULY 15

Ludendorff's 100 Days

Operation Michael *begins, Ludendorff's last desperate throw. Starts offensive against the British Third and Fifth Armies, the French on their left, the Americans on their right, north and south of the Somme, reinforced by troops released from Russia, aiming at Amiens.*

I awoke to a tremendous start conscious of noise, incessant and almost musical, so intense that it seemed as if 100 devils were dancing in my brain. All seemed vibrating – the ground, my dugout, my bed.

                    Arthur Behrend

Gough's Fifth Army retreats 30 miles. 100,000 British casualties, the worst yet, in perhaps the greatest defeat any British army had hitherto known – its effects threatening to rival the disasters that had lost Britain the United States in 1777.

APRIL 14

Ludendorff's second blow pushes back the British and Portuguese. His third blow drives French back to the Marne, and prepares his final effort – with mauled, depleted troops – against the French at Rheims, July 15.

At the Front

The bombardment on our trenches started around dawn on the 21st March and was sheer hell – shells, trench mortars, the lot, gradually cutting down our platoon. During this time our lieutenant-colonel, the captain, and his runner came along the trenches to see how things were. At that time there were only about three or four of us alive but no order was given to draw back or pull out. While we were discussing what to do – there being nobody in charge – my pal was hit with a piece of shell which sliced his head completely off. You can imagine how I felt. All the rest were dead by now, mostly having lost their limbs, so I decided to go along the trenches to see if I could find anybody alive. This was not easy as parts of the trench were blown in . . . Giving up all hope of survival and feeling hopping mad, I waited with my Lewis gun for the enemy to come over the top.

                    Rifleman E. Chapman

A British Prisoner of War

Another man and I were led to a wounded German who had been laid on a waterproof sheet which we made into a makeshift sling. As we got nearer to the dressing stations, a battery of our heavy guns put on a barrage down in front of us and, as splinters started to fly around, our escort decided that we should use a badly damaged communication trench. As we made our way along this, our casualty's leg, which was smashed and hanging out of the sling, knocked against the churned-up ground and, whenever that happened, he let out a squeal of agony. I felt that this was a sure way of upsetting his mate and was half expecting to get his bayonet in my backside, but he seemed unconcerned and, when we had gone a hundred yards or so, decided that we should sit down and rest. After he had had a drink, he passed his water bottle round. This kind of behaviour among front-line troops and their prisoners was not uncommon in the first war, a sort of camaraderie I suppose, and it was not until we came in contact with troops who lived in safe areas well away from the fighting that we received any rough treatment. We duly delivered our casualty and then had to carry another stretcher case into St Quentin.

Sapper F. E. Waldron

MARCH 26

Behind the Lines

In the crisis of near-catastrophe Ferdinand Foch is appointed Supreme Commander of the Allied Armies as Ludendorff's armies push towards Amiens.

Clemenceau laid before the meeting the note he had hurriedly drafted: 'General Foch is appointed by the British and French Governments to co-ordinate the action of the Allied Armies on the Western Front. To this end, he will come to an understanding with the two Generals-in-Chief, who are requested to furnish him with all necessary information.'

After a few minor modifications had been made, the final draft of the note was read out and signed by Milner and Clemenceau. The tense atmosphere now changed to one of cordiality. The French saw their realization of a long-cherished dream; the British saw a rapid supply of French reserves. As Clemenceau left the Town Hall, he declared to General Mordacq, 'That's almost worth a victory over the Germans.' And Mordacq made the comment, 'It certainly was a victory – but over the English.'

P. J. Bouman

It is a hard job you now offer me. A compromised situation, a dissolving front, a battle in full progress turning against us. Nevertheless, I accept.

Ferdinand Foch

MARCH 31

Death of Isaac Rosenberg

They crept out into the uncertain darkness, feeling their way across the cratered and treacherous ground. Whether they came across an unexploded shell, or whether an alert German sniper spotted them, they did not return. Rosenberg's body was never found.

      Jean Liddiard

APRIL 2

Air Power

Since yesterday the 'lutte', as they say, has continued. Gunfire last evening – and at 3.15 this morning one woke to hear the air screaming. That is the effect of these sirens; they have a most diabolical sound. I dressed and went down to the cave. Everybody else was there – the place was packed with hideous humanity: so hideous indeed that one felt a bomb on them wouldn't perhaps be as cruel, after all. I don't think I can go to the cave again. The cold and agony of those stone dusty steps and these filthy people smoking in that air. I crept back to bed and to sleep and woke to a perfect deafening roar of gunfire. It was followed by the sound of people running in the streets. I got up again and went to look. Very ugly, very horrible. The whole top of a house as it were bitten out – all the windows broken, and the road of course covered with ruin. There were trees on both sides of the street and these had just come into their new green. A great many branches were broken, but on the others strange bits of clothes and paper hung. A nightdress, a chemise, a tie – they looked extraordinarily pitiful, dangling in the sunny light.

One thing which confirms me again in my dreadful feeling that I live wherever I am in another Sodom and Gomorrah . . . this. Two workmen arrived to clear away the débris. One found, under the dust, a woman's silk petticoat. He put it on and danced a step or two for the laughing crowd . . . That filled me with such horror that I'll never get out of my mind the fling of his feet and his grin and the broken trees and the broken house.

      Katherine Mansfield

APRIL 11

Crisis

There is no other course open to us but to fight it out. Every position must be held to the last man. There must be no retirement. With our backs to the wall and believing in the justness of our cause, each one of us must fight on to the end.

> Douglas Haig

APRIL 22

Rittmeister von Richthofen scored his eightieth victory yesterday.

> Herbert Sulzbach

I am a hunter. My brother, Lothar, is a butcher. When I have shot down an Englishman my hunting passion is satisfied for a quarter of an hour.

> Manfred von Richthofen

APRIL 24

Richthofen has really been killed in action! I am completely shattered by the news. No words will suffice to do justice to his deeds, or to describe the grief which every German feels at the loss of this national hero; it is just impossible to grasp; he has been buried by the British with the highest military honours, for he crashed the British lines. Six British flying officers bore his coffin, and a British chaplain presented the sermon and sang his praises as an enemy hero, a British plane with mourning pennants circled the burial ground during the funeral, and showed the highest honour to this fallen enemy. The British are indeed truly chivalrous, and we must thank them all for honouring our great airman.

> Herbert Sulzbach

I hope he roasted the whole way down.

> 'Mick' Mannock, the top British fighter ace (with 73 victims), on hearing of Richthofen's death in 1918. Mannock was himself killed the same year.

APRIL 28

Life Continues in the East

The Revolution demands in the interests of socialism that the masses unquestionably obey the single will of the leaders, the Labour process.

> Lenin

MAY

Life Continues in the West

If the enemy does not want peace, then we must bring peace to the world by destroying, with an iron fist and a flaming sword, the portals of those who do not want peace.

> Kaiser Wilhelm II

Guns

'The guns?' said Betty Flanders, half asleep, getting out of bed and going to the window, which was decorated with a fringe of dark leaves.

'Not at this distance,' she thought. 'It is the sea.'

Again, far away, she heard the dull sound, as if nocturnal women were beating great carpets. There was Morty lost, and Seabrook dead; her sons fighting for their country. But were the chickens safe? Was that someone moving downstairs? Rebecca with the toothache? No. The nocturnal women were beating great carpets. Her hens shifted slightly on their perches.

> Virginia Woolf

The Allied blockade, now biting into the Central Powers, was to continue for six months after the cease-fire, with widespread havoc amongst hungry and sick Central Europeans, particularly children.

By June 1918 there were 1,437,930 American soldiers in France. 'Raw necks' the German rulers contemptuously named them.

JUNE

Americans on the Western Front

Everyone felt that the Americans were present at the magical operation of blood transfusion. Life arrived in torrents to revive the mangled body of a France bled white by the countless wounds of four years.

Jean de Pierrefeu

Conscription Continues

I was called up in the war and sent to a hospital. I dressed wounds, applied iodine, gave enemas, did blood transfusions. If the doctor ordered, 'Brecht, amputate a leg!' I would reply, 'Certainly, Your Excellency!' and cut off the leg. If I was told, 'Perform a trepanning!' I opened the man's skull and messed about with his brains. I saw how they patched fellows up, so as to cart them back to the Front as quickly as they could.

Bertolt Brecht

Battlefield

Quite near, we notice that some mounds of earth aligned along the ruined ramparts of this deep-drowned ditch are human. Are they dead – or asleep? We do not know; in any case, they rest. Are they German or French? We do not know. One of them has opened his eyes, and looks at us with swaying head. We say to him, 'French?' – and then, 'Deutsch?' He makes no reply, but shuts his eyes again and relapses into oblivion. We never knew what he was. We cannot decide the identity of these beings, either by their clothes, thickly covered with filth, or by their head-dress, for they are bareheaded or swathed in woollens under their liquid and offensive cowls; or by their weapons, for they either have no rifles or their hands rest lightly on something they have dragged along, a shapeless and sticky mass, like a sort of fish. All these men of corpse-like faces who are before us and behind us, at the limit of their strength, void of speech as of will, all these earth-charged men who you would say were carrying their own winding-sheets are as much alike as if they were naked. Out of the horror of the night, apparitions are issuing from this side and that who are clad in exactly the same uniform of misery and filth. It is the end of all. For the moment it is the prodigious finish, the epic cessation of the war.

I once used to think that the worst hell in war was the flame of shells; and then for long I thought it was the suffocation of the caverns which eternally confine us. But it is neither of these. Hell is water.

The wind is rising, and its icy breath goes through our flesh. On the wrecked and dissolving plain, flecked with bodies between its worm-shaped chasms of water, among the islands of motionless men stuck together like reptiles in this flattening and sinking chaos there are some slight indications of movement. We see slowly stirring groups and fragments of groups, composed of beings who bow under the weight of their coats and aprons of mud, who trail themselves along, disperse, and crawl about in the depths of the sky's tarnished light. The dawn is so foul that one would say the day was already done.

These survivors are migrating across the desolated steppe, pursued by an unspeakable evil which exhausts and bewilders them. They are lamentable objects; grotesque, for the overwhelming mud from which they still take flight has half unclothed them.

As they pass by their glances go widely around. They look at us, and discovering men in us they cry through the wind, 'It's worse down yonder than it is here. The chaps are falling into the holes, and you can't pull them out. All them that trod on the edge of a shell-hole last night, they're dead. Down there where we're coming from you can see a head in the ground, working its arms, embedded. There's a hurdle-path that's given way in places and the hurdles have sunk into holes, and it's a man-trap. Where there's no more hurdles there's two yards deep of water. Your rifle? You couldn't pull it out again when you'd stuck it in. Look at those men, there. They've cut off all the bottom half of their greatcoats – hard lines on the pockets – to help 'em get clear, and also because they hadn't strength to drag a weight like that. Dumas' coat, we were able to pull it off him, and it weighed a good eighty pounds; we could just lift it, two of us, with both our hands. Look – him with the bare legs; it's taken everything off him, his trousers, his drawers, his boots, all dragged off by the mud. One's never seen that, never!'

Scattered and straggling, the herd takes flight in a fever of fear, their feet pulling huge stumps of mud out of the ground. We watch the human flotsam fade away, and the lumps of them diminish, immured in enormous clothes.

      Henri Barbusse

JUNE 3

Prison

Brixton

To my brother Frank

Existence here is not disagreeable, but for the fact that one can't see one's friends. The one fact does make it, to me, very disagreeable – but if I were devoid of affection, like many middle-aged men, I should find nothing to dislike. One has no responsibilities, and infinite leisure. My time passes very fruitfully. In a normal day, I do four hours' philosophical writing, four hours' philosophical reading, and four hours' general reading – so you can understand my wanting a lot of books. I have been reading Madame Roland's memoirs and have come to the conclusion that she was a very over-rated woman: snobbish, vain, sentimental, envious – rather German type. Her last days before her execution were spent in chronicling petty social snubs or triumphs of many years back. She was a democrat chiefly from envy of the noblesse. Prisons in her day were more cheerful than now: she says if she were not writing her memoirs she would be painting flowers or playing an air. Pianos are not provided in Brixton. On the other hand, one is not guillotined on leaving, which is in some ways an advantage. – During my two hours' exercise I reflect upon all manner of things. It is good to have a time of leisure for reflection and altogether it is a godsend being here. But I don't want too much godsend!

I am quite happy and my mind is very active. I enjoy the sense that the time is fruitful – after giving out all these last years, reading almost nothing and writing very little and having no opportunity for anything civilized, it is a real delight to get back to a civilized existence. But oh I shall be glad when it is over! I have given up the bad habit of imagining the war may be over some day. One must compare the time with that of the Barbarian invasion. I feel like Apollinaris Sidonius – The best one could be would be to be like St. Augustine. For the next 1000 years people will look back to the time before 1914 as they did in the Dark Ages to the time before the Gauls sacked Rome. Queer animal, Man!

>   Your loving brother
>   Bertrand Russell

JUNE 5

Respite

Nine miles short of Amiens, General Byng finally halts Ludendorff.

JUNE 15

In the East

Austria, nearing collapse, mounts the Battle of Piave against Italy, but, after initial successes, the attack crumbles.

An English Historian, as an Ambulance Worker on the Italian Front

The best stunt I had in the battle was the day the Austrians retired over the big bridge at Ponte di Piave. I went to the Italian end of it and we were told that there were six Austrian wounded in a dug-out in the bank some way along the actual river side, who had been lying there without any care or anything to eat for several days, forgotten by their Austrian comrades, but now the Italians had come they were being kind to them. But the Italians were too tired and too busy fighting to carry them out along the slippery mud-bank under fire. So to save their lives four of us (including Philip Noel-Baker, later Olympic athlete and Cabinet Minister) went to carry the Austrians to our ambulances, and when we turned up on the river bank the Italians holding the line were so pleased at our coming there and so sorry for the Austrian wounded that the good fellows helped us to carry them all the long mile along the river bank, up and down mud-banks, though they were dead tired with fighting. Two out of the six died on the way but we saved the others.

> G. M. Trevelyan, *to Humphrey Trevelyan*

JULY 15

Relief

Ludendorff stopped for ever, on the Marne.

JULY 16

Tsar Nicholas II, his wife and children, murdered at Ekaterinburg in 'the house of Special Purpose', Commissar Yourkovsky commanding.

We like this specimen the least of all.

   Tsar Nicholas II's last entry in his diary

Foch's 100 days: July 18–November 11

Foch successfully counter-attacks on the Marne. The British, under Rawlinson, thrust General von der Marwitz back to the Somme. August 8 was, according to Ludendorff, 'the black day of the German Army'. Haig attacks east of Amiens with French and American support. 430 Allied tanks in action. Five German defeats. The British take the Hindenburg Line on September 26 and three days later Ludendorff suffers a stroke. He had already recognised his failure and was demanding that the Kaiser should accept the loss of the war. On October 26 Ludendorff formally resigns.

Ludendorff never had any knowledge of human nature, otherwise he could never have been at the mercy of those influences that ruined him.

   Frau Ludendorff

Ludendorff, an early supporter of Hitler, died in 1937 having become obsessed with old German gods and blaming world difficulties on international conspiracies of Jews, Jesuits and Freemasons.

What was the factor that made Ludendorff opt for peace after his first defeats? It was the Americans – not the handful of divisions in the line but the huge growing reserve of well-fed, unwearied and unshaken men they supplied . . . It was not the present that was impossible but the future. The British and French had won the battles of 1918 but it was the Americans who won the War. The German army was never 'stabbed in the back'. By the beginning of 1918, because of the growth of American military and technological strength and because of the British blockade, Germany and her allies were steadily, inevitably losing the War, with consequent effects of moral disintegration at home and in the forces.

   Corelli Barnett

In the victorious period from July to November 11, the French suffered no less than 531,000 casualties themselves, and inflicted 414,000 upon the enemy. That an army and a nation engaged at their full strength from the beginning of the war, which had sustained 700,000 casualties in the first three weeks, and nearly 3 millions in the first three years, should have been capable of so noble an effort at the end will ever command the admiration and gratitude of their Ally.

> Winston Churchill

JULY 15

Start of the Battle of Rheims. The Germans' great hammer-blows fail to smash the Allied Armies. The Kaiser watches.

The arrival of the Imperial train at a wayside station; the supreme War Lord's meeting with his Generals, Hindenburg solemn, deferential, vague; Ludendorff preoccupied, tense, reserved, the man at the wheel . . . the Imperial trappings are becoming threadbare. These men are grappling with doom. They do not seek to add a third to their confidence. The Emperor is ceremoniously relegated to a tall wooden tower specially constructed in a wood, from whose platform above the level of the tree-tops the All-Highest would be in the most favourable position to witness what might happen. And here with his immediate retinue he must dwell perched for six whole days, eye glued to telescopes that show nothing but distant fumes and blurs and smudges; while his throne totters and his people's fortune is decided, utterly helpless and useless, a prey to the worst anxieties, but at any rate out of the way.

> Carl Rosner, paraphrased by Winston Churchill

All these talks and speeches and theories of Wilson's are most dangerous, and more dangerous to England than to anyone else and are also dangerous to France. This 'League of Nations'. What folly! You, you, you, you English . . . what are you about? Why should you take risks by creating nations such as Czechoslovakia and I know not what? . . . You did one very clever thing in recognizing the King of the Hedjaz. But beware! You and France combined will provide material for a Holy War if you go on as at present.

> ex-Empress Eugénie, *to Colonel Verner*

JULY 21

Counter-Attack

The Great German reverse.
Huns Forced to Retreat Across the Marne.

> *Sunday Evening Telegraph*, London

The building is beginning to crack. Everyone to battle.

> Ferdinand Foch

AUGUST

The Inches

See that little stream – we could walk to it in two minutes. It took
the British a month to walk to it – a whole empire walking very
slowly, dying in front and pushing forward behind. And another
empire walked very slowly backward a few inches a day, leaving the
dead like a million bloody rags. No European will ever do that again
in this generation.

> F. Scott Fitzgerald

The Poet on the Western Front

Night was a perpetual tangle. If one went forward patrolling, it was
almost inevitable that one would soon creep round some hole or
suspect heap or stretch of wired posts, and then, suddenly one no
longer knew which was the German line, which our own. Puzzling
dazzling lights flew up, fell in the grass beside and flared like
bonfires; one heard movements, saw figures, conjectured distances,
and all in that state of dilemma. Willow trees seemed moving men.
Compasses responded to old iron and failed us. At last by luck or
some stroke of recognition one found oneself; but there was danger
of not doing so; and the battalion which relieved us sent a patrol out,
only to lose it that way. The patrol came against wire and bombed
with all its skill; the men behind the wire fired their Lewis gun with
no less determination, and, when the killed and wounded amounted
to a dozen or more, it was found that the patrol and the defenders
were of the same battalion. I knew the officer who led that patrol, he
was by temperament suited for a quiet country parsonage, and

would usually have mislaid his spectacles.

The parapets were thin and treacherous in this place. One afternoon a sentry of ours was hit in the head and killed while he stood quite out of observation. I was in my tiny dugout reading Mr Masefield's *Good Friday* when I heard that shot.

> Edmund Blunden

The Hand

This morning in lovely sunlight I went for a little crawl by myself and had rather fun. I found an arm sticking out of the earth. I don't know what impulse made me take off the glove. The arm had been there a long time and there was little left except bones. The hand was beautiful, thin and delicate like the hand of a woman . . . it must always have been a small hand and I think the owner must have been proud of it because gloves are not usually worn at the war. The hand was raised and the fingers curved in rather an affected gesture – I wish I could have kept the glove. My brother-officers were amazed at my lack of squeamishness in removing the glove from a corpse, and yet they would think nothing of treading on a beetle.

> Duff Cooper, *to his wife*

August 8

All you write about S.S. [Siegfried Sassoon] is interesting and poignant. I know so well the indignation he suffers from – I have lived in it for months, and on the edge of it for years. I think that one way of getting over it is to perceive that others might judge oneself in the same way, unjustly, but with just as good grounds. Those of us who are rich are just like the young women whose sex flourishes on the blood of soldiers. Every motor-tyre is made out of the blood of negroes under any lash, yet motorists are not all heartless villains. When we buy wax matches, we buy a painful and lingering death for those who make them . . . War is only the final flower of the capitalist system, but with an unusual proletariat. S.S. sees war, not peace, from the point of view of the proletariat. But this is only politics. The fundamental mistake lies in wrong expectations, leading to cynicism when they are not realised. Conventional morality leads us to expect unselfishness in decent people. This is an error. Man is an animal bent on securing food and propagating the species.

One way of succeeding in these objects is to persuade others that one is after their welfare – but to be really after any welfare but one's own and one's children's is unnatural. It occurs like sadism and sodomy, but is equally against nature. A good social system is not to be secured by making people unselfish, but by making their own vital impulses fit in with other people's. This is feasible. Our present system is at fault; but it is a weakness to be disgusted with people because they aim at self-preservation. One's idealism needs to be too robust for such weaknesses. It doesn't do to forget or deny the animal in man. The God in man will not be visible, as a rule, while the animal is thwarted. Those who have produced stoic philosophies have all had enough to eat and drink. The sum total of the matter is that one's idealism must be robust and must fit in with the facts of nature; and that which is horrible in the actual world is mainly due to a bad system. Spinoza, always is right in all these things, to my mind.

Bertrand Russell, *to Ottoline Morrell*

AUGUST 13

From a Pacifist, in Wormwood Scrubs Prison

I hear the Bishop of London marked his satisfaction at the beginning of the fifth year of the war by consecrating a war shrine in Hyde Park! I could not help wondering whether it was near the Albert Memorial and the architecture of similar taste! By the way, the other Sunday I went through all the lessons (morning and evening) for the holy days and Sundays throughout the year in the book of Common Prayer, and in *no* case has *any* lesson *any* reference to the Sermon on the Mount! No wonder there is not much Christianity when that is how the Established Church treats the whole basis of Christ's teaching.

C. H. Norman

AUGUST 27

Prison Reading

I have been reading Marsh on Rupert [Brooke]. It makes me very sad and very indignant. It hurts reading of all that young world now swept away – Rupert and his brother and Keeling and lots of others – in whom one foolishly thought at the time that there was hope for the world – they were full of life and energy and truth – Rupert himself loved life and the world – his hatreds were very concrete, resulting from some quite specific vanity or jealousy, but in the main he found the world lovable and interesting. There was nothing of humbug in him. I feel that after the war-mongers had killed his body in the Dardanelles they have done their best to kill his spirit by ——'s lies . . . When will people learn the robustness of truth? I do not know who my biographer may be, but I should like him to report 'with what flourish his nature will' something like this: 'I was not a solemn stained-glass saint, existing only for purposes of edification; I existed from my own centre, many things that I did were regret- table, I did not respect respectable people, and when I pretended to do so it was hum-bug. I lied and practised hypocrisy, because if I had not I should not have been allowed to do my work; but there is no need to continue the hyprocrisy after my death. I hated hypoc- risy and lies: I loved life and real people, and wished to get rid of the shams that prevent us from loving real people as they really are. I believed in laughter and spontaneity, and trusted to nature to bring out the genuine good in people, if once genuineness could come to be tolerated.' Marsh goes building up the respectable legend, making the part of youth harder in the future, so far as lies in his power – I try so hard not to hate, but I do hate respectable liars and oppressors and corruptors of youth – I hate them with all my soul, and the war has given them a new lease of power. The young were shaking them off, but they have secured themselves by setting the young to kill each other. But rage is useless; what is wanted is to carry over into the new time something of the gaiety and civilised outlook and genial expansive love that was appearing when the war came.

Bertrand Russell, *to Ottoline Morrell*

Execution

He could see Victor's epitaph:

GENERAL ROUTINE ORDERS
by
F.M. Sir Douglas Haig, G.C.B., G.C.V.O., K.C.I.E.,
C. in C. British Armies in France.
Adjutant-General's Branch.
Courts Martial

No. 89507 Private V. F. J. Nevin as tried by Field General Court
Martial on the following charge:

'When on Active Service, deserting His Majesty's Service.'

The accused absented himself from near the front line in
November 1915, and remained absent till apprehended in a place
behind the line in September 1918; he was then in civilian clothes,
without identity-disc or pay-book.

The sentence of the court was 'To suffer death by being shot.'

The sentence was duly carried out at 5.51 a.m. on September 27
1918.

But now he must go on parade, with his face turned to wood, and
pump Immals while he was there to be pumped: for Victor might
have said something, left some message – a letter perhaps.

Immals was saying how 'in this Army' the plan was to blindfold
the prisoner by putting a gas-mask over his head, with the eye
windows round at the back. 'It's much more use than a hanky.
Covers the whole of his face, so the men can't see the face working.
Sure to put 'em off if they do. As a matter of fact, it's what happened
today.'

'Did he say things?' Auberon asked. With conscious cunning he
aped the laboured callousness of Immals' puny courtiers.

'Lord, no! We've stopped all that in this Army, ages ago. Some of
'em used to make a hell of a noise – praying and talking. It put the
men off. So now we put cotton-wool in their mouths.'

'What did go wrong, then?' the A.D.C. breathlessly asked.

'The blighter's face kept working,' Immals said. His voice was
changing. 'Flicking like hell,' he snarled, with a queer, rising fury.
'Putting the men off – the scab! so that only one bullet hit him –
one out of eight – and that only in the shoulder! The swine was not
even stunned! Wide-awake as I am, and that bloody face of his,
working!'

'And then?' Auberon asked. Once driven to it, he acted morbid-
curiosity quite decently well.

'Usual routine. March the men off. A.P.M. finishes prisoner.
Revolver well into the mouth – muzzle turned slightly upwards, I
didn't take long with the cur.'

Just for an instant Auberon closed his eyes, to see the brains that
had spun Victor's delicate fabrics of fancy and wit bespatter the wall
of the slaughterer's yard. The chubby Staff-lieutenant may have had

imagination too, for he went quickly to one of the open windows, put his head out and was sick over a Malmaison rose that grew against the south wall. But Auberon had business in hand. 'He said nothing at all?' he asked Immals again.

'We don't ask 'em,' said Immals, 'to make a last speech from the cart.'

Without making the action uncivilly pointed, Auberon fetched a bottle from the sideboard. 'A bit drappie?' he asked Immals politely, and Immals held out his tumbler.

'Say when,' said Auberon, as he poured, but Immals fell into abstraction till the common strength of grog had been well passed: then he suddenly said, 'Enough! enough!' like a man rebuking some excess that nobody could have expected. While Immals added soda-water with a frugal hand, Auberon said, 'He left no message, or letter, or anything? Some of 'em do, I suppose?'

'Some of 'em – yes. Only the other day there was one – a second-lieutenant – we shot him for cowardice. He sat up writing letters by a flash-lamp, all the night before – four long uns, all to his mother, with dates on ahead, full of all sorts of lies about the great time he was having. He asked my Sergeant-Major to post 'em, at intervals of a week. "That'll give her a good month."'

> C. E. Montague

SEPTEMBER 13

The Allies Still Advance

Franco-American Attack on Front of 20 Miles.
Successful Onslaught On Famous St Michael's Salient South of Verdun.
Germans Falling Back Before Blow.

> *The Daily Mirror*, London

The entry into the line of the magnificent American Army must be considered as an essential factor in the operations of tomorrow. That army will not take the place of the British or French Armies, but will appear by their side on the field of the second great battle of the nations which will decide the destinies of the world, probably for several centuries.

> *Le Matin*, Paris

The Reichstag Deputy Wildgrube declared Admiral Von Scheer had said to him, 'You may say to the country with a good conscience that I do not doubt for a moment that we shall bring England to her knees by our submarine warfare, only I will not bind myself to the definite date.'

  Cologne Gazette

SEPTEMBER 14

British Soldiers and German Prisoners of War, Clapham Junction

As soldiers both are caught in the toils of a war which neither had done anything to cause, and that unhappy fate brought them together in a spirit of comradeship. They began fraternizing at once. The Germans smiled, waved their hands and called out 'Kamerad!' The Tommies started hilariously shouting 'Good old Jerries!' and jumping out of their carriages they threw at the Germans, not bombs, but packets of tobacco and chocolate.

  Michael Macdonagh

SEPTEMBER 15

The Volunteer

When war was declared L. B. Namier volunteered for the British Army. He was evidently not a perfect soldier. Some intelligent person took him out of the army, and put him into the Foreign Office as adviser on Polish affairs attached to the Historical Adviser to the Foreign Office, Sir John Headlam-Morley. 'I remember,' said Namier to me, 'the day in 1918 when the Emperor Karl sued for peace, I said to Headlam-Morley: 'Wait.' Headlam-Morley said to Balfour: 'Wait.' Balfour said to Lloyd George: 'Wait.' Lloyd George said to Wilson: 'Wait.' And while they waited, the Austria-Hungarian Empire disintegrated. I may say that I pulled it to pieces with my own hands.'

  Isaiah Berlin

SEPTEMBER 17

U.S. Rejects Austrian Offer of 'Peace' Parley.
British Strike on Flanders Line as Americans Capture Stronghold.
Serbian and French Win Front Held 2½ Years.

> *The Detroit Free Press*

Worry Whitens Hair of Kaiser

> *The Detroit Free Press*

SEPTEMBER 25

The German Officer: Portent

I had the depressing experience of meeting a soldier on the street
who was very obvious about not saluting me.

> Herbert Sulzbach

OCTOBER 12

Wartime in America

A distinguished entertainment for the benefit of Queen
Margherita's Fund for the Blinded Soldiers of Italy was given at the
Metropolitan Opera House at which we were honoured by the
presence and deep interest of President and Mrs Wilson, and it was
while he sat in his box that evening that the President received the
first hopeful word from Germany in response to his conditions of
peace. For that occasion was sent this touching message, which I
forwarded in the Sender's autograph to the Naples hospital for the
Blinded Soldiers, to be placed there as a word of perpetual cheer:

'From my land of darkness and silence my heart and voice call out
in appeal for the blinded soldiers of Italy. I send them my message
of courage, hope, victory. Helen Keller.' This benefit realised more
than 40,000 dollars, including subscriptions to the fund made during
the performance. These were most generous, even in the case of a
certain 'society woman' with a German name who subscribed 1000
dollars, which no amount of persistence on our part could get her to
pay.

> Robert Underwood Johnson

OCTOBER 23

Magyar and Slav mutinies in Habsburg armies.

OCTOBER 28

Sea Power

Mutinies begin in German fleet at Kiel, when the fleet is ordered at last to 'venture out against the British'. Mutineers empty the boilers, kill some officers, and some in their turn are killed. Within a week thousands of sailors and soldiers are holding Kiel under the Red flag.

Johann Spiess, the veteran commander of the U-boat war was waiting to take his new U-135 to sea when the mutiny erupted and he was immediately ordered to report to Kommodore Michelsen's office. The first question Michelsen put was a clear indication of what the authorities had in mind.

'Are you absolutely sure of your crew?'

Edwyn A. Gray

I don't rack my brains very much about the problem of good and evil, but on the whole I have not found much of the 'good' in people. Most of them are in my experience riff-raff, whether they proclaim themselves adherents of this or that ethical doctrine, or of none at all.

Sigmund Freud, *to Oskar Pfisler*

OCTOBER 30

I would not dream of abandoning the throne because of a few hundred Jews and a thousand workers.

Kaiser Wilhelm II

Savagery in the East

Italians rout Austrians at Vittorio Veneto. In years to come Italian schoolchildren would face a wall caption: 'Mussolini won the War at the Battle of Vittorio Veneto.'

Helped with a timely stiffening of French and English divisions, the Italian army under a new leader (Armando Diaz) stood its ground on the Piave, and, gathering force and confidence from successive encounters, ultimately, in the last months of the war, delivered upon the field of Vittorio Veneto the decisive punishment to a crumbling and demoralized army, which brought the Austrian Empire to the ground. To this national triumph the Italians with pardonable exaggeration are wont to attribute not only the downfall of the Habsburgs, but the final victory of the allied cause. For a service so tremendous, and for losses greater in proportion than those won by any other continental Power, they opine that they received at the Peace a grudging and insufficient reward.

H. A. L. Fisher

NOVEMBER 3

Finally, on 3 November, the Austro-Hungarian high command, negotiating in the name of an Empire which no longer existed, concluded an armistice of surrender with the Italians. After the armistice had been signed, but before it came into force, the Italians emerged from behind the British and French troops, where they had been hiding, and captured hundreds of thousands of unarmed, unresisting Austro-Hungarian soldiers in the great 'victory' of Vittorio Veneto – rare triumph of Italian arms. The bulk of the Austro-Hungarian army fell to pieces, each man finding his way back to his national home as best he could amid the confusion and chaos.

A. J. P. Taylor

An American at the Italian Front

The Italian I had with me had bled all over my coat, and my pants looked like somebody had made currant jelly in them and then punched holes to let the pulp out . . . I wanted to see my legs, though I was afraid to look . . . so we took off my trousers and the old limbs were still there but gee they were a mess. They couldn't figure out how I had walked 150 yards with a load with both knees shot through and my right shoe punctured in two big places, also over 200 flesh wounds.

Ernest Hemingway, *to his parents*

I was always embarrassed by the words sacred, glorious, and sacrifice and the expression in vain. We heard them, sometimes standing in the rain almost out of earshot, so that only the shouted words
came through, and had read them, on proclamations that were
slapped up by billposters over other proclamations, now for a long
time, and I had seen nothing sacred, and the things that were
glorious had no glory and the sacrifices were like the stockyards at
Chicago if nothing was done with the meat except bury it. There
were many words that you could not stand to hear and finally only
the names of places had dignity . . . Abstract words such as glory,
honor, courage, or hallow were obscene.

     Ernest Hemingway

Collapse in Austria

When I woke up I was a soldiers' councillor.

    What changes had there been? Many caps no longer bore the
imperial cockade, but as before the officers rode along the verges,
as before the drivers lashed their horses, as before the columns
rattled onwards in orderly progress. Gas masks, steel helmets,
ammunition boxes lay in the ditches, so much useless junk now that
the war was over. Yet each individual knew that on his own he
would be lost, only as a mass could we get through, our final
destination, home. First meeting of the soldiers' council. And lo,
who should come riding up astride a donkey, clad only in shirt and
long drawers, ankle tapes aflutter, plumage plucked by pretty women, trounced and pillaged by peasants, but Colonel Kraus, sorry
remnant of a dictatorial commanding officer. Although they
laughed, the men felt sorry for him, bundled him into a greatcoat,
placed a cap on his head; and thus arrayed he appeared before us,
the assembled soldiers' council, to hold forth in a croaking voice
with genuine emotion, unctuous solemnity, faithful to his oath of
allegiance to His Imperial Majesty . . . bound to his regiment by
ties of loyalty and duty . . . with his regiment through thick and
thin. Tears were coursing down the cheeks of the plucked, pillaged
Colonel Kraus, back once more in the bosom of his regiment.

     Ernst Fischer

I expect dreadful things in Germany . . . Just think of the dreadful tension of these four and a half years and the awful disappointment now that this is suddenly released. That Wilhelm is an incurably romantic fellow; he misjudges the revolution just as he did the war. He doesn't know that the age of chivalry ended with Don Quixote . . . As for the downfall of old Austria I can only feel deep satisfaction.

Sigmund Freud, *to Ferenczi*

NOVEMBER 7

Revolution

In the last few days, Munich has lost some of its nothingness and stillness, the tensions of this time are evident even here . . . Everywhere, vast assemblies in beer-halls nearly every evening, speakers everywhere, of whom Professor Jaffé is evidently excellent, and where halls are inadequate, gatherings in thousands under the open sky. I also was one of the thousands on Monday night in the rooms of the Hotel Wagner. Professor Max Weber of Heidelberg was speaking, a political economist rated one of the best of intellects and a fine orator, and then, discussing the anarchy and the fatiguing strain, more students, fellows from four years at the front – all so simple and frank, 'men of the people'. And though we sat round the beer-tables and between them so that the waitresses could only penetrate the dense human mass like weevils – it was not at all oppressive, not even for the breath; the fumes of beer and smoke and bodies did not seem oppressive, we barely noticed, so important was it and so obvious that things could be uttered whose time had at last arrived, and that the simplest and truest of these, in as much as they were presented more or less intelligently, were taken up by the huge crowd with heavy, massive acclamation. Suddenly a pale young worker stood up, spoke quite simply. 'Have you or you or you, have any of you offered an armistice? And yet we are those who should have done so, not these gentlemen at the top; if we could take over a radio station and speak as common folk to the common folk on the other side, peace would come immediately.'

I cannot say it half as well as he did, but suddenly when he had spoken this, a difficulty occurred to him, and with a moving gesture at Weber, Quidde and the other professors standing on the stage beside him, he went on: 'Here, these professor chaps, they know French, they'll help us say it right, as we mean it.' Such moments are marvellous, there have been all too few in Germany, where only intransigence found voice, or submission, itself in its own way only a participation in violence by the under-dogs . . . We have a remarkable night behind us. Here also a council of soldiers, peasants and workers has been established with Kurt Eisner as the first President . . . the Bavarian Republic declares that the people are promised Peace and Security . . . It only remains to be hoped that this extraordinary upheaval will provoke reflection in people's minds and not a fatal intoxication once all is over.

> Rainer Maria Rilke, *to Clara Rilke*

NOVEMBER 8

Finish

'Mercy, mercy', shouts a German ex-waiter on the left, as he sees the cold steel of a North Staffordshire potter quivering above his head, for he has been felled by a rifle butt swung by a Wolverhampton striker of past four and forty years. 'Mercy be damned,' shouts the potter, whose blood is up, as he thrusts to the wind-pipe in the most up-to-date manner.

The time is short. It is now 11 am. on 8th November, 1918.

> Brigadier General F. P. Crozier

GERMAN ARMIES SPLIT. GREAT AMERICAN VICTORY RESULTS IN ENTRY INTO SEDAN.

Hamburg Follows Kiel. All Power in Revolutionaries' Hands.
Red Flag Hoisted In Other Ports.
Processionists Armed With Machine Guns, Bayonets and Revolvers.

> *The Daily Chronicle*, London

If the Kaiser had the least sense of personal dignity he would leave the throne instead of waiting for the people to push him off.

> *Frankfurter Zeitung*

Proclamation: a thousand-year-old monarchy falls

FELLOW CITIZENS

In order to rebuild after long years of destruction, the people has overthrown the power of the civil and military authorities and has taken the regime in hand. The Bavarian Republic is hereby proclaimed. Elected by the Citizens and provisionally instituted until a definite representation of the people is created, the Council of Workers, Soldiers, and Peasants is the highest authority. It has law-giving power.

The entire garrison has placed itself at the disposal of the republican regime. The General Command and the Police Presidium stand under our direction. The Wittelsbach dynasty is deposed.

Long live the Republic!

Kurt Eisner

NOVEMBER 9

'The army will return home in peace and discipline under its commanders, but not under Your Majesty's leadership, for it no longer stands behind Your Majesty.' The Kaiser's eyes lit up in anger. He stretched himself to his full height. He moved towards General Gröner and spoke with a sharp vibrato: 'Sir, I demand that you put that statement in writing. I want the statements of all my active generals in black and white that the armies no longer stand behind their supreme war-lord. Has not every soldier sworn me an oath of allegiance?'

'It is now only a fiction,' replied the General.

Lieutenant Colonel Alfred Niemann

Treason, gentlemen, barefaced treason!

Kaiser Wilhelm II

NOVEMBER 10

End of the Hohenzollerns.
Kaiser Abdicates.
Imperial and Prussian Thrones Renounced.
Crown Prince Also Goes.
Revolution All Over Germany.

> *Sunday Times*, London

Wilhelm II blames the collapse on the Jews and the Socialists.

I acknowledge in advance the decision to be adopted by German
Austria, as to the future form to be taken by the State. The people,
through these its representatives, have assumed the Government. I
renounce all part in affairs of State.

> Karl, Emperor of Austria, King of Hungary

NOVEMBER 11

The Great War ends, after 1561 days. Total German surrender.

If it is possible I should like above all a cup of hot English tea.

> Kaiser Wilhelm II, arriving in exile, at Count Bentinck's
> castle at Amerongen, Holland

In peace the Kaiser was a war lord, in war he avoided taking
decisions, and in defeat he fled.

> Prince von Bülow

Rejoicing

Madame Curie was never to speak of the hardships and dangers in
which she engrossed herself during those four years. She spoke
neither of her tremenduous fatigues, of the risk of death, nor of the
cruel effect of X-rays and radium upon her damaged organism. She
showed her working companions a careless and even a gay face –
gayer than it had ever been. The war was to teach her that good
humour which is the finest mask of courage. She had very little joy
in her soul, just the same . . . the memory of the thousands of
hacked-up bodies she had seen, of the groans and shrieks she had

heard, was to long darken her life. The armistice guns surprised her in her laboratory. She wanted to dress flags on the Institute, and took her collaborator Marthe Klein with her to search neighbour-hood shops for French flags. There were none left anywhere, and she ended by buying some bits of stuff in three colours . . . trembling with nervousness and joy she could not remain still. She and Mlle Klein got into the radiological car, battered and scarred by four years of adventure. An attendant drove them up and down the streets, to and fro, through the eddying mass of a people both happy and grave. In the Place de la Concorde the crowd stopped the car. People clambered onto the fenders of the Renault and hoisted themselves on to the roof. When Marie's car resumed, it carried off a dozen such extra passengers.

> Eve Curie

A Question

These preparations for Festivity are too odious. In addition to my money complex I have a food complex. When I read of the prepara-tions that are being made in all the workhouses throughout the land – when I think of all those toothless old jaws guzzling for the day – and then of all that beautiful youth feeding the fields of France – Life is almost too ignoble to be borne. Truly one must hate human-kind in the mass, hate them as passionately as one loves the few, the very few. Ticklers, squirts, portraits eight times as large as life of Lloyd George and Beatty blazing against the sky – and drunkenness and brawling and destruction. I keep seeing all these horrors, bathing in them again and again (God knows I don't want to) and then my mind fills with the wretched little picture I have of my brother's grave. What is the meaning of it all?

> Katherine Mansfield

A Look at the Future

I dare say that in these pages I have made some bad prophecies, but one I recall, namely that the tramp of the first American battalions upon the soil of France was the premonitory rumblings of the earthquake in which Prussia and her bloody doctrines were to go down living to the Pit. Without America I believe we should have fallen, but some madness made the Germans stake their all upon a policy of sea murder, and bring in the great Republic on our trembling line. Now it must be the task of the Allies to make sure it is never built again to span the river of human destinies.

So it comes about that our nation emerged from the struggle more potent, more splendid than ever she has shone before, laughing at all disloyalties, with mighty opportunities open to her grasp. How she will use them in the years to come, I shall never see. The Germans will neither forgive nor forget; neither money nor comfort will tell with them henceforth. They have been beaten by England and they will live and die to smash England – she will never have a more deadly enemy than the new Germany. My dread is that in future years the easy-going, self-centred English will forget that just across the sea is a mighty, cold-hearted and remorseless people waiting to strike her through her heart. For strike they will one day, or so I believe.

> H. Rider Haggard

From 'AND THERE WAS A GREAT CALM'

Breathless they paused. Out there men raised their glance
To where had stood those poplars lank and lopped,
As they had raised it through the four years' dance
Of Death in the now familiar flats of France;
And murmured, 'Strange, this! How? All firing stopped?'

Aye; all was hushed. The about-to-fire fired not,
The aimed-at moved away in trance-lipped song.
One checkless regiment slung a clinching shot
And turned. The Spirit of Irony smirked out, 'What?
Spoil peradventures woven of Rage and Wrong?'

Thenceforth no flying fires inflamed the gray,
No hurtlings shook the dewdrop from the thorn,
No moan perplexed the mute bird on the spray;
Worn horses mused: 'We are not whipped to-day;'
No weft-winged engines blurred the moon's thin horn.

Calm fell. From Heaven distilled a clemency;
There was peace on earth, and silence in the sky;
Some could, some could not, shake off misery:
The Sinister Spirit sneered: 'It had to be!'
And again the Spirit of Pity whispered, 'Why?'

> Thomas Hardy

AFTERMATH

PEACE AND WAR

People always make war when they say they love peace.
The loud love of peace makes one quiver more than any battle-cry.
Why should one love peace? It is so obviously vile to make war.
Loud peace propaganda makes war seem imminent.
It is a form of war, even, self-assertion and being wise for other
    people.
Let people be wise for themselves. And anyhow
nobody can be wise except on rare occasions, like getting married or
    dying.
It's bad taste to be wise all the time, like being at a perpetual
    funeral.
For everyday use, give me somebody whimsical, with not too much
    purpose in life,
then we shan't have war, and we needn't talk about peace.

>   D. H. Lawrence

*There had been 10 million European and Asiatic deaths, 30 million
missing or wounded. Another 10 million died of influenza, 1918–19.
America lost 800,000.*

But that's what the young men are there for.

>   Adolf Hitler

Survivor: a Villager

I just went when they called me; I didn't mind. A lot of us went from
the village but we soon got split up. I never saw most of them again.

All the time I was in France I only saw three boys I knew. It was a funny thing, but when I came home on leave the women would say, 'Did you meet my George out there? My John? He's in the Artillery, you know. You must have seen him.' They thought we were all fighting in one big old meadow, I suppose.

The war changed me – it changed us all. You could call it experience. It broadened your mind and one thing and another. Everybody ought to have this military training. It would do them good and make them obedient. Some of the young men now, they need obedience. They don't know what it is. Our lives were all obedience.

I was home on leave when the Armistice was signed. I came to the village on the Friday and the Armistice was signed on the Monday. I went back to France but now it was like a holiday. I was now in a Scottish regiment – the glorious 51st. The officer tried to persuade me to stay in the army but I said, 'No sir!' I wanted to get home. We all did. We were fed up, you know. And we had seen terrible things.

Samuel Gissing, *to Ronald Blythe*

Another Survivor

A lot of farmers hid their horses during the Great War, when the officers came round. The officers always gave good money for a horse but sometimes the horses were like brothers and the men couldn't let them go, so they hid them. I wasn't called up. Nothing happened to me and I didn't remind them. We didn't really miss the men who didn't come back. The village stayed the same.

John Grout, *to Ronald Blythe*

Après la Guerre – Air: 'Sous les Ponts de Paris'

Après la guerre finie,
Soldat anglais parti;
Mam'selle Fransay boko pleuray
Après la guerre finie.

Après la guerre finie,
Soldat anglais parti;
Mademoiselle in the family way,
Après la guerre finie.

Après la guerre finie,
Soldat anglais parti;
Mademoiselle in the family way:
Boko pic-a-nin-ee.

Mademoiselle can go to hell
Après la guerre finie.

NOVEMBER 20, 1918

Chaplin's 'Shoulder Arms'

A wonderful spoof on World War One heroics which still managed
to convey the tragedy of war without holding up any of the fun . . .
Its best sequences – Charlie's pantomime as he duels with an unknown sniper, his adventures in a flooded dug-out, his masquerade as
a tree in order to penetrate the enemy lines – are still hilariously
funny.

> Joe Franklin

NOVEMBER 23, 1918

On the Proposed League of Nations

A product of men who want everyone to float to heaven on a sloppy
sea of universal mush.

> T. H. Roosevelt, *to Rudyard Kipling*

*The Blockade continues, despite Winston Churchill's proposal to
send twelve food ships to a Germany threatened by Bolshevism.*

And all the profiteers who had lived so long in clover
Fell a-sighing and a-sobbing when they heard the war was over,
For they'd all made their bit in the Great War, Daddy.

DECEMBER 1918

From the Dock, Before Sentence of Ten Years' Imprison-
ment for Violating the United States Espionage Law

Your Honor, years ago I recognised my kinship with all living
beings, and I made up my mind that I was not one bit better than the

meanest of earth. I said then, and I say now, that while there is a lower class, I am in it, while there is a criminal element I am of it, and while there is a soul in prison, I am not free.

Eugene Debs

Peace

Meanwhile in Paris, the nucleus of a wild, international, pleasure-crazy crowd, the Big Four were making a desert and calling it peace. When I thought about these negotiations at all – which was only when I could not avoid hearing them discussed by Oxford dons or Kensington visitors – they did not seem to me to represent at all the kind of 'victory' that the young men whom I had loved would have regarded as sufficient justification for their lost lives. Although they would no doubt have welcomed the idea of a League of Nations, Roland and Edward certainly had not died in order that Clemenceau should outwit Lloyd George, and both of them bamboozle President Wilson, and all three combine to make the beaten, blockaded enemy pay the cost of the War. For me the 'Huns' were then, and always, the patient, stoical Germans whom I had nursed in France, and I did not like to read of them being deprived of their Navy, and their Colonies, and their coal-fields in Alsace-Lorraine and the Saar Valley, while their children starved and froze for lack of food and fuel. So, when the text of the Treaty of Versailles was published in May, after I had returned to Oxford, I deliberately refrained from reading it; I was beginning already to suspect that my generation had been deceived, its young courage cynically exploited, its idealism betrayed, and I did not want to know the details of that betrayal. At an inter-collegiate debate a Hindu student remarked that here, at any rate, was 'the Peace that passeth all understanding' – and I left it at that.

Vera Brittain

Storm helmets, machine guns, field kitchens, flags. Splendid troops, No red emblems. I shouted bravo.

Gerhart Hauptmann

War alone brings to its highest tension all human energy and puts the stamp of nobility upon those nations who have the courage to

face it. All other tests are substitutes, which never really place men
in the position where they are forced to make a great choice – the
alternative of life and death.

       Benito Mussolini

The stupendous impression produced on me by the war – the
greatest of all impressions. For that, individual interest – the interest of one's own ego – could be subordinated to the common
interest, that the great heroic struggle of our people demonstrated
in overwhelming fashion.

       Adolf Hitler

This war was a commercial and industrial war. It was not a political
war.

       President Woodrow Wilson

There are strange Hells within the minds War made
Not so often, not so humiliatingly afraid
As one would have expected – the racket and fear guns made.
One Hell the Gloucester soldiers they quite put out:
Their first bombardment, when in combined black shout
Of fury, guns aligned, they ducked lower their heads
And sang with diaphragms fixed beyond all dreads,
That tin and stretched-wire tinkle, that blither of tune:
'Après la guerre fini' till Hell all had come down,
Twelve-inch, six-inch, and eighteen pounders hammering Hell's
    thunders.

Where are they now, on State-doles, or showing shop-patterns
Or walking town to town sore in borrowed tatters
Or begged. Some civil routine one never learns.
The heart burns – but has to keep out of face how heart burns.

       Ivor Gurney

Years later, I often asked myself why I had joined the Army. The
usual explanations were no good. I was not hot with patriot feeling,
I did not believe that Britain was in any real danger. I was sorry for
'gallant little Belgium' but did not feel that she was waiting for me to
rescue her. The legend of Kitchener, who pointed at us from every

hoarding, had never captured me. I was not under any pressure from public opinion . . . the white feathers came later. I was not carried to the recruiting office in a herd rush of chums, nobody thinking, everybody half-plastered; I went alone . . . this was no escape to freedom and independence; I may not have known much about military life, but I was not so green. And I certainly did not see myself as a hero, whose true stature would be revealed by war; that had never been one of my illusions. What is left then to supply a motive?

Nothing, I believe now, that was rational and conscious . . . I went at a signal from the unknown . . . There came out of the unclouded blue of that summer, a challenge that was almost like a conscription of the spirit, little to do really with King and Country and flag-waving and hip-hip-hurrah, a challenge to what we felt was our untested manhood. Other men, who had not lived as easily as we had, had drilled and marched and borne arms – couldn't we?

> J. B. Priestley

Myself, I valued the Kaiser's war as having given me not only an unsurpassable standard of danger, discomfort and horror by which to judge more recent troubles, but a confidence in the golden-heartedness and iron endurance of my fellow-countrymen (proved again during Hitler's war), which even the laxity of this new plastic age cannot disturb.

> Robert Graves

I had entered the holocaust still childish and I emerged tempered by my experience, but with my illusions intact, neither shattered nor cynical.

> Lord Avon (Anthony Eden)

The War was good, by drawing over our depths that hot surface wish to do or win something.

> T. E. Lawrence

. . . those who lolled on the wires – to be blanched or gay –
    painted by fumes – to be cindered by fires.

> Rudyard Kipling

JUNE 28, 1919

*The Versailles Treaty is signed in the Hall of Mirrors where Wilhelm I
had been proclaimed Emperor of Germany in 1871.*

This is not peace, it is an armistice for twenty years.

   Ferdinand Foch

The World War of 1914–18 was the greatest moral, spiritual and
physical catastrophe in the entire history of the English people – a
catastrophe whose consequences, all wholly evil, are still with us.

   Paul Johnson

The Second World War took place not so much because no one won
the First, but because Versailles did not acknowledge this truth.

   Paul Johnson

Statesmen at Versailles

At dinner, Balfour told Nicolson that after the official opening of
the Conference, Balfour walked down the steps with Clemenceau.
A.J.B. wore a top hat: Clemenceau wore a bowler. A.J.B.
apologised for his top hat. 'I was told', he said, 'that it was obligat-
ory to wear one.' 'So', said Clemenceau, 'was I.'

   Charles L. Mee

AUGUST 5, 1919

MEMORANDUM TO CENTRAL COMMITTEE

The road to Paris and London lies via the towns of Afghanistan, the
Punjab and Bengal.

   Trotsky

A New Order?

He is always in the technical sense mad – that is, his mind is tilted
from its balance, and since we live by balance he is a wrecker, a
crowbar in the machinery. His power comes from the appeal he

makes to the imperfectly balanced, and as these are never the
majority his appeal is limited. But there is one kind of fanatic whose
strength comes from balance, from a lunatic balance. You cannot
say that there is any one thing abnormal about him, for he is all
abnormal. He is as balanced as you or me, but, so to speak, in a
fourth-dimensional world. That kind of man is brilliantly sane.
Take Lenin for instance. That's the kind of fanatic I'm afraid of.

John Buchan

1923

But at night you feel strange things stirring in the darkness, strange
feelings stirring out of this still-unconquered Black Forest. You
stiffen your backbone and you listen to the night. There is a sense of
danger. It is not the people. They don't seem dangerous. Out of the
very air comes a sense of danger, a queer, bristling feeling of
uncanny danger.

Something has happened. Something has happened which has
not yet eventuated. The old spirit of the old world has broken, and
the old, bristling, savage spirit has set in. The war did not break the
old peace-and-production hope of the world, though it gave it a
severe wrench. Yet the old peace-and-production hope still governs, at least the consciousness. Even in Germany it has not quite
gone. But it feels as if, virtually, it were gone. The last two years
have done it. The hope in peace-and-production is broken. The old
flow, the old adherence is ruptured. And a still older flow has set in.
Back, back to the savage polarity of Tartary and away from the
polarity of civilized Christian Europe. This it seems to me, has
already happened. And it is a happening of far more profound
import than any actual event. It is the father of the next phase of
events.

D. H. Lawrence

The modern dictatorship arises amid the ruins of an inherited social
and political structure, in the desolation of shattered loyalties – it is
the desperate shift of communities shifted from their moorings.

L. B. Namier

Christmas, 1924

'Peace upon earth!' was said. We sing it,
And pay a million priests to bring it.
After two thousand years of mass
We've got as far as poison gas.

> Thomas Hardy

The politician, dead and turned to clay,
Will make a clout to keep the wind away.
I am not fond of draughts, and yet I doubt
If I could get myself to touch that clout.

> Hilaire Belloc

The study of war has taught me that almost every war was avoidable
and that the outbreak was most often produced by statesmen losing
their heads or their patience, and putting their opponent in a
position where he could not draw back without serious loss of face.

> Basil Liddell Hart

1935

Don't put Winston in the Government – it will mean war at home
and abroad. I know the depths of Winston's disloyalty – and you
can't know how he is distrusted by *all* the electors of this country.

> Nancy Astor, *to Stanley Baldwin*

I together with the Duce, am the only head of government in
Europe who knows the war as it really was, I mean for the front line
crock.

> Adolf Hitler

AFTERMATH

Have you forgotten yet? . . .
For the world's events have rumbled on since those gagged days,
Like traffic checked awhile at the crossing of city-ways:
And the haunted gap in your mind has filled with thoughts that flow
Like clouds in the lit heaven of life; and you're a man reprieved to
    go,
Taking your peaceful share of Time, with joy to spare.
But the past is just the same – and War's a bloody game . . .
Have you forgotten yet? . . .
*Look down, and swear by the slain of the war that you'll never
    forget.*

Do you remember the dark months you held the sector at Mametz –
The nights you watched and wired and dug and piled sandbags on
    parapets?
Do you remember the rats; and the stench
Of corpses rotting in front of the front-line trench –
And dawn coming, dirty-white, and chill with a hopeless rain?
Do you ever stop and ask, 'Is it all going to happen again?'

Do you remember that hour of din before the attack –
And the anger, the blind compassion that seized and shook you then
As you peered at the doomed and haggard faces of your men?
Do you remember the stretcher-cases lurching back
With dying eyes and lolling heads – those ashen-grey
Masks of the lads who once were keen and kind and gay?

Have you forgotten yet? . . .
*Look up, and swear by the green of the spring that you'll never
    forget.*

      Siegfried Sassoon

APPENDIXES

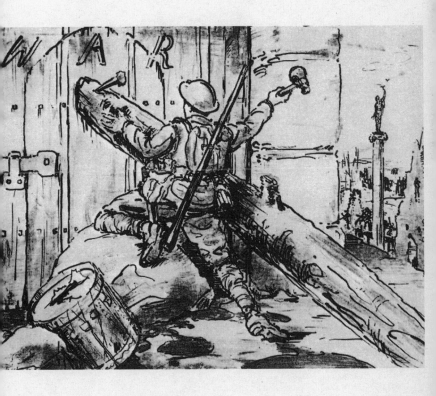

LIST OF CONTRIBUTORS

ADLER, Victor, Austrian Social Democrat leader

AKHMATOVA, Anna, Russian poetess

ALBERT, Duke of York, later George VI

ALBERTINI, L., Italian journalist and scholar

ALEXANDRA, Tsarina of Russia

ANGELL, Norman, British pacifist, won the Nobel Peace Prize in 1933

APOLLINAIRE, Guillaume, poet of Polish/Italian birth, educated in France, fought in the French army and died of influenza, 1918

ARCOS, René, French poet and novelist

ASQUITH, Cynthia, writer, daughter of Herbert H. Asquith

ASQUITH, Herbert H., British Liberal statesman, Prime Minister during the war

ASQUITH, Raymond, eldest son of Herbert H. Asquith, killed in action, 1916

ASTOR, Nancy, American-born politician and political hostess, the first woman to take a seat in the House of Commons, 1919

ATTLEE, Clement, English Labour statesman, Prime Minister 1945–51

AVON, Lord, see EDEN

BALFOUR, Arthur, British statesman and philosopher, Foreign Secretary 1916–19, responsible for the Balfour Declaration (1917), proposing Zionists a national home in Palestine

BALFOUR, Michael, biographer and historian

BARBUSSE, Henri, French novelist

BARNETT, Corelli, British writer and war historian

BEATTY, David, 1st Earl, British Admiral, Commander-in-Chief of the Grand Fleet, 1916

BECKMANN, Max, German painter and engraver

BEHREND, Arthur, German soldier

BELLOC, Hilaire, Anglo-French biographer, poet, essayist, historian, traveller

BENNETT, Arnold, English novelist and critic

BERLIN, Isaiah, British philosopher

BETHMANN-HOLLWEG, T. T. F. A. von, German Chancellor

BLOK, Alexander, Russian poet, initially supported the 1917 Revolution although later disillusioned

BLUNDEN, Edmund, English poet and critic

BLYTHE, Ronald, British writer

BOTTOMLEY, Horatio, English journalist and financier, Member of Parliament 1906–11

BOUMAN, P. J., Dutch social historian

BOWRA, C. M., British scholar and critic

BRECHT, Bertolt, German playwright and poet

BRITTAIN, Vera, V.A.D. 1914–18, English writer

BROOKE, Reginald, Lieutenant-Colonel in the British army

BROOKE, Rupert, English poet, died in 1915 on his way to the Dardanelles

BROOME, F. N., Captain in the British army

BROPHY, John, English lexicographer and novelist

BRYANT, Sir Arthur, British historian and biographer

BUCHAN, John, Scottish novelist, biographer and war historian

BUCHANAN, Sir George, British diplomat, ambassador to Russia during First World War

BÜLOW, Prince Bernhard von, German statesman

CAREW, Tim, British military writer

CAVELL, Edith, English nurse, executed 1915

CHAPMAN, E., Rifleman in the British army

CHURCHILL, Winston, British statesman, 1911 1st Lord of the Admiralty, 1917 Minister of Munitions, Prime Minister 1940–45

CLEMENCEAU, Georges, French statesman, premier 1906–9, 1917–20

COHEN, Joseph, American literary critic

COLDSTREAM, Sir William, British painter

CONQUEST, Robert, British poet, literary and political critic, historian

COOPER, Alfred Duff, British politician, served with the Grenadier Guards 1914–18

COOPER, Ernest Read, British writer

CROZIER, F. P., General in the British army

CURIE, Eve, musician and writer, daughter of Marie Curie

CURIE, Marie, Polish scientist, 1910 isolated polonium and radium, 1911 won Nobel Prize

DARWIN, Bernard, English golfer, journalist and biographer

DEBS, Eugene, American politician, socialist candidate for presidency 1900, 1912, 1920, pacifism led to his imprisonment 1918–21

DEVLIN, Patrick, American historian

DOYLE, Sir Arthur Conan, British doctor, publicist, legal reformer, writer of detective stories, historical romances and war history

EDEN, Anthony, British statesman, Prime Minister 1955–57

EISNER, Kurt, German revolutionary politician and journalist, murdered 1919

ELLIS, John, British social historian

EUGÉNIE, widow of Napoleon III, Emperor of the French

FERDINAND, Franz, Archduke, heir to Emperor Franz-Josef of Austria

FISCHER, Ernst, Austrian art and literary critic, political activist in the Comintern

FISHER, Lord, British admiral. First Sea Lord, 1904–10 and 1914–15.

FISHER, H. A. L., British historian

FITZGERALD, F. Scott, American novelist

FOCH, Ferdinand, French Marshal, Generalissimo of the Allied armies from March 1918

FORD, Ford Madox, English novelist and poet. His *Tietjans* trilogy, much concerned with the Great War, though unrepresented here, has been considered of outstanding importance

FORD, Henry, American automobile engineer and manufacturer

FORSTER, Edward Morgan, English novelist

FRANKLIN, Joe, American cinema historian

FRANZ FERDINAND, Archduke of Austria, whose murder precipitated the war

FREEMAN, Joseph, American journalist, former editor of *New Masses*

FREUD, Sigmund, Austrian founder of psychoanalysis

FRÖLICH, Paul, German journalist and politician

FULLER, J. F. C., British General and military writer, prominently associated with the Tank Corps during the war

GALLIENI, Military Governor of Paris, 1914

GAUDIER-BRZESKA, Henri, Polish sculptor, killed serving in the British army on the Western Front

GEORGE V, King of England 1910–36

GERARD, James W., American diplomat, ambassador to Germany 1913–17

GISSING, Samuel, English farm-worker

GORKY, Maxim, Russian novelist and playwright

GRAY, Edwyn A., British naval writer

GREENE, Graham, English novelist

GRENFELL, Julian, English poet

GREY, Lord, British statesman, Foreign Secretary 1905–15

GROUT, John, English farmer

GUEDALLA, Philip, English biographer and historian

GURNEY, Ivor, British poet

HAGGARD, H. Rider, English novelist, journalist, agriculturalist, imperial administrator

HAIG, Douglas, British Field-Marshal

HANKEY, Lord, British soldier, civil servant and minister

HARCOURT, William, British Liberal statesman

HARDINGE, Lord, British Viceroy of India 1910–16

HARDY, Thomas, English poet and novelist

HARRISON, Arthur, British schoolmaster

HASTE, Cate, American journalist

HAUPTMANN, Gerhart, German playwright

HEMINGWAY, Ernest, American author and war correspondent

HENLEY, W. E., English poet, playwright, critic and editor

HESSE, Hermann, German novelist and poet

HINDENBURG, Paul von, German Field-Marshal, later President of the Republic

HITLER, Adolf, German soldier in First World War, later Nazi dictator of Germany

HODDIS, Jakob van, German expressionist poet

HOEHLLING, A. A., and HOEHLLING, Mary, American journalists

HORNE, Alistair, British journalist and historian

HOUSMAN, Alfred Edward, English scholar and poet

HUGHES, C. J. Pennethorne, British historian

HULSE, Edward, Captain in the British army

INNES, H. McLeod, of Trinity College, Cambridge

JACKSON, J. Hampden, English historian and biographer, authority on the Baltic states and Finland

JAMES, Henry, American novelist

JOFFRE, Joseph, French General, became President of the Allied War Council in 1917

JOHNSON, Paul, historian, social critic and journalist

JOHNSON, Samuel, English lexicographer, critic and poet, 1709–84

KARL, Emperor of Austria, King of Hungary 1887–1922, nephew of Archduke Franz Ferdinand

KEEGAN, John, British military historian

KERENSKY, Alexander, leader of the Mensheviks during the Russian revolution

KIPLING, Rudyard, poet, novelist, short-story writer and regimental historian

KITCHENER, Horatio Herbert, 1st Earl, Kitchener of Khartoum, English soldier and statesman, Secretary of War 1914 until his death in 1916

KÖBES, Albin, German sailor, a leader of the sailors' mutiny, 1917, shot after its suppression

KOKOSHKA, Oskar, Austrian artist, became British citizen in 1947

KOLLONTAI, Alexandra, Russian reformer and politician, member of Lenin's Cabinet

KOURAKOFF, Sergei, Russian writer

KRAUS, Karl, Austrian satirist and poet. His Great War masterpiece, *The Last Days of Mankind*, is unrepresented here through translation difficulties

LANCE, David, British writer on military matters

LANSDOWNE, Marquess of, Liberal politician, Minister in Asquith's Cabinet

LAWRENCE, David Herbert, English poet, novelist and critic

LAWRENCE, Thomas Edward (Lawrence of Arabia), British soldier and writer

LEGER, William St, British soldier

LENIN, Vladimir Ilyich, led Bolsheviks in Russia, 1917

LERSNER, German Foreign Office official

LEWIS, Percy Wyndham, artist, writer and critic, founded with Ezra Pound the Vorticist magazine *Blast*

LIDDELL HART, Basil Henry, military journalist and historian

LIDDIARD, Jean, British biographer

LISSAUER, Ernst, German poet and novelist

LLOYD GEORGE, David, Liberal statesman of Welsh parentage, 1908–15 Chancellor of the Exchequer, 1915–16 Minister of Munitions, 1916–22 coalition Prime Minister

LOURIE, Arthur Sergevitch, Russian composer and musicologist

LUCAS, E. V., English essayist and biographer

LUDENDORFF, Erich, German General, early supporter of Adolf Hitler

LUDWIG III of Bavaria, reigned from 1913 until his abdication in 1918

LUXEMBURG, Rosa, German revolutionary of the left, imprisoned 1915–16 for attacks on the army, kept in 'preventive detention' 1916–18, murdered 1919

MACDONAGH, Michael, writer

MACDONALD, James Ramsay, British Labour politician, active member of the anti-war I.L.P.

MACMILLAN, Harold, British statesman, served with the Grenadier Guards during the war

MANDELSHTAM, Osip, Russian poet, disappeared under Stalin's rule

MANN, Heinrich, German novelist, best known as the author of *Professor Unrat* which was later filmed as *The Blue Angel*

MANN, Julia, mother of Heinrich and Thomas Mann

MANN, Thomas, German novelist, best known as the author of *Buddenbrooks*, *The Magic Mountain* and *Dr Faustus*

MANNING, Frederick, New Zealand novelist

MANNOCK, Mick, British airman

MANSFIELD, Katherine, short-story writer, born in New Zealand, settled in England

MARIENHOF, Anatoly, Russian poet

MAUROIS, André, French novelist and biographer, liaison officer with the British army during the war

MAY, Ernest R., American historian

MAYAKOVSKY, Vladimir, Russian poet, supporter of the Bolsheviks in 1917

MEE, Charles L., American historian and journalist

MEYER, Jacques, French combatant at Verdun

MOLTKE, General von, German General, nephew of the victor of the 1870 war against France

MONTAGUE, C. E., essayist, drama critic and novelist, on the staff of the *Manchester Guardian* 1890–1925

MONTGOMERY, Bernard Law, British soldier, served with the Royal Warwickshire Regiment during the war, later became 1st Viscount Montgomery of Alamein, site of his famous victory in the Second World War

MOOREHEAD, Alan, British journalist, historian, traveller and biographer

MORAN, Lord, British physician

MORTON, A. L., British historian

MOSLEY, Nicholas, British novelist

MUMFORD, Lewis, American architectural critic and social historian

MUNRO, Ethel, sister to Hector Munro

MUNRO, Hector Hugh 'Saki', British novelist and short-story writer, killed in action 1916

MUSSOLINI, Benito, Italian soldier during the war, later Fascist dictator of Italy

NAMIER, Lewis Bernstein, Polish-born Oxford historian

NANSEN, Fridtjof, Norwegian explorer, diplomat, humanitarian, active in the League of Nations

NASH, Paul, English painter, official war artist from 1917

NICHOLAS II, Tsar of Russia from 1894, executed by the Red Guards in 1918

NIEMANN, Alfred, German officer

NORMAN, C. H., British pacifist, imprisoned during the Great War

O'BRIEN, Conor Cruise, Editor-in-Chief of the *Observer* from 1978, pro-Chancellor of the University of Dublin from 1973

O'CALLAGHAN, D., Major-General in the British army

OWEN, Wilfred, English poet, killed in action on the Western Front 1918

PARTRIDGE, Eric, British lexicographer, served in the war

PEARSE, Padraic, Irish writer and nationalist, led Easter rising of 1916 and proclaimed President of the provisional government and later executed

PECKELSHAIM, Kapitänleutnant Baron von und zu, German naval officer

PICHON, Stephen Jean Marie, French statesman and journalist, Minister of Foreign Affairs 1917–20

PIERREFEU, Jean de, French historian

POPE, Jessie, writer

PORTER, Cathy, historian, translator and biographer, specialising in modern Russian history

POSTGATE, Margaret, writer

POUND, Ezra, American poet and translator, co-editor of *Blast*, the Vorticist journal, 1914–15

POWELL, Enoch, British politician, poet and scholar

POWYS, John Cowper, British poet, essayist and novelist

PRÉVERT, Jacques, French poet

PRIESTLEY, John Boynton, English novelist, playwright and critic

PRITCHETT, V. S., British novelist, short-story writer and critic

PROUST, Marcel, French novelist and critic

RAE, John, headmaster of Westminster School, novelist and journalist

RASPUTIN, Gregory, Russian peasant mystic, powerful in the Tsar's court

READ, Herbert, English poet, critic and art historian, officer in the Great War

REED, John, American journalist, Communist organiser, indicted for sedition in America, died in Russia and buried in the Kremlin, author of *Ten Days that Shook the World*

RHONDDA, Viscountess, journalist, founder of *Time and Tide*

RICHTHOFEN, Manfred von, German airman noted for his numerous aerial victories (eighty in all)

RICKWORD, Edgell, poet and critic

RILKE, Rainer Maria, Austrian poet, born in Prague of German-speaking parents

ROCKWELL, Kiffin, an original member of the American *Escadrille Americaine*, later *Lafayette Escadrille*, killed June 1916

RODZIANKO, President of the Russian Duma

ROLLAND, Romain, French author and pacifist, wrote from Switzerland during the war

ROOSEVELT, Theodore, 26th President of the United States

ROSENBERG, Isaac, poet and painter

ROSNER, Carl, German novelist

RUSSELL, Bertrand, British pacifist, philosopher and mathematician, imprisoned during the war for breaking the Defence of the Realm Act

SAKI, *see* MUNRO

SANDBURG, Carl, American poet

SASSOON, Siegfried, poet

SCHWEITZER, Albert, Alsatian medical missionary, theologian, musician and philosopher

SMILLIE, Bob, Scottish Labour politician, President of the Scottish Miners' Federation during the war

SQUIRES, James Duane, American journalist

STAMFORDHAM, Lord, British civil servant, Private Secretary to George V

STERN, J. P., Czech-born scholar, literary critic, biographer

STRACHEY, Lytton, English biographer and literary critic

STRAMM, August, German poet

SULZBACH, Herbert, German volunteer 1914, refugee from Hitler 1937, commissioned in British army 1945

TAYLOR, A. J. P., English historian

THOMAS, Edward, English poet and critic, killed at Arras 1917

THOMPSON, Leonard, English farm-worker

THOMPSON, P. A., Captain in the British army

TILLYARD, E. M. W., British historian

TOLLER, Ernst, German poet and playwright

TOYNBEE, Arnold, historian

TOYNBEE, Philip, novelist, poet and journalist

TRAKL, Georg, German poet

TREVELYAN, George Macaulay, historian

TROTSKY, Leon, Russian revolutionary, helped to organise the October Revolution

TSVETAYEVA, Marina, Russian poet

TZARA, Tristan, Romanian dadaist poet, in Zurich during the Great War

UNGARETTI, Giuseppe, Italian poet

VANSITTART, Robert Gilbert, British diplomat and peer, later uncompromising opponent of Nazi Germany

WALDRON, F. E., British sapper

WALPOLE, Sir Hugh Seymour, English novelist

WEBER, Max, German sociologist

WEIZMANN, Chaim, Jewish statesman, active proponent of Zionism, first President of Israel

WELLS, Herbert George, English novelist, short-story writer and journalist

WERFEL, Franz, Austrian poet, playwright and novelist

WEST, Rebecca, British novelist and critic

WILHELM II, 3rd German Emperor reigning from 1888 until his abdication in 1918

WILHELM, Crown Prince of Germany

WHEELER-BENNETT, Sir John, British historian

WILSON, T. P. Cameron, British soldier and poet, killed 1918

WILSON, Thomas Woodrow, American statesman, elected President of the United States in 1912 and 1916

WOOLF, Virginia, English novelist and critic

WYLIE, Elinor, American poet and novelist

YEATS, William Butler, Irish poet and dramatist

ZIMMERMANN, German politician, Foreign Secretary from November 1916 to August 1917

ZSCHULTE, Helmut, German writer, served in the Great War

ZWEIG, Stefan, Austrian poet, translator, biographer, short-story writer and novelist

ACKNOWLEDGMENTS

Grateful thanks are due to Michael Levien and Dr Frederick Grubb for valuable help; to Maisie Boothman for patient typing and, above all, to Valerie Buckingham for editorial assistance.

All pictures are reproduced by kind permission of the Imperial War Museum, London. They are: *Prelude*, 'K.O.S.B. "Fagged"' by William Orpen; *1914*, 'Bringing in Prisoners' by Eric Kennington; *1915*, 'Banking at 4000 feet' by C. R. W. Nevinson; *1916*, 'Road Menders' by Adrian Hill; *1917*, 'Gavrelle Trench' by Adrian Hill; *1918*, 'An Advanced Cage for German Prisoners, 1917' by Adrian Hill; *Aftermath*, 'A Shell Bursting, Passchendaele' by Paul Nash; *Appendixes*, 'The End of the War' by William Nicholson.

The author and publishers are indebted to the copyright holders for permission to reproduce material as follows:

ANNA AKHMATOVA: extracts from *Poems of Akhmatova*, Selected, Translated and Introduced by Stanley Kunitz and Max Hayward. 'July 1914' (p. 14) © 1967 by Stanley Kunitz and Max Hayward, first appeared in the *Nation*; 'When in the Throes of Suicide' (p. 199) © 1972 by Stanley Kunitz and Max Hayward, first appeared in *Arian's Dolphin*. Reprinted by permission of Collins, and Little, Brown and Company in association with the Atlantic Monthly Press.

L. ALBERTINI: extract from *The Origins of the War of 1914*, translated and edited by Isabella M. Massey, 1952, reprinted by permission of Oxford University Press

GUILLAUME APOLLINAIRE:	extracts from *Selected Poems*, © Gallimard 1927, reprinted by permission of Editions Gallimard
RENÉ ARCOS:	extract from 'The Dead' reprinted by permission of the translator, Christopher Middleton
HENRI BARBUSSE:	extracts from *Under Fire*, translated by Fitzwater Wray, Everyman's Library, reprinted by permission of J. M. Dent & Sons Ltd
CORELLI BARNETT:	extracts from *The Sword Bearers* reprinted by permission of David Higham Associates Ltd
MAX BECKMANN:	extracts from *Letters of the Great Artists* by Richard Friedenthal reprinted by permission of Thames & Hudson
HILAIRE BELLOC:	extract from *Collected Verse* reprinted by permission of Gerald Duckworth & Co.
ARNOLD BENNETT:	extracts from *The Journals of Arnold Bennett* reprinted by permission of the Estate of Arnold Bennett and A. P. Watt Ltd
ISAIAH BERLIN:	extract from *Personal Impressions* reprinted by permission of the author and the Hogarth Press Ltd
EDMUND BLUNDEN:	extracts from *Undertones of War* and *Poems 1914–20* reprinted by permission of A. D. Peters & Co. Ltd
RONALD BLYTHE:	extracts from *Akenfield*, Allen Lane, reprinted by permission of David Higham Associates Ltd
C. M. BOWRA:	extract from *Poetry and Politics 1900–1960* reprinted by permission of Cambridge University Press
VERA BRITTAIN:	extracts from *Testament of Youth* by Vera Brittain are included with the permission of Paul Berry, her Literary Executor
F. N. BROOME:	extract from *The Kaiser's Battle* by Martin Middlebrook reprinted by permission of Penguin Books Ltd
JOHN BROPHY:	extracts from *Soldiers' Slang*, Scholartis Press, © John Brophy and Eric Partridge, reprinted by permission of Anthony Sheil Associates Ltd

SIR ARTHUR BRYANT: extracts from *English Saga* reprinted by permission of the author

JOHN BUCHAN: extracts from *Greenmantle* and *The Three Hostages* reprinted by permission of Lord Tweedsmuir of Elsfield, Hodder & Stoughton Ltd and A. P. Watt Ltd

TIM CAREW: extracts from *Wipers* reprinted by permission of Hamish Hamilton Ltd

E. CHAPMAN: extract from *The Kaiser's Battle* by Martin Middlebrook reprinted by permission of Penguin Books Ltd

WINSTON CHURCHILL: letter to Arthur Conan Doyle reprinted by permission of Winston S. Churchill; extract from *My Early Life* on p. 12 reprinted by permission of the Hamlyn Publishing Group Ltd; extracts from *The World Crisis* on pp. 149, 163, 164, 237 top, reprinted by permission of Eyre Methuen Ltd

JOSEPH COHEN: extract from 'The Three Roles of Siegfried Sassoon' published in *Tulane Studies in English*, 1957, reprinted by permission of the author

ROBERT CONQUEST: extract from *We and They* reprinted by permission of Maurice Temple Smith Ltd

LADY DIANA COOPER: extract from *Autobiography* reprinted by permission of the author

ERNEST READ COOPER: extract from *People at War*, edited by Michael Moynihan, reprinted by permission of David & Charles

BRIGADIER GENERAL F. P. CROZIER: extracts from *A Brass Hat in No Man's Land*, Jonathan Cape, reprinted by permission of the Estate of Brigadier General Frank Percy Crozier

EVE CURIE: extracts from *Madame Curie* reprinted by permission of William Heinemann Ltd

BERNARD DARWIN: extract from *W. G. Grace* reprinted by permission of Gerald Duckworth & Co.

PATRICK DEVLIN: extracts from *Too Proud to Fight*, 1974, reprinted by permission of Oxford University Press

ARTHUR CONAN DOYLE: extracts from *The British Campaigns in Europe 1914–18* reprinted by permission of Geoffrey Bles Ltd

ANTHONY EDEN: extract from *Another World 1897–1917* reprinted by permission of Penguin Books Ltd

T. S. ELIOT: extract from *Collected Poems 1909–1962* reprinted by permission of Faber and Faber Ltd

JOHN ELLIS: extract from *Eye-Deep in Hell* reprinted by permission of Croom Helm Ltd

ERNST FISHER: extracts from *An Opposing Man* reprinted by kind permission of Curtis Brown Ltd, London

H. A. L. FISHER: extracts from *A History of Europe* reprinted by permission of Edward Arnold

F. SCOTT FITZGERALD: extracts from *The Bodley Head Scott Fitzgerald, Vol. 2* reprinted by permission of The Bodley Head

FORD MADOX FORD: 'The Old Houses of Flanders' reprinted by permission of Secker & Warburg Ltd

E. M. FORSTER: extracts from *Abinger Harvest* reprinted by permission of Edward Arnold

JOE FRANKLIN: extract from *Classics of the Silent Screen* reprinted by permission of Citadel Press

RALPH FREEDMAN: extracts from *Hermann Hesse: Pilgrim of Crisis*, Jonathan Cape, reprinted by permission of the author

SIGMUND FREUD: extracts from *Sigmund Freud: Life and Work* by Ernest Jones reprinted by permission of the author's Literary Estate and the Hogarth Press Ltd

PAUL FRÖLICH: extract from *Rosa Luxemburg* first published in Paris, 1939; published in London by the Left Book Club, 1940; third revised edition published 1967 in Germany by Europäische Verlagsanstalt; this translation first published 1972 in London by Pluto Press, copyright © 1972 Pluto Press. Reprinted by kind permission of Pluto Press, London

J. F. C. FULLER: extracts from *The Decisive Battles of the*

Western World reprinted by permission of David Higham Associates Ltd

JAMES W. GERARD: extracts from *My Four Years in Germany*, © 1917 by George H. Doran Company, reprinted by permission of Doubleday & Company, Inc.

MAXIM GORKY: extracts from *Fragments From My Diary*, first published in 1924 by P. Allan (new translation by Maura Budberg 1972), published by Allen Lane, reprinted by kind permission of Tanya Alexander

EDWYN A. GRAY: extracts from *The Killing Time* reprinted by permission of Frederick Warne (Publishers) Ltd

GRAHAM GREENE: extract from *A Sort of Life*, The Bodley Head, reprinted by permission of Laurence Pollinger Ltd

JULIAN GRENFELL: extracts from *Julian Grenfell: his life and times* by Nicholas Mosley reprinted by permission of Weidenfeld & Nicolson

PHILIP GUEDALLA: extract from *The Two Marshals*, Hodder & Stoughton, reprinted by permission of David Higham Associates Ltd

IVOR GURNEY: extracts from *Selected Poems of Ivor Gurney*, edited by P. J. Kavanagh, Oxford University Press 1982, reprinted by permission of Oxford University Press

LORD HANKEY: extract from *The Supreme Command, 1914–1918*, Allen & Unwin, reprinted by permission of David Higham Associates Ltd

LORD HARDINGE: extract from *Old Diplomacy* reprinted by permission of John Murray (Publishers) Ltd

CATE HASTE: extract from *Keep the Home Fires Burning* reprinted by permission of Penguin Books Ltd

ERNEST HEMINGWAY: extract from *A Farewell to Arms*, Jonathan Cape, reprinted by permission of the Executors of the Ernest Hemingway Estate

JAKOB VAN HODDIS: extract from *The Cabaret* by Lisa Appignanesi reprinted by permission of the author

A. A. and
MAY HOEHLLING: extract from *The Last Journey of the Lusitania* reprinted by permission of Longman Group Ltd

ALISTAIR HORNE: extracts from *The Price of Glory* reprinted by permission of Macmillan, London and Basingstoke

A. E. HOUSMAN: 'Here we dead lie because we did not choose' (Poem XXXVI) reprinted by permission of the Society of Authors as the literary representative of the Estate of A. E. Housman and Jonathan Cape Ltd, publishers of A. E. Housman's *Collected Poems*

PAUL JOHNSON: extracts from *The Offshore Islanders* reprinted by permission of Weidenfeld & Nicolson

JOHN KEEGAN: extract from review, published 21 August 1980 and titled *The Nondescript who Promised Revenge*, reprinted by permission of the *Guardian*

RUDYARD KIPLING: 'A Drifter at Tarentum', 'Gethsemane' and extracts from *Poems 1886–1929* reprinted by permission of the National Trust, Eyre Methuen Ltd and A. P. Watt Ltd

OSKAR KOKOSHKA: extracts from *My Life*, Thames & Hudson, 1974, reproduced by permission of F. Bruckmann Kg

HAROLD KURTZ: extract from *The Empress Eugénie* reprinted by permission of Hamish Hamilton Ltd

DAVID LANCE: extracts from *The Tank: Theory and Practice 1916–39* reprinted by permission of the Imperial War Museum

D. H. LAWRENCE: letters to Cynthia Asquith (p. 85, 2 November 1915) and Catherine Carswell (p. 117, 9 July 1916) from *The Collected Letters of D. H. Lawrence*; poem (p. 257) from *The Complete Poems of D. H. Lawrence*; extract (p. 264) from 'A Letter From Germany' from *Phoenix* are all published by William Heinemann Ltd and are reprinted by permission of Laurence Pollinger Ltd and the

Estate of the late Mrs Frieda Lawrence
Ravagli

T. E. LAWRENCE: extracts from *Seven Pillars of Wisdom*, Jonathan Cape, reprinted by permission of the Seven Pillars Trust and the author

WILLIAM ST LEGER: extract from *People at War*, edited by Michael Moynihan, reprinted by permission of David & Charles

P. WYNDHAM LEWIS: extract from *Blasting and Bombardiering* reprinted by permission of John Calder (Publishers) Ltd

BASIL LIDDELL HART: extract from *Through the Fog of War*, Faber and Faber, reprinted by permission of David Higham Associates Ltd

JEAN LIDDIARD: extract from *Isaac Rosenberg: the half-used life* reprinted by permission of Victor Gollancz Ltd

E. V. LUCAS: extract from *Swollen Headed William* reprinted by permission of Eyre Methuen Ltd

G. D. K. MCCORMICK: extract from *Pedlar of Death: the Life of Sir Basil Zaharoff*, Macdonalds, reprinted by permission of David Higham Associates Ltd

HAROLD MACMILLAN: extract from *Winds of Change* reprinted by permission of Macmillan, London and Basingstoke

OSIP MANDELSHTAM: poems on pp. 9, 157, 223 from *Selected Poems*, translated by Clarence Brown and W. S. Merwin, 1973, reprinted by permission of Oxford University Press

THOMAS MANN: extracts from *The Brothers Mann*, published by Secker & Warburg, reprinted with the kind permission of the author, Nigel Hamilton

FREDERICK W. MANNING: extract from *Her Privates We* reprinted by permission of Peter Davies Ltd

ANDRÉ MAUROIS: extracts from *Call No Man Happy* reprinted by kind permission of Curtis Brown Ltd, London, on behalf of the Estate of André Maurois

CHARLES MEE: extract from *The End of Order: Versailles 1919* reprinted by permission of Secker & Warburg

ALAN MOOREHEAD: extract on p. 70 from *Churchill and His World* reprinted by permission of Thames and Hudson; extract on pp. 164–5 from *The Russian Revolution*, Harper & Brothers, © 1958 by Time Inc. Used with permission

LEWIS MUMFORD: extracts from *The Condition of Man* reprinted by permission of Harcourt Brace Jovanovich, Inc.

L. B. NAMIER: extract from *Vanished Supremacies* reprinted by permission of Hamish Hamilton Ltd

PAUL NASH: extract from *Letters of the Great Artists* by Richard Friedenthal reprinted by permission of Thames and Hudson

HAROLD NICOLSON: extracts from *George V* reprinted by permission of Constable Publishers

CONOR CRUISE   extract from article published in 1978 by
O'BRIEN: permission of the *Observer*

WILFRED OWEN: extracts from *War Poems and Others: A Selection*, edited by Dominic Hibberd, reprinted by permission of the Owen Estate and Chatto and Windus Ltd

ERIC PARTRIDGE: extracts from *Soldiers' Slang*, Scholartis Press, © John Brophy and Eric Partridge, reprinted by permission of Anthony Sheil Associates Ltd

CATHY PORTER: extract from *Alexandra Kollontai*, published by Virago Press 1980, reprinted by permission of Virago Ltd

EZRA POUND: extracts from *The Cantos of Ezra Pound* reprinted by permission of Faber and Faber Ltd; extract from *Gaudier-Brzeshka* reprinted by permission of the Marvell Press

ENOCH POWELL: extract from an article published in *Books and Bookmen*, April 1979, reproduced by permission of Brevet Publishing Ltd

JOHN COWPER POWYS: extract from *Autobiography*, Pan Books Ltd, reprinted by permission of Laurence Pollinger Ltd and the Estate of the late John Cowper Powys

JACQUES PRÉVERT: extract from *Spectacle*, © Editions Gallimard 1951, reprinted by permission of Editions Gallimard

J. B. PRIESTLEY: extracts from *Margin Released* reprinted by permission of William Heinemann Ltd

V. S. PRITCHETT: extract from *London Perceived* reprinted by permission of the author, Chatto and Windus Ltd and William Heinemann Ltd

MARCEL PROUST: extract from *Letters of Marcel Proust*, edited by Mina Curtiss, reprinted by permission of the editor and Chatto and Windus Ltd

JOHN RAE: extract from *Conscience and Politics*, 1970, reprinted by permission of Oxford University Press

HERBERT READ: extracts from *Collected Poems*, Faber and Faber, reprinted by permission of David Higham Associates Ltd

JOHN REED: extract from *Ten Days That Shook the World* reprinted by permission of Lawrence and Wishart Ltd

EDGELL RICKWORD: extracts from *Behind the Eyes: Selected Poems and Translations* reprinted by permission of Carcanet Press Ltd

RAINER MARIA RILKE: extract from *Selected Poems* translated by J. B. Leishman, reprinted by permission of St John's College, Oxford and the Hogarth Press Ltd

ISAAC ROSENBERG: extracts from *The Collected Works of Isaac Rosenberg*, edited by Ian Parsons, reprinted by permission of the author's Literary Estate and Chatto and Windus Ltd

BERTRAND RUSSELL: extracts from *Autobiography of Bertrand Russell* reprinted by permission of George Allen & Unwin

CARL SANDBURG: extract from *Cornhuskers*, © 1918 by Holt, Rinehart and Winston, Inc.; © 1946 by Carl

Sandburg, reprinted by permission of Harcourt Brace Jovanovich, Inc.

SIEGFRIED SASSOON: extracts from *Collected Poems* reprinted by permission of George T. Sassoon

ALBERT SCHWEITZER: extract from *My Life and Thought* reprinted by permission of George Allen & Unwin

J. P. STERN: extracts from *Hitler, the Führer and the People* reprinted by permission of the Harvester Press Ltd

LYTTON STRACHEY: extract on pp. 42–3 from *Lytton Strachey* by Michael Holroyd, published by William Heinemann Ltd, 1967, © The Strachey Trust, reprinted by permission of Michael Holroyd

AUGUST STRAMM: extract from *German Poetry 1910–75*, published by Carcanet Press, translation © Michael Hamburger, reprinted by kind permission of Michael Hamburger

HERBERT SULZBACH: extracts from *With the German Guns* reprinted by permission of Frederick Warne (Publishers) Ltd

A. J. P. TAYLOR: extracts from *The Course of German History, Europe: Decline and Grandeur* and *The Habsburg Monarchy* reprinted by permission of Hamish Hamilton Ltd

EDWARD THOMAS: extracts from *Collected Poems* reprinted by permission of Mrs Myfanwy Thomas and Faber and Faber; letter to Robert Frost reprinted by permission of Mrs Myfanwy Thomas

E. M. W. TILLYARD: extract from *The Elizabethan World Picture* reprinted by permission of Mr Stephen Tillyard and Chatto and Windus Ltd

ARNOLD TOYNBEE: extract from *Acquaintances*, 1967, reprinted by permission of Oxford University Press

PHILIP TOYNBEE: extract from *Two Brothers* reprinted by permission of Mrs Toynbee

G. M. TREVELYAN: extract from *George Macaulay Trevelyan* by Mary Moorman reprinted by permission of Hamish Hamilton Ltd

MARINA TSVETAYEVA: extract from *Selected Poems*, translated by Elaine Feinstein, 1971: revised edition 1981; reprinted by permission of Oxford University Press

F. E. WALDRON: extract from *The Kaiser's Battle* by Martin Middlebrook reprinted by permission of Penguin Books Ltd

HUGH WALPOLE: extracts from *Hugh Walpole* by Rupert Hart Davis reprinted by permission of Sir Rupert Hart Davis

CHAIM WEIZMANN: extract from *Chaim Weizmann*, edited by Meyer W. Weisgal and Joel Carmichael, reprinted by permission of Weidenfeld and Nicolson

H. G. WELLS: extracts from *Experiment in Autobiography* reprinted by permission of the Estate of H. G. Wells and A. P. Watt Ltd

REBECCA WEST: extracts from *Black Lamb, Grey Falcon* reprinted by permission of A. D. Peters & Co. Ltd

JOHN WHEELER-BENNETT: extracts from *Knaves, Fools and Heroes* reprinted by permission of Macmillan, London and Basingstoke

VIRGINIA WOOLF: extract from *Jacob's Room* reprinted by permission of the author's Literary Estate and the Hogarth Press Ltd

ELINOR WYLIE: 'Doomsday' © 1932 by Alfred A. Knopf, Inc., and renewed 1960 by Edwina C. Rubenstein. Reprinted from *Collected Poems of Elinor Wylie*, by Elinor Wylie, by permission of Alfred A. Knopf, Inc.

W. B. YEATS: 'On Being Asked for a War Poem' from *Collected Poems* reprinted by permission of M. B. Yeats, Anne Yeats, Macmillan, London Ltd and A. P. Watt Ltd

HELMUT ZSCHULTE: extract from *Eye-Deep in Hell* by John Ellis reprinted by permission of Croom Helm Ltd

STEFAN ZWEIG: extract from *The World of Yesterday* reprinted by permission of Williams Verlag AG

BIBLIOGRAPHY

Unless otherwise indicated the place of publication is London.

ALBERTINI, L., *The Origins of the War of 1914*, O.U.P., 1952

APOLLINAIRE, G., *Selected Poems*, Penguin, 1965

APPIGNANESI, L., *The Cabaret*, Studio Vista, 1976

ASQUITH, C., *Diaries 1915–18*, Hutchinson, 1968

ASQUITH, C. and SPENDER, J. A., *Life of Herbert Henry Asquith, Lord Oxford and Asquith*, Hutchinson, 1932

ASQUITH, M., *The Autobiography of Margot Asquith*, Butterworth, 1922

BALFOUR, M. L. G., *The Kaiser and his Times*, Cresset Press, 1964

BARBUSSE, H., *Under Fire*, Everyman, 1926

BARNETT, C., *The Sword Bearers*, Eyre & Spottiswoode, 1963

BARNSTONE, W. (ed.), *Modern European Poetry*, New York, Bantam Books, 1966

BELLOC, H., *Collected Verse*, Duckworth, 1954

BENNETT, A., *The Journals of Arnold Bennett*, Penguin, 1954

BERLIN, I., *Personal Impressions*, Hogarth Press, 1980

BLUNDEN, E., *Poems 1914–20*, Cobden-Sanderson, 1930
        Undertones of War, Cobden-Sanderson, 1928

BLYTHE, R., *Akenfield*, Allen Lane, 1969

BOUMAN, P. J., *Revolution of the Lonely*, New York, McGraw Hill, 1951

BOWRA, C. M., *Poetry and Politics 1900–1960*, C.U.P., 1966

BRITTAIN, V., *Testament of Youth*, Gollancz, 1933

BROOKE, R., *Collected Poems*, Sidgwick and Jackson, 1918

BROPHY, J. and PARTRIDGE, E., *Songs and Slang of the British Soldier: 1914–18*, Scholartis Press, 1931

BROWN, C., *Mandelstam*, C.U.P., 1973

BRYANT, A., *English Saga 1840–1940*, Collins with Eyre & Spottiswoode, 1940

BUCHAN, J., *Greenmantle*, Hodder and Stoughton, 1916

The Three Hostages, Hodder and Stoughton, 1924
BÜLOW, Prince von, *Denkwürdigkeiten*, Berlin, 1930
CAREW, T., *Wipers*, Hamish Hamilton, 1974
CARMICHAEL, J. and WEISGAL, M. W. (eds), *Chaim Weizmann*, Weidenfeld and Nicolson, 1962
CHAPMAN, G. (ed.), *Vain Glory*, Cassell, 1937
CHURCHILL, W., *My Early Life*, Macmillan, 1930
    The World Crisis, Thornton Butterworth, 1923–31
CLARK-KENNEDY, A. E., *Edith Cavell*, Faber, 1978
COHEN, J., *Journey to the Trenches*, Robson Books, 1975
    The Three Roles of Siegfried Sassoon, New Orleans, Louisiana, Tulane University, 1957
CONQUEST, R., *We and They*, Temple Smith, 1980
COOKE, W., *Edward Thomas*, Faber and Faber, 1970
COOPER, D., *Autobiography*, Michael Russell, 1979
CROZIER, F. P., *A Brass Hat in No Man's Land*, Jonathan Cape, 1930
CURIE, E., *Madame Curie*, Heinemann, 1938
DARWIN, B., *W. G. Grace*, Duckworth, 1934
DEVLIN, P., *Too Proud to Fight*, O.U.P., 1974
DOYLE, A. Conan, *The British Campaigns in Europe 1914–18*, Geoffrey Bles, 1928
EDEN, A., *Another World 1897–1917*, Allen Lane, 1976
ELLIS, J., *Eye-Deep in Hell*, Croom Helm, 1976
ELLIS, P. B., *H. Rider Haggard*, Routledge & Kegan Paul, 1978
FIELD, A., *Picture Palace*, Gentry Books, 1974
FISCHER, E., *An Opposing Man*, Allen Lane, 1974
FISHER, H. A. L., *A History of Europe*, Arnold, 1936
FITZGERALD, F. Scott, *The Beautiful and the Damned*, Collins, 1922
    Tender is the Night, Chatto and Windus, 1934
FORSTER, E. M., *Abinger Harvest*, Arnold, 1936
FRANKLIN, J., *Classics of the Silent Screen*, New York, Citadel Press, 1959
FREEDMAN, R., *Hermann Hesse*, Jonathan Cape, 1979
FREEMAN, J., *An American Testament*, Gollancz, 1938
FRIEDENTHAL, R., *Letters of the Great Artists*, Thames and Hudson, 1963
FRÖLICH, P., *Rosa Luxemburg*, Gollancz, 1940
FULLER, J. F. C., *The Decisive Battles of the Western World*, Eyre & Spottiswoode, 1954
GERARD, J. W., *My Four Years in Germany*, Hodder and Stoughton, 1917
GORKY, M., *Fragments from my Diary*, P. Allan, 1924
GRAY, E. A., *The Killing Time*, Seeley, Service and Co., 1974
GREENE, G., *A Sort of Life*, Bodley Head, 1971
GRENFELL, J., *Battle*, Flanders, 1915
GUEDALLA, P., *The Second Empire*, Constable, 1922
    The Two Marshals, Hodder and Stoughton, 1943
GURNEY, I., *The Poems of Ivor Gurney 1890–1937*, Chatto and Windus, 1973
HAMILTON, N., *The Brothers Mann*, Secker and Warburg, 1978

HANKEY, Lord, *The Supreme Command, 1914–1918*, Allen and Unwin, 1961

HARDINGE, C., *Old Diplomacy*, John Murray, 1947

HARDY, T., *The Collected Poems*, Macmillan, 1952

HARRISON, A., *How was that Sir*, I.A.P.S., 1975

HART DAVIS, R., *Hugh Walpole*, Macmillan, 1952

HASTE, C., *Keep the Home Fires Burning*, Allen Lane, 1971

HAYWARD, M. and KRUNITZ, S., *Poems of Akhmatova*, Collins/Harvill, 1974

HEMINGWAY, E., *A Farewell to Arms*, Jonathan Cape, 1929

HENLEY, W. E., *Poems*, D. Nutt, 1898

HINDENBURG, P. von, *Aus Meinem Leben*, Leipzig, 1920

HITLER, A., *Mein Kampf*, Munich, 1925–27

HOEHLLING, A. A. and HOEHLLING, M., *The Last Journey of the Lusitania*, Longman, 1957

HOLROYD, M., *Lytton Strachey*, Heinemann, 1967

HORNE, A., *The Price of Glory*, Macmillan, 1962

HOUSMAN, A. E., *The Collected Poems of A. E. Housman*, Jonathan Cape, 1939

HUGHES, C. J. Pennethorne, *The Nineteenth Century and the World War*, Gollancz, 1935

HULSE, E. H. W., *Letters Written from the English Front in France between September 1914 and March 1915*, 1916

HYAM, A., *The Rise and Fall of Horatio Bottomley*, Cassell, 1972

JACKSON, J. Hampden, *England since the Industrial Revolution*, Gollancz, 1936

JOFFRE, J. J. C., *Mémoires du Maréchal Joffre 1910–17*, Paris, 1932

JOHNSON, P., *The Offshore Islanders*, Weidenfeld and Nicolson, 1972

JOHNSON, R. U., *Remembered Yesterdays*, Allen and Unwin, 1924

JOLLIFFE, J., *Raymond Asquith: Life and Letters*, Collins, 1980

JONES, E., *Sigmund Freud: life and work*, Hogarth Press, 1953–57

KIPLING, R., *Poems 1886–1929*, Macmillan, 1929

KISCH, C., *Alexander Blok: Prophet of Revolution*, Weidenfeld and Nicolson, 1960

KOKOSHKA, O., *My Life*, Thames and Hudson, 1974

KOLLONTAI, A., *A Diary*, Leningrad, 1924
      Who Needs War, Moscow, 1916

KOURAKOFF, S., *Savage Squadrons*, Harrap, 1937

KRUNITZ, S., *see* HAYWARD

KURTZ, H., *The Empress Eugénie*, Hamish Hamilton, 1964

LANCE, D., *The Tank: Theory and Practice 1916–39*, Imperial War Museum, 1969

LAWRENCE, D. H., *The Letters of D. H. Lawrence*, Heinemann, 1932
      Selected Essays, Penguin in association with Heinemann, 1950

LAWRENCE, T. E., *Seven Pillars of Wisdom*, Jonathan Cape, 1935

LEWIS, W., *Blasting and Bombardiering*, Calder and Boyars, 1967

LIDDELL HART, B., *Through the Fog of War*, Faber, 1938

LIDDIARD, J., *Isaac Rosenberg: the Half-used Life*, Gollancz, 1975

LINDSAY, J. (ed.), *Modern Russian Poetry*, Vista Books, 1960

LLOYD GEORGE, D., *War Memoirs of David Lloyd George*, Ivor Nicholson and Watson, 1933–6

LUCAS, E. V., *Swollen-headed William*, Methuen and Co., 1914

LUDENDORFF, E., *My War Memories*, Berlin, 1920

LUXEMBURG, R., *The Crisis of Social Democracy*, Berlin, 1916

McCORMICK, G. D. K., *Pedlar of Death: the Life of Sir Basil Zaharoff*, Macdonald, 1965

MACDONAGH, M., *In London During the Great War*, Eyre & Spottiswoode, 1935

MACKWORTH, M. H., *This Was My World*, Macmillan, 1933

MACMILLAN, H., *Winds of Change*, Macmillan, 1966

MANDELSTAM, O., *Selected Poems*, O.U.P., 1973

MANNING, F. W., *Her Privates We*, Peter Davies, 1930

MANSFIELD, K., *Letters to John Middleton Murry*, Constable, 1951

MAUROIS, A., *Call No Man Happy*, Jonathan Cape, 1943

MAY, E. R., *The World and American Isolation*, Harvard University Press, 1959

MAYAKOVSKY, V., *Poems*, trs. Dorian Rottenberg, Progress Publishers, Moscow, 1972

MEE, C. L., *The End of Order: Versailles, 1919*, Secker and Warburg, 1981

MIDDLEBROOK, M., *The Kaiser's Battle*, Allen Lane, 1978

MONTAGUE, C. E., *Rough Justice*, Chatto and Windus, 1926

MOOREHEAD, A., *Churchill*, Thames and Hudson, 1960
    Montgomery: a Biography, Hamish Hamilton, 1946
    The Russian Revolution, Collins with Hamish Hamilton, 1958

MOORMAN, M., *George Macaulay Trevelyan*, Hamish Hamilton, 1980

MORAN, Lord, *The Anatomy of Courage*, Eyre & Spottiswoode, 1945

MORTON, A. L., *A People's History of England*, Gollancz, 1938

MOSLEY, N., *Julian Grenfell: his life and times*, Weidenfeld and Nicolson, 1976

MOYNIHAN, M. (ed.), *People at War*, David and Charles, 1973
    A Place Called Armageddon, David and Charles, 1975

MULGAN, J. (ed.), *Poems of Freedom*, Gollancz, 1938

MUMFORD, L., *The Condition of Man*, Secker and Warburg, 1944

MUNRO, H. H., *see* SAKI

NAMIER, L. B., *Vanished Supremacies*, Hamish Hamilton, 1958

NEUMANN, R., *Zaharoff the Armament King*, Allen and Unwin, 1938

NICOLSON, H., *George V*, Constable, 1952

NIEMANN, A., *Kaiser und Revolution*, Berlin, 1918

NORDAU, P., *Conan Doyle*, Murray, 1976

O'CALLAGHAN, Major General, *The Young Officer's 'Don't' or Hints to Youngsters on Joining*, London, 1907

OWEN, W., *War Poems*, Chatto and Windus, 1973

PANICHAS, G. A. (ed.), *Promise of Greatness*, Cassell, 1968

PARTRIDGE, E., *see* BROPHY

PECKELSHAIM, Baron von, *War Diary of U-202*

PIERREFEU, J. de, *Plutarque a menti*, Paris, 1922

BIBLIOGRAPHY

PORTER, C., *Alexandra Kollontai*, Virago, 1980

POUND, E., *Collected Cantos*, Faber, 1935
  Gaudier-Brzeska, Marvell Press, 1960

POWYS, J. Cowper, *Autobiography*, New York, Simon and Schuster, 1934

PRÉVERT, J., *Spectacle*, Paris, Gallimard, 1951

PRIESTLEY, J. B., *Margin Released*, Heinemann, 1964

PRITCHETT, V. S., *London Perceived*, Chatto and Windus with Heinemann, 1962

PROUST, M., *Letters of Marcel Proust*, Chatto and Windus, 1950

RAE, J., *Conscience and Politics*, O.U.P., 1970

READ, H., *Collected Poems*, Faber and Faber, 1966

REED, J., *Ten Days that Shook the World*, New York, Boni and Liveright, 1919

REYNOLDS, E. E., *Nansen*, Geoffrey Bles, 1932

REYNOLDS, R., and STOCK, A. L., *Prison Anthology*, Jarrolds, 1938

RHONDDA, Viscountess, *see* MACKWORTH

RICKWORD, E., *Behind the Eyes*, Manchester, Carcanet, 1976
  Collected Poems, Bodley Head, 1947

RILKE, R. M., *Letters*, Wiesbaden, Insel Verlag, 1935
  Selected Poems, Hogarth Press, 1941

ROLLAND, R., *Above the Battle*, Paris, 1915

ROSENBERG, I., *The Complete Works*, Chatto and Windus, 1937

ROSNER, C., *Der König*, Berlin, 1920

RUSSELL, B., *Autobiography*, Allen and Unwin, 1967

SAKI (MUNRO, H. H.), *The Bodley Head Saki*, Bodley Head, 1963

SANDBURG, C., *Complete Poems*, Jonathan Cape, 1951

SASSOON, S., *Collected Poems*, Faber, 1947

SCHWEITZER, A., *My Life and Thought*, Allen and Unwin, 1933

SILKIN, J. (ed.), *The Penguin Book of First World War Poetry*, Penguin, 1979

SPENDER, J. A., *see* ASQUITH

SQUIRES, J. D., *British Propaganda at Home and in the United States from 1914 to 1917*, Cambridge, Mass., Harvard Historical Monographs, 1935

STERN, J. P., *Hitler: the Führer and the people*, Harvester Press, 1975

STOCK, A. L., *see* REYNOLDS

SULZBACH, H., *With the German Guns*, Leo Cooper, 1973

SYMONS, J. (ed.), *An Anthology of War Poetry*, Pelican, 1942

TAYLOR, A. J. P., *The Course of German History*, Hamish Hamilton, 1945
  Europe: Grandeur and Decline, Penguin in association with Hamish Hamilton, 1967
  The Habsburg Monarchy, Hamish Hamilton, 1948

THOMAS, E., *Collected Poems*, Faber, 1936

THOMPSON, P. A., *Lions Led by Donkeys*, Werner Laurie, 1927

TILLYARD, E. M. W., *The Elizabethan World Picture*, Chatto and Windus, 1943

TOLAND, J., *No Man's Land*, Eyre Methuen, 1980

TOYNBEE, A., *Acquaintances*, O.U.P., 1969

TOYNBEE, P., *Two Brothers*, Chatto and Windus, 1964

TROTSKY, L., *The History of the Russian Revolution to Brest-Litovsk*, Allen and Unwin, 1919

TSVETAYEVA, M., *Selected Poems*, Oxford, O.U.P., 1971

UNGARETTI, G., *Il Porto Sepolto*, Udine, 1916

WAVELL, A. P., *Other Men's Flowers*, Jonathan Cape, 1944

WEISGAL, M. W., *see* CARMICHAEL

WELLS, H. G., *Experiment in Autobiography*, Gollancz, 1934

WERFEL, F., *The Hidden Child*, Jarrolds, 1930

WEST, R., *Black Lamb, Grey Falcon*, Macmillan, 1944

WHEELER-BENNETT, J., *King George VI: his Life and Reign*, Macmillan, 1958

   Knaves, Fools and Heroes, Macmillan, 1974

WILLIAMS, I. (ed.), *Newspapers of the First World War*, Newton Abbot, David and Charles, 1970

WOOLF, V., *Jacob's Room*, Hogarth Press, 1922

WYLIE, E., *Collected Poems*, New York, Alfred A. Knopf, 1932

YEATS, W. B., *Collected Poems*, Macmillan, 1950

ZEMAN, Z. A. B., *A Diplomatic History of the First World War*, Weidenfeld and Nicolson, 1971

   Germany and the Revolution in Russia, 1915–18, O.U.P., 1958

ZWEIG, S., *The World of Yesterday*, Cassell, 1943

INDEX